We Confess!

The Civil War, the South, and the Church

Deborah Brunt

WestBow Press books may be ordered through booksellers or by contacting:

WestBow Press
A Division of Thomas Nelson
1663 Liberty Drive
Bloomington, IN 47403
www.westbowpress.com
1-(866) 928-1240

ISBN: 978-1-4497-3178-6 (sc)
ISBN: 978-1-4497-3179-3 (hc)

Library of Congress Control Number: 2011960571

Printed in the United States of America

WestBow Press rev. date: 11/21/2011

For my mother—
a beautiful lady
ravaged by generational strongholds
she did not see nor escape.

Mama, you have stirred a passion in me to see
blind eyes opened
and captives set free.

Contents

Forward

The wise King Solomon in the book of Proverbs tells us that there are three things that a person should not be without and they are knowledge, understanding, and wisdom; each, a stepping stone to the other.

Knowledge is the facts of the truth. Understanding is being under the correct view of the truth, and wisdom is the proper application or usage of what one understands.

I greatly appreciate the boldness, courageousness and tenderness with which Deborah Brunt brings the reader face to face with truth in her book, *We Confess: The Civil War, the South, and the Church.* For too long, as the Old Testament prophet Isaiah once said, "judgment is turned away backward, and justice standeth afar off: for truth is fallen in the street, and equity cannot enter."

This is a thoroughly documented book and will be referenced time and time again by those who are truth seekers and true champions for righteousness.

I highly recommend this book.

Apostle Willie F. Wooten
Author, *Breaking the Curse off Black America*

Acknowledgments

I'm deeply indebted to each of the prayer partners who have stood with me and labored with me to bring this book to birth. Especially, I want to thank Ruthie and Billy Joe Young for seeing God at work in a still-wounded woman with a glimmer of startling new insight. To help me find what God was uncovering, you went where no one else would go. What's more, you held me accountable: to stay before the Lord until I had the whole picture, to complete the healing process, and to speak from that place in love.

Belated but heartfelt thanks to Henry Blackaby for meeting with me in March 2005 and for publicly affirming me before the entire staff of the SBC entity where I worked. Your encouragement helped me keep putting one foot in front of the other during those difficult days when I first began seeing what I was seeing.

I also deeply appreciate Dr. John Benefiel, of Oklahoma City, for first giving me a platform to speak this message in December 2010 and for encouraging me not to hold back.

Much thanks to Phil and Erin Ulrich, 520 Media, and to the IT volunteers at Church on the Rock, OKC, for overcoming all manner of extraordinary technical difficulties to produce "We Confess! The Civil War, the South, and the Church" on DVD. Thanks also to the first responders to this message, who heard it in person or on the DVD. You helped me know what I needed to explain better and more fully. You affirmed that I'm not making this confession alone.

Dr. Willie Wooten, Christy Lilly, and Marion Neill read portions of various drafts of this manuscript and gave feedback. Thank you, thank you! Your insights were extremely helpful. Many thanks also to Sally

Mishkin for her expertise in copy-editing the manuscript. In the midst of pressing family and work responsibilities, Sally carved out time to devote to this project.

Special thanks to James Nesbit, an anointed artist who designed the incredible cover art before I even asked! Special thanks, as well, to Charlie Jenkins of CJ Three Photography for the delightful outdoor photo shoot in Memphis' Memorial Gardens and the amazing author photo you produced.

I'm deeply grateful to my parents, for loving me and for loving God. Somehow, in the midst of all you inherited, you opened the way for me to walk in truth.

How can I begin to express my love and gratitude to my husband, Jerry, our two daughters, Megan and Amanda, and their husbands—our *beaux-fils*—Logan and Sam? You have loved me and walked with me through all God has required. I don't have words, except: *I love you. Thank you.*

May the blessings with which you've *all* blessed me be multiplied back to each one of you.

Most of all, I thank and praise *HaShem*, in Hebrew, "the Name." Father, Son, Spirit, you are one Lord. You are my Lord. You are the God of the covenant Name—the Name we don't know how to pronounce, and yet, you insist that we know. Thank you for revealing to your people who *you* are and who *we* are. It is only in your light that we see.

1—Celebration

Why don't we do what we have not done? Why don't we, who most tend to gravitate to the word "celebrate" when talking of the Civil War, instead throw all caution to the wind—and *confess*?

I will cleanse them of bloodguilt which I have not yet cleansed.
—Joel 3:21 CJB

Today, I sit in silence, deeply grieved over what I read. Tomorrow, I will celebrate, profoundly grateful for what God has promised.

As I start the first draft of this chapter, it's February 2011. An online search of the topic "celebrating the 150th anniversary of the Civil War" has produced 220,000 hits. Scanning the top listings, I find such headlines as:

- "Southerners Celebrate 150th Anniversary of the Civil War"[1]
- "State [Tennessee] Prepares to Celebrate 150th Anniversary of Civil War"[2]
- "Mississippi to Celebrate 150th Anniversary of Civil War with Several Events"[3]
- "South Carolinians Celebrate 150th Anniversary of Secession"[4]
- "Events Celebrate 150th Anniversary of Civil War" [in Texas][5]
- "Upcoming Events Celebrating the 150th Anniversary of the Civil War" [in Virginia][6]

- "Celebrating 150th Anniversary of the Civil War: Events and Reenactments Recall Florida's Role in the War between the States"[7]
- "Peterboro [New York] to Celebrate 150th Anniversary of Civil War"[8]
- "Plymouth [Michigan] Historical Museum Celebrates 150th Anniversary of the Civil War with New Exhibit"[9]
- "History Channel to Celebrate 150th Anniversary of Civil War"[10]
- "Is Celebrating the Civil War's 150th Anniversary PC [politically correct]?"[11]
- "Commemorate, Don't Celebrate Civil War's 150th"[12]
- "Celebrate or Commemorate: Debate Rages over Civil War Anniversary"[13]

Certainly an event so major, so cataclysmic, should be remembered and pondered. A century-and-a-half after the war, many people and groups are doing so. Civil War buffs, re-enactors, and historians, along with US states that participated in the Confederacy and states and localities where Civil War battles were fought—these and others have four years of events in the works, because the war itself lasted four years. Some events started even before the anniversary arrived.

We need to remember. We need to re-examine. But *celebrate*?

Political correctness aside, what other *war* do we celebrate? Can you imagine a headline reading, "Events Celebrate WWII," or "Celebrating 60th Anniversary of the Korean War"? So why in the world would we celebrate the one war that shredded our nation so thoroughly? The one war that cost by far the largest number of American lives—and at the hands of fellow Americans? The war that, more than any other, bequeathed to us, "the staggering burden of needless bloodshed" (1 Sam. 25:31)?

In November 1860, Abraham Lincoln was elected President of the United States. Shortly afterward, South Carolina seceded from the Union, followed in quick succession by Mississippi, Florida, Alabama, Georgia, Louisiana, and Texas. War began when Southerners fired on US troops at Ft. Sumter, South Carolina, April 12, 1861. Soon after, four more states seceded: Virginia, Arkansas, Tennessee, and North Carolina.

By the time Robert E. Lee surrendered to Ulysses S. Grant, April 9, 1865, at Appomattox Courthouse, Virginia, Americans had fought Americans in some 10,500 armed conflicts. The 381 costliest battles occurred in 25 states plus D.C. Of these battles, 293 were fought in the 11 Confederate states, including 123 battles in Virginia alone.

Two slaves states that did not secede but remained deeply divided throughout the war, Missouri and Kentucky, saw a total of 38 battles. Fifteen major battles were fought in West Virginia, formed from Virginia during the war in order to remain in the Union.

The 35 battles fought in other states included one in Colorado, one in Idaho, two in Minnesota, two in New Mexico, two in North Dakota, four in Kansas, and seven in Oklahoma.

Only two battles took place in Pennsylvania, but one of them was the costliest of the war. The Battle of Gettysburg, fought July 1–4, 1863, claimed more than 51,000 lives on both sides.[14]

Total Civil War casualties have been estimated at 620,000, exceeding the nation's losses in all its other wars, from the Revolution through Vietnam.

Our least resolved conflict

Katharine Seelye of the *New York Times* has called the Civil War, "the most wrenching and bloody episode in American history ... America's deadliest conflict—and perhaps its least resolved."[15]

"This was a war that split the country, that pit brother against brother, and whose effects are still being felt around the nation," said a TakeAway.com host, as she introduced an interview with Jeff Antley, spokesperson for Sons of Confederate Veterans and the Confederate Heritage Trust, sponsors of the 2010 secession ball held in Charleston, South Carolina.[16]

Articles published in late 2010 and early 2011 previewed the ball and other planned events:

Bruce Smith of Associated Press wrote,

> At South Carolina's Secession Gala, men in frock coats and militia uniforms and women in hoop skirts will sip mint juleps as a band called Unreconstructed plays "Dixie." In Georgia, they will re-enact the state's 1861 secession convention. And Alabama will hold a mock swearing-in of Confederate President Jefferson Davis.
>
> Across the South, preparations are under way for the 150th anniversary of the Civil War. And while many organizations are working to incorporate both the black and the white experiences, there are complaints that some events will glorify the Old South and the Lost Cause while overlooking the fundamental reason for the war: slavery.[17]

Harold Jackson of the Philadelphia *Inquirer* wrote,

> Special events are being held in at least 21 states, including Pennsylvania, to mark the 150th anniversary of the Civil War... Cadets from the Citadel, South Carolina's historic military college, fired cannons on Morris Island in Charleston Harbor to reenact the January 1861 shelling of a ship that had tried to reinforce U.S. troops at Fort Sumter.
>
> In my home state of Alabama, Civil War reenactors are planning to parade through Montgomery to the state Capitol on Feb. 19 to re-create the swearing-in of Davis. They will also raise a Confederate flag.
>
> Mississippi began its commemoration of the Civil War this month with a reading at Vicksburg National Military Park of that state's Ordinance of Secession and a reenactment of rebels in 1861 firing from the bluffs of Vicksburg on a commercial steamboat that they believed was carrying U.S. troops.
>
> In observing the war's sesquicentennial, Virginia is taking pains to note that although Richmond succeeded Montgomery as the capital of the Confederacy, the state originally voted by a 2–1 ratio not to secede. Paul Levengood, president of the Virginia Historical Society, told the Richmond *Times-Dispatch* that the moment of secession should be recognized, but not celebrated.

> Commemorate, don't celebrate. I like that perspective for how the former Confederate states should observe the war's anniversary.[18]

Yes. Commemorate.

Ah, but "commemorating the Civil War has never been easy," Katharine Seelye aptly observed, quoting former Atlanta mayor Andrew Young: "We don't know what to commemorate because we've never faced up to the implications of what the thing was really about."[19]

Indeed, 14 states still annually commemorate the Civil War, eight of them officially, all of them honoring the Confederacy. In some states, the day is called Confederate Memorial Day; in Tennessee, Confederate Decoration Day; in Texas, Confederate Heroes Day.

True to their Confederate roots, each state or statewide organization that hosts a Confederate memorial day has chosen its own date for its own reasons. Of the eight states that officially observe such a day, Texas does so in January (with a second unofficial observance in April); Alabama, Florida, Georgia, and Mississippi, in April; North and South Carolina, in May; and Tennessee, in June.

The states with April dates do so to commemorate the second and final major surrender of the war. The first surrender, and the one history books most often equate with the war's end, was Lee's surrender to Grant, April 9, 1865. Seventeen days later, Confederate General Joe Johnston surrendered to Union General William Sherman near Greensboro, North Carolina.

The surrender to Sherman took place April 26. Even now, Florida and Georgia annually memorialize the Confederacy on that date. Texas does so unofficially. To commemorate the same event, Alabama observes the fourth Monday in April; Mississippi, the last Monday in April. Thus, only rarely do all four states (five, including Texas' unofficial observance) take place on April 26. Yet in 2011, April 26 fell on a Monday, so all five commemorations converged.

Indeed, a host of tributes to the Confederacy converged in April 2011, since that month also marked the 150th anniversary for the start of the Civil War.

The very fact that we're still celebrating the war and commemorating the Confederacy reveal that we truly have not "faced up to the implications of what the thing was really about." Ignoring those implications has created many other issues we haven't wanted to see, and we who are the most blinded are also the most in bondage as a result.

So why don't we do what we have not done? Why don't we, who most tend to gravitate to the word "celebrate" when talking of the Civil War, instead throw all caution to the wind—and *confess*?

Confess what? you ask. A lot, really. Specifics will unfold in the pages of this book. Confession requires vision. To *say* a thing, to declare from our hearts that it is true, we first have to *see* it. In the decades since the Civil War, Southerners and, in particular, Southern Christians have said a lot about who we are and what in the world our ancestors were doing. But we didn't so much confess as defend. All too often, we expressed, not grief, but pride.

"One old Confederate veteran put it colorfully on his tombstone," wrote Charles Reagan Wilson in *Baptized in Blood*: "An unreconstructed Johnnie, who never repented, who fought for what he knew to be right from '61 to '65 and received one Mexican dollar for two years' service. Belonged to the Ku Klux Klan, a deacon in the Baptist Church and a Master Mason for forty years."[20]

Even when we have tried to confess, it's seemed only to keep stirring up the hornets' nest. Our confessions have fallen short because we haven't seen what we needed to see in order to deal fully, deeply, and decisively with the underlying issues. We haven't seen because we felt it would be too painful to look, and we thought that doing so would only make matters worse. In our attempt to avoid further pain and trauma, we've instead prolonged and increased both. We've tiptoed around the hornets' nest, trying to pretend it's no longer there, instead of working together to remove it.

Trail of blood

Tiptoeing no more, let's face up to the Civil War's *bloodshed*. We might confess the needlessness of the bloodshed and the wrong responses generations of white Southerners have made to it—if, of course, we saw either or both to be true.

- *Needless bloodshed.* Everything positive that the Civil War accomplished, especially the freeing of slaves, should have been accomplished without war—and the church should have led the way in accomplishing it.
- *Wrong responses to bloodshed.* The chilling words of Ezekiel 35:6 make very clear that the right response to bloodshed is to hate it: "Therefore as surely as I live, declares the Sovereign Lord, I will give you over to bloodshed and it will pursue you. Since you did not hate bloodshed, bloodshed will pursue you."[21]

In a sin-riddled world, extreme measures are sometimes required to save lives and defend justice. We can honor and thank those who regularly put themselves in harm's way in order to protect a land and its people. Yet always, we must guard against needless bloodshed and the use of force for less-than-just purposes. And always, the righteous response to bloodshed is to hate it.

"Since you did not hate bloodshed, bloodshed will pursue you." With Ezekiel's strong warning in mind, picture a US map with the southeastern quadrant highlighted, and glimpse a stunning trail of blood that has plagued our own history.

1539–1542

Spanish explorer Hernando De Soto led the first European expedition through much of the region that eventually became the Confederacy, a region then peopled by different native tribes. Though already extremely wealthy and powerful, De Soto was obsessed with finding gold. He and his 600 men proudly identified themselves and their expedition as *Christian.* At the same time, they used trickery, brutality, extortion, enslavement, pillage, and bloodshed to get information, supplies, and safe passage from the tribes. De Soto's cruelty resulted in the deaths of thousands of Indians and about half his own men. De Soto himself died of fever on the east bank of the Mississippi River somewhere in modern-day Arkansas. Before his death, the man destroyed by his own obsession did not repent but rather proclaimed himself the sun god. After his death, De Soto's frightened followers took his wrapped and weighted body by night and threw it into the Mississippi.

1830–1858

In the first three decades of the 1800s, settlers poured into the region that would become the Deep South states. Many settlers and land speculators wanted the lands held by the "Five Civilized Tribes" of the region—Choctaws, Creeks, Chickasaws, Cherokees, and Seminoles. The tribes became "civilized" as they adopted various aspects of American culture in hopes of retaining their lands. At the same time, some tribal leaders violently defended what white encroachment threatened to take away. Settlers in the midst of a Second Great Awakening paid more attention to greed and fear than to God. They clamored for the young US government to get the Indians out. Thus, in 1830, President Andrew Jackson signed into law the Indian Removal Act. In theory, the act allowed tribes east of the Mississippi to relocate voluntarily to lands in modern-day Oklahoma and Kansas—lands considered uninhabitable by whites and conveniently named by them, Indian Territory. In reality, the country's first peoples relocated under duress. Tens of thousands died in forced marches westward or in fighting that arose when some would not move.

1861–1864

A South that proclaimed itself Christian and linked its identity to cotton refused to admit the wrong of slavery or to seek workable economic solutions that did not depend on slavery. Seceding states formed a Confederacy, deceived themselves as to why they were doing so, and chose to provoke war and to declare until the bitter end, "We will never yield." By the war's end, Americans had taken more than 600,000 American lives. In the aftermath, devastated Southern fathers and mothers could not admit that they had sacrificed their sons on the altar of needless bloodshed. Maintaining that the South, though defeated, was *right*, they built thousands of monuments glorifying the shed blood of the Confederate soldiers. Even today, some Southerners try to attach noble motives to the forming of the Confederacy and the resulting war. Even today, denial prompts us to justify and glorify the bloodshed, rather than hating it.

1619–1960s

Slavery came to the British colonies with a few Africans brought to Jamestown, Virginia, in 1619. By 1860, when US census figures counted nearly four million slaves, the states north of the Mason-Dixon line had abolished slavery; the southern states had not. No exact count exists as to the number of violent deaths attributable to the slavery system, but estimated numbers are staggering. In addition to the millions who died en route to slave owners in the US, many more succumbed to the brutality of the system, the brutal conditions under which many slaves worked, and the deadly revolts the system triggered.

After slavery was abolished in 1863, a new system of "Jim Crow" laws was implemented first in the South and later across much of the nation. These laws, designed to disfranchise African Americans and segregate them from whites, also gave silent assent to extra-legal means of keeping blacks "in their place." According to "The History of Jim Crow" website, "Violence against African Americans spread like an epidemic across the South until the 1930s, with the most extreme expressions of racism taking the form of lynchings and urban riots. During the Jim Crow era, the word lynching came to mean mob violence against African Americans, capital punishment without the sanction of law, ritualized torture, and explosive race riots that erupted in nearly every part of the country. More often than not the alleged crimes committed by lynching victims were trumped up and even imaginary."[22] More bloodshed accompanied the overturning of segregation in the 1960s, and much of the white church in the South fought against desegregation, instead of leading the battle for it.

1973–today

On the heels of the Civil Rights turmoil of the 1960s—and a century after the South began memorializing the Civil War from a less-than-honest perspective—the US legalized abortion. In the nearly 40 years since then, Americans have taken more than 52 million American lives. As in a Deep South opting for secession and war, millions of desperate mothers and fathers, who've convinced themselves there is no other solution, have sacrificed their own children on the altar of needless bloodshed. However, this time, the blood shed is not only needless, but also innocent.

From De Soto (thousands), to Indian Removal (tens of thousands), to Civil War (hundreds of thousands), to slavery and racial violence (millions), to abortion (tens of millions), we've tried to glorify, or at least to justify, the bloodshed in an attempt to convince ourselves it was not needless.

By doing so, have we not trapped ourselves in the place Ezekiel 35:7 describes? "Since you did not hate bloodshed, bloodshed will pursue you."

April 2011

Today, I sit in silence, deeply grieved over what I read. Tomorrow, I will celebrate, profoundly grateful for what God has promised.

As I draft this section of this chapter, it's May 2011. Last month and this, a series of disasters has plagued the South. In April, devastating droughts sparked wildfires in Texas and Oklahoma. Meanwhile, five severe weather outbreaks lashed the eastern half of the nation, breaking numerous records in terms of severity, destruction, and deaths. In the words of newscasters themselves, the month's storms took the heaviest toll in "Dixie." On the heels of the storms came the Great Flood of 2011. The Mississippi River overflowed its banks from Illinois to the Gulf Coast, nearing and topping 100-year flood levels and causing billions of dollars of damage, most of it in the Deep South.

Of these disasters, the tornadoes produced by far the greatest loss of life. A record-breaking 751 tornadoes occurred in April alone—209 tornadoes more than the previous monthly record, set in May 2003. The two storm systems that primarily hit the Midwest caused great destruction, but no fatalities. Conversely, the three storm systems that plowed through the Deep South resulted in escalating numbers of casualties. April 4–5, nine people died; April 14–16, 43 died; April 25–28, about 340 died.

The April deaths from tornadoes or straight-line winds took place in these states (from greatest to least number of fatalities): Alabama, Mississippi, Tennessee, Georgia, North Carolina, Arkansas, Virginia, Oklahoma, Louisiana, and Kentucky.

The month's last storm system, occurring April 25–28, spawned one of the worst tornado outbreaks in US history. April 27, 2011, became the single deadliest tornado day in the nation since 1925.

Can it be coincidence that April 2011 launched four years of celebrations of Civil War bloodshed? Can it be coincidence that, in the 150th anniversary month, the deadliest tornado day in generations left a staggering death toll across the Deep South, but especially in Alabama, Mississippi, and Georgia—*the day after* those three states and two others commemorated Confederate Memorial Day? Can it be coincidence that *all* the month's storm-related deaths took place in former slave states or territories and the vast majority of them in states that still officially commemorate the Confederacy?

Can it be coincidence? Or might we be reaping consequences of not hating bloodshed? Might the Lord himself be shouting, warning, that we as a region, as a nation—and more specifically, as the church in both—must address an issue we haven't even considered, and certainly haven't considered as pertaining to us?

God knows what we have not: There is no statute of limitations on bloodshed. Unresolved, undealt-with bloodshed produces bloodguilt not yet cleansed.

Persons and cultures

To see what God is showing us, we must understand: The Lord deals with *individuals*, and he deals with *peoples*. Scripture teaches that the God who created us knows us by name. He wants each of us, personally, to know him. The New Testament makes clear that a person's eternal destiny depends solely on salvation by grace through faith in the Lord Jesus Christ. And yet, all of Scripture, all history, and the clear voice of the Spirit of God cry out that, in this world, the Lord acts in regard to whole groups of people, as well as individuals. He blesses and curses, raises up and puts down, reproves and corrects persons. He moves in similar ways in regard to whole cultures. He does so, not by whim or caprice, but in righteousness, holiness, and love. Further, this Creator-Redeemer God is great, wise, and loving enough to deal justly with an entire culture and, at the same time, deal justly with every individual in it.

In Romans 11, the apostle Paul spoke in terms of two very broad groups, Jews and Gentiles. Addressing a group of Gentile believers, he wrote, "You will say then, 'Branches were broken off so that I could be grafted in.' Granted. But they [Jews] were broken off because of unbelief, and you [Gentiles] stand by faith" (vv. 19–20). Did Paul mean that all Jews had forfeited salvation through Christ? Not at all. Paul himself was Jewish. So were all the original apostles and most of the first believers. Today, the Messianic Jewish community is growing. But as a whole, as a culture, the Jewish people have not yet embraced Christ. Did Paul mean that all Gentiles are saved? Obviously not. Yet over the centuries, spiritual awakenings have swept through many non-Jewish cultures as people en masse received the Lord Jesus Christ by faith.

Paul then addressed non-Jewish people groups who had embraced Christ: "Do not be haughty, but fear. For if God did not spare the natural branches, He may not spare you either. Therefore consider the goodness and severity of God: on those who fell, severity; but toward you, goodness, if you continue in His goodness. Otherwise you also will be cut off" (Rom. 11:20–22 NKJV).

What a strong warning! The New Testament includes it, not because God is a bully, but rather just the opposite. The Lord does not want to have to exercise severity toward *any* person or group. He especially doesn't want a culture that's known and embraced him to turn away from him. Remember: He can and does show his goodness to *individuals* within a *culture* that has provoked his severity. But as with Esther, he doesn't want us to hide out in that place of favor, confident he'll save *us* while the world goes to hell around us. He wants individuals to receive his goodness and to so cooperate with him that whole groups do likewise.

In the US, where we're consummately proud of our individualism, God has to do some profound renewing of our minds to get us to see: In this life, every person lives and moves inside a culture, or a composite of several cultures. The collective choices of a culture dramatically affect the lives of the persons in it. Further, the collective choices of a culture dramatically affect the generations that come after. But also the choices of the individuals within a culture can dramatically affect the course of the whole culture. The choices of one person can impact a family line for generations to come. And any generation, no matter how negatively impacted by wrong choices of previous generations, can rise up to turn the tide.

The path of your life, the influence you wield (for good or bad), and the legacy you leave to future generations depend in large measure on the collective choices of your forebears and of the people among whom you live—*and on the ways you respond to those choices.*

You may want to believe undealt-with issues of previous generations have nothing to do with you. You may want to believe that bloodguilt, in particular, is an Old Testament matter, irrelevant to the Christian of today. Yet God is revealing massive evidence to the contrary. He's uncovering a trail of blood incredibly long and deep. To be free, you need to see: The blood still crying out from the ground impacts your life and family today in ways you have not dreamed.

Bloodguilt

Both old and new testaments teach the concept of *bloodguilt*, a particularly grave type of guilt we can knowingly or unknowingly bring on ourselves. Tragically, whole peoples and nations can invite bloodguilt, and one person or group can bring bloodguilt on the generations that come after. A certain type of bloodguilt can decide a person's eternity. All bloodguilt wreaks destruction in lives, nations, and generations.

John Wesley, who with his brother Charles founded the Methodist movement, spoke passionately of the bloodguilt associated with slavery: "The blood of thy brother crieth against thee from the earth: oh, whatever it costs, put a stop to its cry before it is too late—instantly, at any price, were it the half of thy goods, deliver thyself from blood guiltiness. Thy hands, thy bed, thy furniture, thy house and thy lands, at present are stained with blood. Surely it is enough—accumulate no more guilt, spill no more blood of the innocent. Whether thou art a Christian or not, show thyself A MAN."[23]

Scripture names specific sins that produce bloodguilt. As you might imagine, most of those sins have to do with wrongfully shedding blood. Shedding of innocent blood produces bloodguilt (Deut. 19:10). So does needless bloodshed.

In 1 Samuel 25, a foolish man named Nabal railed against David, even though David and his followers had been kind to Nabal. Uncharacteristically, David vowed to kill Nabal and every one of his men before nightfall. Nabal's wife Abigail interceded, urging David not to take such rash action so he would "not have on his conscience the staggering burden of needless bloodshed" (1 Sam. 25:31).

David responded, "Blessed be the LORD, the God of Israel, who sent you to meet me today! Blessed be your good sense, and blessed be you, who have kept me today from bloodguilt and from avenging myself by my own hand!" (vv. 32–33 NRSV).

Nabal's men were innocent. They hadn't participated in or agreed with Nabal's actions. Nabal did wrong, yet to kill Nabal for humiliating David's men would have been sin. So God used Abigail to protect David both from shedding innocent blood and from needless bloodshed.

Deuteronomy 22:8 speaks of the bloodguilt homeowners could unintentionally bring on themselves by not building a parapet, or low wall, around the edge of a flat roof. The Amplified rendering of Ezekiel 7:23 decries those who shed blood intentionally, thinking they can use the justice system to cover their tracks: "the land is full of bloodguiltiness [murders committed with pretended formalities of justice]."

In Matthew 23:34–35, Jesus spoke of the incredible bloodguilt that would accrue to people who kill and persecute those sent out with the gospel: "Therefore, behold, I am sending you prophets and wise men and scribes; some of them you will kill and crucify, and some of them you will scourge in your synagogues, and persecute from city to city, so that upon you may fall the guilt of all the righteous blood shed on earth, from the blood of righteous Abel to the blood of Zechariah, the son of Berechiah, whom you murdered between the temple and the altar" (NASU).

Shortly after Jesus spoke those words, as a crowd fomented by religious leaders pressed for his crucifixion, Pilate cried, "I am innocent of this man's blood." "All the people answered, 'His blood is on us and on our children!'" (Matt. 27:24–25).

Such statements as, "His blood be on us," and, "Your blood will be on your own head," are pronouncements of bloodguilt. The people who called for Jesus' crucifixion, by their own words, accepted a staggering burden of bloodguilt on themselves and their generations. Meanwhile, Pilate proclaimed himself innocent of the blood of Jesus—as he released Jesus to be crucified.

Pilate tried to sidestep bloodguilt, but he did not. His words couldn't negate his choices. Conversely, when someone says, "Your blood be on your head," those words don't necessarily make it so. Bloodguilt only accrues where the choices have been made that invited it.

Shedding of innocent blood, shedding blood needlessly, and *not hating bloodshed* all bring bloodguilt. So do certain sins that wreak havoc in a person's *bloodline.* The most surprising of these sins, to our thinking, is identified in Leviticus 20:9: "If there is anyone who curses his father or his mother ... his bloodguiltiness is upon him" (NASU).

Cuss words produce bloodguilt? Not exactly. In Scripture, curses aren't just foul language. They are pronouncements of evil that can bring severe consequences, impacting generations. God knows parents can do terrible things to their children. He will not overlook those wrongs or fail to deal with them properly. But to curse your parents will not right the wrongs they have done. Quite the opposite. To curse your parents is to aim a gun at yourself and your progeny, calling down upon all your heads whatever evil you pronounce against your mom and dad. Thus, *cursing parents* produces bloodguilt.

According to Leviticus 20, acts of *sexual immorality* also produce bloodguilt. These include homosexuality and bestiality, but also incest and adultery.

Yet, of all the sins that cause bloodguilt, the ones God considers most heinous are *sins against the blood by which we're atoned.* Here, we might sigh with relief, assuming only people who reject the redemptive sacrifice of Jesus Christ accrue such bloodguilt. We might think Christians exempt. But that's not true.

God's people—old testament and new—become his people by choosing to enter blood covenant with him.

In the Old Testament, God's people could bring bloodguilt upon themselves by slaughtering any of the animals used for his holy sacrifices, rather than bringing those animals to the priests. Whether the person slaughtered the animal in order to offer it to another god, or whether he simply wanted for himself the part of the animal God had designated for the priests, he sinned against the blood that covered his guilt and sin.

In the New Testament, Jesus himself became our sacrifice. Once we identify ourselves with him and with the covenant made on the basis of his shed blood, anything we embrace that devalues or competes with that covenant produces bloodguilt.

In 1 Corinthians, Paul wrote, "Is not the cup of thanksgiving for which we give thanks a participation in the blood of Christ? And is not the bread that we break a participation in the body of Christ? ... So then, whoever eats the bread or drinks the cup of the Lord in an unworthy manner *will be guilty of sinning against the body and blood of the Lord*" (10:16; 11:27).[24]

Hebrews 10 speaks at length of the sufficiency of the blood sacrifice of Jesus and of the new covenant we enter by his blood. Yet the same chapter contains one of the strongest warnings of Scripture, directed to those "who have trampled the Son of God underfoot, who have treated as an unholy thing the blood of the covenant that sanctified them, and who have insulted the Spirit of grace." Lest we think the warning applies solely to those who reject Christ, consider: Do Christians ever insult the Spirit of grace? Also notice: Christ's covenant sanctifies those who receive it (not those who reject it)—and the Hebrews writer speaks specifically of those who have "treated as an unholy thing the blood of the covenant *that sanctified them*." Further, the Scripture adds: "The Lord will judge *his people*" (vv. 29, 30).

We'd like to ignore those strong words or to explain them away. But they were written to warn us—to stand in our path and halt us—so that we might not continue to reap the deadly consequences of bloodguilt.

Promise of cleansing

Tornadoes happen when two strong fronts collide, when a violent wind that's blown unhindered from one direction meets a new, powerful wind blowing the opposite way. That's true physically, and it's true spiritually. The Spirit of grace prefers to blow gently. He woos with great tenderness and patience. Yet when he sees that we've set our sails to catch a contrary wind, and now are being driven relentlessly before it, he will blow as hard as it takes to stop us in our tracks.

Once he's gotten our attention, he makes clear what it will take for us to go the other way. Not only does he show us how to reverse course, he provides the wind for us to do it.

Today, I grieve over the destruction that hit just as the South again began "celebrating" and wrongly "commemorating" the Civil War. Yet I celebrate this promise that the God of covenant love holds out to us: "I will cleanse them of bloodguilt which I have not yet cleansed" (Joel 3:21 CJB).

What a promise! What a God! He confronts our wrong courses in order to deliver us. He exposes our bloodguilt in order to cleanse us.

That cleansing *frees*. It frees us. It frees those we love and those we've hated. It frees generations not yet born. It breaks cycles of immorality and bloodshed that past generations never escaped. It washes away blame, shame, and despair. That cleansing *heals*. It heals relationships. It heals lives. It eradicates the three biggest causes of disease: bitterness, rejection, and fear. That cleansing *blesses*. It breathes life into dry bones. It radically transforms our desires and attitudes. Where before, curses and death pursued us, now goodness and love chase us down.

God's promise of healing, freeing, life-giving cleansing is ours for the taking.

But laying hold of the promise begins with confessing the deeply soiled areas that need to be cleansed.

It's incredibly hard for good people to admit to grievous sins. It's rather easier for the ax murderer to confess than for the upstanding citizen to do so. But King David shows us: It can be done.

David was the most upstanding of kings. By God's own admission, David was a man after God's own heart. Yet even David at times greatly dishonored and misrepresented God. During one season in his life, David committed grievous sins—sins that included adultery and the shedding of innocent blood. When confronted, he confessed. He confessed privately to God. More amazing, David confessed publicly. He acknowledged his bloodguilt. He allowed the story of his wrongdoing to be written, and he himself wrote several songs of confession—all of which we can still read in our Bibles today.

One of David's songs, Psalm 51, makes clear the connection between confession and *cleansing*. The biblical introduction to the psalm (not one added later by translators, but one included with the Hebrew manuscripts) identifies the sin: "For the choir director: A psalm of David, regarding the time Nathan the prophet came to him after David had committed adultery with Bathsheba."

This astounding song of confession follows:

> Have mercy on me, O God,
> because of your unfailing love.
> Because of your great compassion,
> blot out the stain of my sins.
> Wash me clean from my guilt.
> Purify me from my sin.
> For I recognize my rebellion;
> it haunts me day and night.
> Against you, and you alone, have I sinned;
> I have done what is evil in your sight.
> You will be proved right in what you say,
> and your judgment against me is just.
> For I was born a sinner—
> yes, from the moment my mother conceived me.
> But you desire honesty from the womb,
> teaching me wisdom even there.
> Purify me from my sins, and I will be clean;
> wash me, and I will be whiter than snow.
> Oh, give me back my joy again;
> you have broken me—
> now let me rejoice.
> Don't keep looking at my sins.
> Remove the stain of my guilt.
> Create in me a clean heart, O God.
> Renew a loyal spirit within me.
> Do not banish me from your presence,
> and don't take your Holy Spirit from me.
> Restore to me the joy of your salvation,
> and make me willing to obey you.
> Then I will teach your ways to rebels,
> and they will return to you.
> Forgive me for shedding blood, O God who saves;
> then I will joyfully sing of your forgiveness.
> Unseal my lips, O Lord,
> that my mouth may praise you. (Ps. 51:1–15 NLT)

It's in confessing the truth, no longer denying or defending our actions, that we're set free: "Then your conscience won't have to bear the staggering burden of needless bloodshed and vengeance" (1 Sam. 25:31 NLT).

Go and celebrate

The Israelites of Ezra's day show us the connection between confession and *celebration*. Having returned from decades in exile, having rebuilt the Jerusalem wall, the people gathered to hear the reading of the "Book of God's Teachings." Ezra the priest and other teachers read "clearly and explained the meaning so that the people could understand what was read" (Neh. 8:8 *GOD'S WORD*).

As the people listened, they saw, for the first time in their lives, the extent to which they and their ancestors had missed and misrepresented their God. In response, all the people wept. Astoundingly, they didn't close their ears or cry for the teachers to stop speaking. Because of wrong choices made by generations before them, their nation had been decimated by war. The people had lived for decades in exile. Now, as the returned exiles began to hear the truth, they pressed in to hear it all.

Twenty-three days later, they gathered to confess. First, they confessed who God is: "Blessed be your glorious name, and may it be exalted above all blessing and praise. You alone are the Lord. You made the heavens, even the highest heavens, and all their starry host, the earth and all that is on it, the seas and all that is in them. You give life to everything, and the multitudes of heaven worship you" (Neh. 9:5–6).

They confessed all the ways God had proven his love and faithfulness to them and to the generations before them, all the ways he had made known his character through his amazing acts.

They confessed the ways their ancestors had responded to God's goodness—and the ways the Lord had in turn responded to them: "But they, our ancestors, became arrogant and stiff-necked, and did not obey your commands. They refused to listen … But you are a forgiving God, gracious and compassionate, slow to anger and abounding in love. Therefore you did not desert them" (Neh. 9:16–17). Even when the people created and worshiped another god, "Because of your great compassion you did not abandon them … You gave your good Spirit to instruct them … you sustained them" (Neh. 9:19–21).

The Israelites of Ezra's day confessed the bondage and distress that their ancestors' stubbornness and their own unrepentant hearts had ultimately brought on them. And they re-covenanted to be the people of God in truth.

But even before they confessed and covenanted, they celebrated. From the moment the people saw who God intended them to be and what they had lost due to sin, their leaders urged them, "Go and celebrate … This is a sacred day before our Lord. Don't be dejected and sad, for the joy of the Lord is your strength!" (Neh. 8:10 NLT).

It was indeed a sacred day. Now that they saw what they did not want to see, they could confess and be cleansed. They could become who God had made them to be.

Promises to keep

Believe me, I know all the reasons why confessing may sound like a lousy idea. But I'll tell you from hard-earned experience: Not confessing is a far, far lousier one.

I also know from experience: You cannot confess what you don't see. That's why, in our day, God is graciously removing the veil. He's showing his people the extent to which we've missed and misrepresented him. Regardless what region we're from, regardless what color our skin, he wants to lift from our shoulders staggering burdens that generations have needlessly carried. He wants goodness, not bloodshed, to pursue us. He wants the forgiveness, cleansing, and restoration that he is holding out to overflow within us and to rise like a river among us, sweeping us all up in its strong, true flow.

The God of covenant love has promises to keep, and this is one: "I will cleanse them of bloodguilt which I have not yet cleansed." He waits and watches for us to see what he is showing us and to press in to hear it all.

As we listen, as we see, we'll give ourselves permission to weep—to finish the grieving aborted so long ago. Paradoxically, we'll celebrate—together, freely, with great joy.

Then, refusing to deny or blame any longer, we will confess.

2—Song of Deliverance

When God reveals our past, he always does so redemptively. Seeing today in light of yesterday, we discover how to open a doorway to tomorrow that has been locked and blocked.

My Beloved, you are not acting like yourself. You're not reflecting who I am because you don't know who you are. Because I love you, I will release you from all that's kept you from becoming who I made you to be.

Sometimes, God delivers you by showing you what you've aligned with.

That's what he did for me.

He took me inside a structure that identifies itself with Jesus Christ, a structure to which I'd been attached all my life. For five-and-a-half years within that structure, I did what my Lord and my leaders instructed. I watched others within the structure seek to serve the Lord. I saw what hindered, what divided, what oppressed, what manipulated them and me.

Yet I still could not see how bound we all were.

Then the enemy said, "To hell with appearances." Flagrant evil leapt out of the closet and blatantly exposed itself. During the months that followed—excruciating months that seemed to stretch forever—God began to open my eyes.

Duplicity I had not recognized became stunningly clear: What purports to promote allegiance to Jesus Christ in fact cultivates a different allegiance altogether. What espouses godliness produces quite the opposite. What loudly declares, "Follow Jesus at all costs," fears most those who do.

In my position within the structure, I urged women to follow Christ fully. I taught the women in the churches to seek *God* as to how they should organize, to seek *him* and follow *him* every step of the way. I did not challenge any accepted doctrines. I urged the women to respect and submit to their leaders' authority.

Even before I taught such—even in places where no one had heard me teach—God was leading women to organize in new ways, to create new wineskins to hold the new wine he was pouring out. Yet something deep and tenacious fought against it. Something shadowy but incredibly strong hindered those trying to go with God. People were laying aside old wineskins—and then, in a sense, reinventing them. Genuine Christ-followers struggled with surprisingly little success to form something truly fresh, supple, and filled to overflowing with God's life.

Meanwhile, leaders of one organization felt threatened because so many churches, so many groups, were abandoning the traditional organizational structures. Perhaps because I was the most visible person giving women "permission" to make such changes, these leaders launched a no-holds-barred assault against me.

The business world has a word for a targeted, repeated, prolonged assault intended to force someone out: *mobbing*. Think "lynch mob"—then substitute an escalating pattern of verbal and emotional abuse for the noose.

In typical mob fashion, the assault against me was instigated by a few and gained momentum, as more and more people actively participated or simply agreed to look the other way. Most who joined the crowd heard the cry for blood without having the slightest clue what I was supposed to have done. Most who participated, actively or passively, did so in order to protect or promote themselves. If they hesitated, if they dissented, what would happen to *their* place in the system? Might the mob turn on *them*? If they cooperated fully—albeit discreetly—might not their status rise?

In the face of such brutal assault, the Lord Jesus has done astounding things. He has guarded me against bitterness. He has overwhelmed me with grace to forgive and to love. And he used what literally could have killed me to catapult me to a place of life and freedom I had never known.

As I catapulted to this new place, the Lord gave me two assignments:

- *Look around* to see what's going on in the church, particularly the conservative American church culture, both evangelical and charismatic.
- *Look back* to find the roots of what is happening today.

For six years, the Lord took me through a deep and profound healing process. At the same time, he guided me step by step to carry out these two assignments.

From the start, I knew the trauma I'd experienced wasn't a single, aberrant occurrence. Even seeing through a glass darkly, I recognized an abusive pattern. Further, what I'd encountered could not be attributed simply to Christian people being human. The source was intentionally, brutally malevolent. It had astounding authority within a Christian context to operate unhindered.

Still, until I looked where the Lord said look, I did not have a clue how pervasive are the things that oppress, divide, and manipulate the Body of Christ—especially that part of the US church that prides itself on its commitment to Jesus and his Word.

Surveying the present, I saw how strong loyalties enmesh with our commitment to Christ—then usurp his place in our lives. Surveying the past, I realized how choices of the Southern church culture in the years leading up to and immediately following the Civil War profoundly affect the US church today.

Now, it's time to tell what I've seen.

What's a church culture?

Throughout this chapter and this book, statements about the "Southern church" and the "Southern church culture" reflect the consensus—the prevailing attitudes, beliefs, and behaviors—of the white-dominated church-going people of the Deep South. Let me be clear: Even when, for brevity, I use the term "Southern church," I'm not describing the true *ecclesia* in the region, but rather the collective choices of all who identify themselves with the church.

Among any group of church-goers, some truly know the Lord; some do not. Some who know him pursue him with all their hearts; some do not. Yet when, for example, the church-goers of the South collectively think and act like a *culture*, demonstrating shared beliefs and behaviors, they have become a "church culture."

We might assume that all the beliefs and behaviors of any given church culture would reflect those of every other church culture and of Christ himself. Yet, that's not the case. The church in any society is influenced by a number of factors, and most notably by the society itself. When examining the history of the church in the South, we can find individuals and even groups in every generation who have believed and behaved very differently from the norm. That's precisely the point. Those persons have acted *counter*-culturally, not only to the society at large, but also to their church culture.

Now, our Lord is revealing a tangled mass of ways that we in this church culture have not followed Christ fully and have not represented him well. What God is uncovering focuses first on the white Southern church because we have led the way into wrongdoing. In so doing, we've deeply hurt "us," and we've gravely wounded whole groups of people we've chosen to label, "them." Most of all, we've defamed our Lord. That's bad news—news we don't want to hear. But here's the good news: Wonderful, healing, life-giving things will happen as we receive what God is revealing and stand together to confess.

Oddly enough, the black church in the South and the conservative church culture beyond the South mirror the white Southern church in many ways. Often, the resemblance results from bitterness, which has itself sprung from woundedness. When nurtured and not uprooted, bitterness teaches us to hate. At the same time, it opens us to become what we hate. As we indulge bitterness, our beliefs, thoughts, and behaviors begin to mirror what so wounded us.

So we all stand before God with no room to point fingers. We all stand before God, desperately needing to see what he's revealing, desperately needing to grieve, to forgive, to confess, to repent. For, wonder of wonders, that narrow way leads us out into a spacious and lovely place.

What we fear will undo us

Ah, I see those raised hands. You're asking questions I've asked myself.

Won't digging up the past just reopen old wounds? Don't we need to let sleeping dogs lie? Aren't we supposed to forget what lies behind and press on toward the future? Haven't we repented enough?

And if some things ***are*** *out of kilter in the church today, doesn't calling attention to them hurt the cause of Christ? By airing our dirty laundry, don't we become accusers of the brethren? In a society already contemptuous of Christianity, don't we call down more contempt on ourselves? Aren't we supposed to focus instead on the positive aspects of the church? Besides, don't our sins pale in comparison with the wickedness around us?*

Personally, I'd like to take each of those very legitimate questions and answer them, one by one. But when I try, I find myself writing in circles.

The Lord will address our questions in his time and his way. But he will not begin there.

Rather, he begins with a true story, followed by a song to his Bride.

The story unfolds through a chapter in Donald Miller's book, *Blue Like Jazz*. In the chapter, titled, "Confession: Coming Out of the Closet," Miller tells of auditing a class on a college campus with a very small Christian population and a very hostile attitude toward Christianity. One weekend each year, the college held a festival so students, says Miller, could party, get naked, and get high.

One year during the festival weekend, Miller joined a handful of Christian students in setting up a confessional booth in the middle of campus. As intrigued students showed up at the booth, they saw a monk-robed fellow student sitting inside. When they sat to begin confessing their sins, they were told: "No, *I'm* going to confess to you."

The Christian students had decided ahead of time: "We are not actually going to accept confessions … We are going to confess to them. We are going to confess that, as followers of Jesus, we have not been very loving; we have been bitter, and for that we are sorry. We will apologize for the Crusades, we will apologize for televangelists, we will apologize for neglecting the poor and the lonely, we will ask them to forgive us, and we will tell them that in our selfishness, we have misrepresented Jesus on this campus. We will tell people who come into the booth that Jesus loves them."[25]

Miller reported, "Many people wanted to hug when we were done. All of the people who visited the booth were grateful and gracious. I was being changed through the process. I went in with doubts and came out believing so strongly in Jesus I was ready to die and be with Him. I think that night was the beginning of change for a lot of us."[26] Further, that night marked the beginning of a new openness to Christ on that campus.

We fear confession will undo us. Actually, it will renew us, and will draw people to our Lord.

And now, the song. The Lord sings to you personally, even as he sings to us collectively. He speaks Spirit to spirit—his Spirit addressing our inmost being, our true identity, our human spirit. To our eyes and our rational mind, the words don't look like a song. Still, your Lord sings to you.

My Beloved, you are not acting like yourself. You're not reflecting who I am because you don't know who you are.

You have my Word; you have my Spirit living in you, to show you who I am and who you are. Yet try as you might, you cannot see clearly; you cannot step fully into all I have for you. Binding entanglements keep you from it. Generational bloodguilt keeps you from fully knowing me.

Come to me. Lay aside denial and offense. Stop being ruled and misled, beaten up and torn apart by logic and emotion. Much of what you think and feel is rooted in who you are ***not****—but have mistakenly believed you are. Come to me. Press in to me, even when it doesn't make sense, when it doesn't feel good. Press in to me, past confusion and pain. I will show you myself. I'll show you who you are in me. I'll reveal what holds you down, what holds you back. And because I love you, I will release you from all that's kept you from becoming who I made you to be.*

I come to you

Is something deep within you responding to God's song? You don't fully understand what he means, but the inmost *you* is stirring, tugging you toward *him*. If so, say it aloud. Even better, throw all caution to the wind, and sing it. Regardless the current state of your relationship with the Lord—how rich or sporadic, how neglected or absent—tell him, "I come to you."

Be forewarned: *Pride* will grab you by one arm and *fear* by the other, to wrestle you down and throw you back. For two centuries, pride and fear have held much of our church culture in a vise. Even if these strongholds usually don't oppress you, expect both to move against you as you pursue the truth about who we are and what we've aligned with.

At the same time, remember: The Lord Jesus Christ has all authority, all power. He is calling you to come, and he will make the way for you to do it.

Cooperate with him. If you sense any defensiveness or smugness, denial or fear rising up within you, acknowledge these attitudes—call them what they are. Then, renounce them, turn from them, and in the name of the Lord Jesus Christ tell them to *go*. If any of these attitudes stubbornly cling to you, don't be deterred. Fix your eyes on Jesus, listen for his voice, and whatever he tells you, do it. He will lead you to freedom. He will draw you to himself.

Don't confuse process with failure. Coming to him is a process. Moving into freedom is a process.

Sometimes in process, it looks like you're going nowhere. Sometimes in process, it looks like you're going backward. Yet behind the scenes, God is putting things into place to move you forward faster and farther than you ever dreamed possible. Regardless what things look like, believe him and lean into him.

Let my people go

When God sent Moses to Egypt to set the Israelites free, Moses told Pharaoh, "This is what the Lord says: Let my people go, so that they may worship me" (Ex. 8:1).[27] Not only did Pharaoh refuse, he also made the Israelites' bondage harder.

At first, Moses wanted to throw up his hands. He cried out, "Why, Lord, why have you brought trouble on this people? Is this why you sent me? Ever since I went to Pharaoh to speak in your name, he has brought trouble on this people, and you have not rescued your people at all" (Ex. 5:22–23).

In response, three times the Lord spoke his covenant Name, the Name no one today knows how to pronounce, the Name that appears in most English translations as "Lord" in all caps. This Lord declared emphatically who he is and what he would do for Israel: "*I am the Lord,* and I will bring you out from under the yoke of the Egyptians. I will free you from being slaves to them, and I will redeem you with an outstretched arm and with mighty acts of judgment. I will take you as my own people, and I will be your God. Then you will know that *I am the Lord* your God, who brought you out from under the yoke of the Egyptians. And I will bring you to the land I swore with uplifted hand to give to Abraham, to Isaac and to Jacob. I will give it to you as a possession. *I am the Lord*" (Ex. 6:6–8).

When Moses repeated what God had said, Pharaoh laughed. The Israelites didn't believe. Yet, against all odds, Moses kept pressing in. He took God at his word. He kept declaring God's command, "Let my people go." With plague after plague, the Lord loosened Pharaoh's grip until, ultimately, Pharaoh had to let go.

For two centuries, pride and fear have held our church culture back from seeing and becoming who we are. Pride delights in a distorted image. It shows us everyone else's sin—and refuses to see our own. It does not build us up according to truth, but instead puffs us up with empty flattery. It looks down its nose at humility—yet can make itself appear quite humble. Fear delights in quenching faith. Fear wears numerous respectable disguises. For example, it can disguise itself as submission to authority or as zeal to defend God. Whatever the pretense, fear keeps us from facing the truth, speaking the truth, daring to trust, to obey, or to change. When we give in to fear or pride, we dishonor the Lord, hinder the flow of his grace—and act out of who we are not.

In Moses' day, the most powerful ruler on earth had every confidence that he could keep an enslaved people enslaved. In our day, the principalities and powers that have held captive a significant segment of the Bride of Christ are equally convinced they will keep her where she is.

Yet God commands, "Let my people go, so that they may worship me!" He has come down to deliver, and he is seeking those who will press in with him as he accomplishes it.

For now, will you take one tiny, but profound, step? Ask the Lord to pour out a spirit of grace and supplication on *you*. Ask him to pour out a spirit of grace and supplication on *us*, his people. Ask in faith. Thank him that he will do it.

Raise your voice like a shofar!

You may have already noticed: This book sounds a *shofar* blast to the people of God.

The shofar, or ram's horn, is the one instrument that doesn't fit with any others. Hard to blow and extremely hard to blow well, the shofar creates a sound that is compelling, but neither beautiful nor soothing. Indeed, no sound grates like a poorly blown shofar, and no sound pierces like a shofar blown with the authority of the Lord. The blast seems to bypass your ears and shoot straight into your gut, reverberating there until your entire inner being rattles. As the blast continues, the jarring sound forcibly, profoundly grips you until you don't know whether to cry for mercy or to cry for more.

The shofar offends your ears to awaken your spirit. It sounds a compelling Spirit-to-spirit call. The shofar never lulls you to sleep. It always summons you to action. In Scripture, different types of shofar blasts call for different responses. Rightly responding requires both a clear call and ears to hear.

We Confess! was not written to give you more head knowledge about history or about the church today. It was written at the command of the Lord: "Shout out loud! Don't hold back! Raise your voice like a *shofar*!" (Isa. 58:1 CJB). It was written to catapult you—spirit, soul, and body—into a new place of freedom in Christ. It was written to free the Bride of Christ to become who she is.

Read it as one hearing and responding to the sound of a shofar.

When you hear the sound of the shofar

Our Lord speaks to us, Spirit to spirit. He communicates by his Spirit into our innermost being, our human spirit. When we first receive in our spirit what he is saying, we may not have words to express it; we may not be able to wrap our emotions around it. In our loud, fast-paced world, we may even ignore and bypass God's quiet deposit to our spirit. But as we wait on the Lord, opening ourselves to him, seeking his face, what first entered our *spirit* wells up into our *soul* and *body*, informing and impacting our thoughts and emotions, our words and actions. Responding in trust and obedience, we follow the Lord fully.

Even as Christians, however, our soul and body can rebel, acting independently of our human spirit and quenching the Spirit of God. At that point, we may know what God is revealing but choose to reject it. Either way—whether we neglect the Spirit's voice or reject what he has said—we come to wrong conclusions. We indulge lying emotions. We speak and act in ways that do not reflect who we are in Christ.

As you read this book, stay in sync—spirit, soul, and body—with the Spirit of God.

If something hits your spirit, pause. Don't just read past it. Notice. What was it that grabbed you, that struck a chord or created a dissonance in you? Even if you can't explain the significance of what you read or why it hit you, hold on to it. Make a note of it. Ponder it. Ask God to give you more light and watch expectantly for him to answer, even as you keep reading or put the book aside and do other things.

As you read, pay attention to your *thoughts*. Some will be from the Lord; some will not. Do not let your thoughts silence your spirit; instead, let the Spirit discern your thoughts. If you find yourself trying to justify or accuse ("It wasn't our fault; it was theirs"), notice and reject that defensiveness. Whenever your thoughts interrupt the flow of reading, notice what you're thinking and what those thoughts are hindering you from seeing. Pray for discernment and respond to whatever God reveals.

For example, if your find yourself mentally reviewing your to-do list, it may be time to put the book down and do something else. Or it may mean that something you read has hit uncomfortably close to home, and your thoughts are taking you a different direction in order to avoid dealing with the very matter God wants to expose. Or your wandering thoughts may spring from an entirely different source. If you ask and truly want to know, God will give you discernment as to where your thoughts originated and what you need to do in response.

As you read, notice your *emotions* and, again, let the Spirit discern them. If you feel anger, grief, or any strong emotion, ask the Lord, "Where is that coming from?" As he identifies the source, ask him, "What do I do with this?" He will tell you what you need to express appropriately, what you need to turn from, what you need to forgive, what you need to leave at his feet.

As soon as you know that God is calling for a certain response, do it—even if you don't understand why, even if you don't feel like it. Acting on one thing God has revealed opens the way for him to reveal the next thing. Failure to act shuts off further revelation.

As you read, you will encounter much that astounds you, much that you wish weren't true, much that you'd rather not know. Some of it may deeply offend you. In fact, you may have already read things that offended you. My purpose is not to create offense. My purpose is to speak the truth in love. That involves revealing some things we've done for generations that deeply offend God.

Truth alert: The enemy loves to use *offense* to keep us from seeing, admitting and turning from our *offenses*. God brings a sin to our attention. Becoming offended, we get defensive. Instead of confessing and repenting, we excuse, blame, and angrily stomp off.

This time, make the enemy's scheme backfire! First, thank the Lord Jesus for what he has done for us: Because of the offense of the cross, our offenses no longer define us and do not have to continue to rule us!

Then, as you read, notice if you begin to feel offended and ask God to pinpoint what specifically is provoking it. Give the Lord permission to steer you past the deception that will try to misdirect you as to the source. Thank the Lord that his shofar blasts offend your mind and emotions in order to awaken your spirit. For Christ's sake, choose to release the offense. Go one step further and ask the Lord, "See if there is any offensive way in me, and lead me in the way everlasting" (Ps. 139:24).

Afterward, be still and notice what God speaks into your spirit. Receive whatever he says. If he's silent, receive that too. In so doing, you show both humility and courage. You call the enemy's bluff, and you position yourself to walk free from strongholds to which offense and defensiveness have lashed generations.

At times as you read, you may feel overwhelmed. If that happens, stop. Sit still before the Lord. Let him minister to you, Spirit to spirit. Let him guide you as to what to do next. Give yourself permission to grieve—to weep and wail, if needed—and in so doing, fully receive his comfort. Take time to sing and worship, to dance and shout. Thank God that he is revealing what needs to *go* in order for more of his righteousness, freedom, and life to *come.*

I urge you: Do not opt for denial, no matter how inviting it seems. You will want to believe I'm overstating things. You will want to believe that what's gone before has nothing to do with you, with your family, or with the church today, especially your segment of the church. You will want to believe we've gotten way past all that. To deflect denial, keep asking God for a spirit of grace and supplication. Let him gently, lovingly, show you what unholy alignments continue to keep *you* from being who you are, continue to keep *us* from being who we are.

Don't avoid the pain the truth brings. Instead, ask the Lord to wrap himself around you and take you through the pain. On the other side, you'll discover more fully the real you, filled with true thoughts and godly emotions, characterized by gracious words and righteous acts. On the other side, we'll become more fully the Bride as God sees her to be—clean, whole, free.

If you don't agree with something I've written, that's okay. I'm seeking with all my heart to represent God accurately, but I haven't got it all right. Some insights that are accurate, I may not have words to express adequately. Test what you read by the Spirit of God and the Word of God. If you still don't agree with something, you are free to lay it aside. Yet, please do not throw out the baby with the bathwater. Do not dismiss the stunning, freeing, life-giving revelations our Lord is giving because you find I haven't expressed them perfectly.

Tell us about past events

This book sounds a shofar call for God's people to move together with him and one another into a new place of freedom, a new place of living out the identity he intended for us from before the foundation of the world. If we're stuck, held in place by something to which our predecessors tied themselves and which still ensnares us, we can't move ahead without discovering and disentangling from that tether. In other words: To go forward, we have to look back.

God does not want us to look back longingly, to try to return to an earlier, "better" time. He does not want us to look back accusingly, to reopen and aggravate old wounds. But he does want us to see clearly what in our past still shackles us. He wants us to see—and take—the way of escape.

Isaiah 41:22 says, "tell us about past events, so that we can reflect on them and understand their consequences" (CJB). Only the true God can reveal the future with 100 percent accuracy. When he gives us glimpses of it, he does so to warn us from taking destructive paths. He does so to give life and hope. Similarly, only the true God can reveal the past in such a way that we see the fruit it continues to bear today.

As the Lord shines his light on choices of past generations, you may suddenly understand entrenched patterns you've observed in your life, your family, your region, your church culture—things rooted in yesterday, still unresolved today. Be strongly encouraged. "What is exposed by his light loses its power to bind you," says intercessor and author Sylvia Gunter.[28]

When God reveals our past, he always does so redemptively. Seeing today in light of yesterday, we discover how to open a doorway to tomorrow that has been locked and blocked.

Five years ago, the Lord began prompting me to delve into the "past events" of the Bible Belt and the denomination most closely linked with it. Other writers have explored the spiritual roots of other peoples and cultures. Some have helped us understand how events that happened millennia ago still impact us today.

This book will explore the relatively recent past of my native region, the Deep South of the United States. Ever since it was settled by the "white man," this region has been associated with evangelical Christianity. We'll examine key facets God is revealing about the region and its Protestant church culture during the decades surrounding the Civil War. This church culture was primarily peopled with Methodists, Baptists, Presbyterians and, to a lesser extent, Episcopalians. We'll look most closely into the history of Southern Baptists, the denomination that chose, from its inception, to identify fully with the South.

Primarily, we'll look at what Southerners and Southern Baptists have confessed about themselves, sometimes deliberately, sometimes without any idea what they were revealing.

Early confessors

In *We Confess!*, you'll meet a number of people whose words and works reveal our past. Some are historians, living or dead. Many of these historians are or were Southern Baptist. Most had more than an academic reason for looking back. They were searching for their own story, their own roots.

Each has discovered and told part of the story of nineteenth-century Southern culture. Some sought to defend. Some personally confessed. In telling the story, these historians may reach conclusions with which you don't agree. Regardless, they expose truth we haven't wanted to see.

May I introduce, in alphabetical order, several whose works you may want to check out for yourself:

Joe W. Burton, a Southern Baptist author, wrote a little book published by Broadman Press in 1976. Titled *Road to Augusta: R. B. C. Howell and the Formation of the Southern Baptist Convention*, Burton's candid account reveals much, not only about the origin of the SBC (in Augusta, Georgia, in 1845), but also about two of the principal men in early SBC life, R. B. C. Howell and James R. Graves.

Luther E. Copeland has written an amazing book provocatively titled, *The Southern Baptist Convention and the Judgment of History: The Taint of an Original Sin*. In the Preface, Copeland confesses himself a descendant of a Confederate soldier on his mother's side and a slaveholder on his father's side. He became Baptist in 1940 and graduated from three Southern Baptist schools. He said, "For over four decades, beginning in 1948, my professional career has been spent almost entirely in the service of several Southern Baptist agencies, as a missionary and a seminary professor."

Then, he stated what motivated him to write such a book: "For some time I have suspected that the origin of the Southern Baptist Convention (SBC) in the defense of slavery, a system which surely all contemporary Southern Baptists recognize as wrong, has infected the major aspects of Southern Baptist life." In the Preface to the Revised Edition, published in 2002, Copeland wrote, "Although I was still a Southern Baptist when this book was first published, I am not any longer."[29]

John Lee Eighmy, also Southern Baptist, wrote another provocatively-titled work, *Churches in Cultural Captivity: A History of the Social Attitudes of Southern Baptists.* A professor at Oklahoma Baptist University, Eighmy suffered a fatal heart attack in 1970 during a faculty-student basketball game. He was 42 years old. The manuscript for *Churches in Cultural Captivity*, "more than 95 percent complete" at the time of his death, was published posthumously in 1972.[30]

Jesse C. Fletcher wrote *The Southern Baptist Convention: A Sesquicentennial History*, the authorized 150-year history of the SBC, published in 1994. When the Lord first told me to "look back," I began by reading the bulk of this work.

Historian, professor, and author **William W. Freehling** wrote a perceptive work titled, *Prelude to Civil War: The Nullification Controversy in South Carolina, 1816–1836.* Thirty years before the war started, South Carolina leaders championed the idea that a state could disregard, or "nullify," a federal law. The state's legislators threatened nullification of an unpopular tariff. *Prelude to Civil War* shows that the nullification crisis hinged as much on Southern sensitivity to the early antislavery movement as on the tariff. Further, this work reveals the grievous change in Southern mindset that snuffed the Second Great Awakening and sent the South rocketing toward war. Freehling documents the role of *silence* and *silencing* in bringing about the changes.

Terry Matthews, adjunct professor at Wake Forest University, in Winston-Salem, North Carolina, posted online the teaching notes for his class, Religion 466: Religion in the South. Matthews' notes proved a gold mine for me as I began my quest for the truth about what happened in our past and why. I particularly appreciate Matthews' probing the bond between the Southern church and the Southern culture, as well as his insights into "spiritual bulimia" and his transparency in confessing his own sins.

Defining *spiritual bulimia* as a pattern of spiritual binging and purging, Matthews described its acceptance into the antebellum Southern church: "Unable to bring themselves to give up the sin of slavery, they found solace in purging themselves of their sin and guilt through intense, emotional, cathartic, religious experiences. A cyclic pattern developed in which Southerners would feast on sin during the week, and go to church on Sunday for an emotional and psychological release."[31] Terry Matthews confessed:

> All Southerners are affected to one degree or another by this disease. I can say that because I grew up as a spiritual bulimic. At one point in my life, I was a card carrying member of something called the "No Smoke, No Drink Club." Raised in a sheltered Southern Baptist home, I was thoroughly convinced that smoking and drinking were two of the worst sins a person could commit. Like many Southerners, I viewed sin as largely a question of personal morality. If I didn't cuss, fuss, smoke or drink, I felt I was a good person. It never occurred to me that there were other sins of which I was guilty, sins that were such an intimate part of my environment that I was blind to their reality. I never questioned the dehumanization of segregation, nor did I appreciate the evil of my own racism. Both segregation and racism were so a part of who I was—and the society to which I belonged—that I was unable to see them for what they really were: social systems completely at odds with the will of God. I thought of myself as morally clean because I abstained from alcohol and tobacco, but the reality was very different. I was so thoroughly tainted by these social and moral abuses, that I was numb to their existence.[32]

James Oakes published a groundbreaking book in 1982 titled, *The Ruling Race: A History of American Slaveholders*. Oakes' chapter on "The Convenient Sin" shows, from the letters, diaries, and papers of slave owners themselves how many of them embraced Christianity, how strongly they were convicted of slavery's sin, and the choices they made in response.

Rufus B. Spain wrote yet another work with provocative title and significant insights, *At Ease in Zion: A Social History of Southern Baptists, 1865–1900.* Originally published in book form in 1967, *At Ease in Zion* was republished in 2003 by the University of Alabama Press.[33]

Young Spain first began to probe the South's past in the late 1950s, a time when such probing simply wasn't done. As a Southern Baptist and a graduate student at Vanderbilt University, he began to wonder: "How could a people whose Baptist heritage stamped them as 'prophetic,' called to challenge ordinary ways of thinking and living because the God of the Bible directed them not to be 'conformed to the things of this world,' be so much at home in their culture? … By definition a restless and even revolutionary people, they were, in fact, 'at ease' in southern culture. They went further than that, to the point of being convinced that their home territory was a modern version of Zion … Rufus Spain wanted to know how these indefensible circumstances came about."[34]

In an attempt to answer his own questions, Spain began combing "the minutes and reports of the Southern Baptist Convention, minutes and reports of the twelve state conventions, and the denominational papers published weekly in each of the Southern states." He confined his research to the 35 years after the Civil War. He reported, "The state papers were the most enlightening sources."[35] Spain's research resulted in a doctoral dissertation, then a book, that includes numerous direct quotations from the Baptists of the era.

And finally, **Charles Reagan Wilson** wrote a stunning book on the post-Civil War South, published in 1980. *Baptized in Blood: The Religion of the Lost Cause, 1865–1920,* deals with much the same time frame as Spain's book. But while Spain focuses solely on Southern Baptists, Wilson quotes leaders of all the major Southern denominations of the time. His study reveals the extreme measures taken in the decades immediately after the War to forge "an alliance between religion and culture" in the South.[36]

Even more compelling than the writings of historians are the words of the people of the era themselves. Thanks to twentieth-century historians, who spent long hours locating and reading nineteenth-century newspapers, books, letters, and manuscripts—and thanks to the amazing research capabilities of today's internet—we can hear the voices and see the exact words of individuals who lived before, during. and immediately after the Civil War. Among them:

Richard Furman, whom Baptist historians have called "the spiritual father of the Southern Baptist Convention." From 1787 until his death in 1825, Furman served as the personable, aristocratic, well-respected and extremely influential pastor of First Baptist Church, Charleston, South Carolina. James A. Rogers' biography of Furman, published 2001, was written at the request of Furman's descendants. Although appreciative and positive, the biography reveals striking paradoxes and a stunning trajectory in Furman's life and ministry.

Furman's own writings also reveal much. Two papers, in particular, show the direction in which the most influential Baptist leader of the day led the Southern church. We'll look at both papers in later chapters. One is Furman's trail-blazing, pro-slavery argument published in 1822 under an extremely long titled shortened here to: "Exposition of the Views of the Baptists, Relative to the Coloured Population in the United States." The second is an "Address to the Churches" Furman gave two years after declaring slavery a positive good and less than a year before his death. In that Address, the man saved as a result of the First Great Awakening, who pastored during three decades of the Second Great Awakening—and who led the denomination perhaps most impacted by both—announced that the Holy Spirit does *not* inspire people today. How then do Christians know what is of God and what is not? To distinguish truth from error, said Furman, we must rely on ministers whose minds have been enlightened by science and the classics.

Denominational newspaper editors, the influential bloggers of the nineteenth-century Deep South. According to Rufus Spain, the Southern Baptist newspapers were the "official organs" of their respective state conventions, yet were privately owned. The editors were most often pastors and denominational leaders who preached via the printed page, as well as the spoken sermon. When the newspaper editors spoke, people listened. But also, when the people spoke, the editors listened. "The continuation of a paper depended on circulation and circulation depended on satisfied subscribers." As we'll also see, the Southern Baptist view almost always reflected the Southern view. So, when you read what a Southern Baptist newspaper editor wrote or allowed to be printed in his paper, you're usually reading a view widely held by Southerners and Southern Christians of the day.

Two of the most influential editors began as friends and ended as arch-rivals. Their story reflects much of the subsequent story of the SBC itself:

R. B. C. Howell moved from Virginia to Nashville in 1835, where he served as pastor of First Baptist Church and exerted enormous influence through the newspaper he founded, originally called *The Baptist* and later, *The Tennessee Baptist*. A proud and dedicated denominational man, Howell served either as a vice president or president of the Southern Baptist Convention every year of his life after its founding in 1845. Also after 1845, Howell expended a huge amount of energy mentoring and then trying to depose his protégé-turned-arch-enemy, J. R. Graves.[37]

James R. Graves moved to Nashville in 1845, took over as editor of the *Tennessee Baptist* paper in 1849 and started the Landmark Movement in 1851.[38] Like me when I began this research, you may never have heard of Landmarkism. And yet its doctrines still taint the bloodstream of Southern Baptists. As to J. R. Graves himself, Luther Copeland has called the man, "a powerful preacher and writer, and at midcentury, possibly the most influential Southern Baptist alive."[39] Do not, however, equate "powerful" with "godly." Graves' book published in 1880, *Old Landmarkism: What Is It?*, gives a stunning look at the reasonings behind the teachings Graves promoted for 30 years as "biblical"—that Baptists alone are the true church.

Finally, I'm eager for you to meet two remarkable nineteenth-century women, one from England, one from the Deep South:

Emily Anne Eliza Shirreff, a British abolitionist. In 1865, when Shirreff published two well-researched, well-written tracts called, "The Chivalry of the South" and "A Few More Words on the Chivalry of the South," she could not have imagined the internet, or that people all over the world would still read her words via that medium nearly 150 years after she wrote them.

The inimitable **Mary Chesnut**, a Southern gentlewoman, avid reader, and prolific writer. Chesnut longed to publish a book, never did during her lifetime—yet won a Pulitzer Prize nearly a century after her death. Historian **C. Vann Woodward** spent years editing her huge unfinished manuscript—a nonfiction account in journal format of the Civil War years. In 1981, Woodward published the award-winning, 836-page epic, *Mary Chesnut's Civil War.*

Chesnut's father, Stephen Miller, was a South Carolina governor and US senator, turned Mississippi plantation owner. Among the first to argue for slavery as a positive good, Miller died in 1838 in Mississippi. Two years later, 17-year-old Mary married James Chesnut, Jr., son of a wealthy South Carolina planter. James was very involved in politics—serving briefly as US Senator, then in a number of political roles in the Confederacy. The couple became very close to Confederate President and Mrs. Jefferson Davis.

From the moment South Carolina seceded from the Union, Mary Chesnut found herself at the epicenter of history as it was being made. She kept detailed journals and, 20 years later, used them to chronicle her experience of the war years. Most remarkable—and what made her complete manuscript "unpublishable" from a Southern perspective for so many years after her death—was her view of slavery as "a *monstrous* system, and wrong and iniquity,"[40] and her astonishing insight, honesty, and humor in portraying the culture and people of the South, including herself and her family members. She was at once a woman deeply immersed in her culture yet willing to hold it at arm's length and to say what she saw.

Our current neediness

All these voices and others help us see what God is revealing today through events long past. Their words uncover much, sometimes on purpose, sometimes unwittingly. God's reasons for showing us such specifics do not include finger-pointing. His reasons do include setting a lot of captives free—captives who may never have lived in the Deep South and may never have identified themselves as Southern Baptist.

Collectively, the US church is stuck. We're sucking air. We're trying to teach the rest of the world about church growth when our country is one of the few where the church is shrinking. Terrified at the direction our nation is going, we swing between a fatalism that sighs, "Things are only going to get worse," and a panic that cries, "For God's sake, do something!"

Biblically, the church is a body. What affects any part, affects all.

We in the US church have typically thought of ourselves as the strong part of the body, the part responsible to help all the rest. We haven't admitted this, even to ourselves; but we've often considered ourselves the head, responsible to lead all the rest. The Lord wants to set things in order. *He* is the head of his church. He's speaking to us, the US church culture rooted in the Bible Belt. He's showing us past events in order to shed light on our current neediness. He's humbling us, exposing what we have not wanted to see in order to cleanse and heal the people and the land.

We've tried to forget the past and go forward. But we cannot go forward without detaching from the things of the past that still hold us. By bringing these entanglements to our attention, God is at work to free us. He is committed to making all his body pure, whole, and able to go forward together. To cooperate with him will require courage and humility far greater than we've previously managed to summon. To summon them now, we need the outpoured Spirit of God and the prayers of the church around the world.

My Beloved, you don't know who you are. The truth you fear so much, the truth your pride cannot bear to hear, will set you free. It will hurt to admit all that has ensnared you for so long. But what a relief to know: None of those things define you! None of those things can hold you when you yield to me! You are my people—my treasure, a kingdom of priests and a holy nation. As you humble yourselves and pray and seek my face and turn from your wicked ways, I will hear from heaven and forgive your sin and heal your land.

3—King Cotton and Mighty Oaks

> Without the South's obsession with cotton, it is hard to imagine that the Civil War would have occurred at all.—*The New Georgia Encyclopedia*

> We may equate the Deep South with cotton, plantations, secession, and Civil War. But what's lasted the longest, what's rooted the deepest, is an oak planted by God himself.

When you think about the Mississippi Delta, what comes to mind? Rich black soil? Intense poverty? Flat land? Stately plantations? Slavery? Southern belles in hoop skirts? Cotton fields stretching as far as the eye can see?

When you think about the Mississippi Delta, what does *not* come to mind?

I'd suggest … forests.

And yet forests—not cotton—covered most of the Delta until after the Civil War.

"A bird's-eye view of the region before the Civil War would have revealed vast stretches of forest broken only at the riverside fringes," writes John C. Willis in *Forgotten Time: The Yazoo-Mississippi Delta After the Civil War.* "In 1883, the wilderness still covered 75 to 80 percent of the Delta, with trees from 2 to 4 feet thick standing 30 to 100 feet tall."[41]

Picture dense forests of pecan, hickory, gum, elm, and cottonwood dominated by oaks in the drier lands and cypress in the marshes. Clinging vines drape the trees. An undergrowth of wild cane stands 10 to 20 feet tall.[42] Now, in your mind, write this caption below that picture: *Mississippi Delta.*

Hard to grasp, isn't it? If someone were to ask, "What plant best epitomizes the Delta?" we'd all with one voice cry, "Cotton!" Indeed, if we were to name one plant most identified with the entire Deep South, we'd say, *cotton.* King Cotton.

That's because recent history has imprinted a man-made identity for the region on our souls. The Mississippi Delta lies at the geographical heart of the former Confederacy. We equate the Delta with cotton. We equate the Deep South with cotton. But, originally, none grew on the land. *People* brought cotton into the region. In the 13 original colonies, only a few farmers planted cotton. The crop was too expensive and labor-intensive to be profitable.

Shortly after the British colonies became the first 13 states, and just as the Northwest Ordinance and the Louisiana Purchase opened vast stretches of land for settlement, Eli Whitney invented the cotton gin. Instantly, cotton became a lucrative crop. As settlers crossed the Appalachians and flooded the South, they planted cotton wherever they could find flat enough land and fertile enough soil. They saw cotton as white gold.

Eventually, cotton *made* the South—and cotton *broke* the South. Landowners didn't diversify enough because they so identified themselves and their success with one crop.

"With cotton came slavery," says the *New Georgia Encyclopedia.* "Since the success of a labor-intensive crop like cotton was directly tied to the ability of a landowner to procure workers, white Georgians bought slaves in record numbers. The promise of a bumper cotton crop not only changed the state's agricultural history but also literally caused the enslavement of hundreds of thousands of men and women. Slaves planted, chopped, and picked cotton; they cleared and dug drainage ditches to create more cotton land. The international slave trade geared up to meet this new labor demand, and as a result, slavery and cotton tightened their grip on the state and left their unmistakable, tragic mark internationally."[43]

Not only in Georgia, but all across the Deep South, the people came to see themselves and their future in terms of cotton. Yet the original identity of the land was much more closely tied to the oak.

An ancient oak

Just as the Mississippi Delta brings to mind pictures of the antebellum South, so does Charleston, South Carolina. And for good reason. Charleston led the way in identifying the South with its cotton. Charleston's gentlemen planters were the elite of the South's cotton aristocracy. Furious over tariffs they considered disastrous to their profits and deeply sensitive to the early rumblings of abolition, "the Carolina chivalry," as they liked to call themselves, provoked the Nullification Crisis that tested the secession waters three decades before the Civil War erupted. Indeed, in Charleston, February 1833, "the South Carolina and federal armies eyed each other nervously across the waters of the harbor, ready for an attack which might lead to civil war."[44]

Eleven years earlier, in 1822, a thwarted slave revolt in Charleston prompted pastor Richard Furman to write, on behalf of the first state Baptist convention, the first biblical apology for slavery that presented the institution as a positive good, rather than a necessary evil. The "Charleston Tradition" Baptists personified by Furman and his protégés profoundly influenced the forming and direction of the Southern Baptist Convention in 1845.

December 20, 1860, South Carolina became the first state to secede from the Union. Due to a smallpox epidemic in Columbia, the state capital, the deed was done in Charleston.

So if any place might equate its identity with King Cotton, it's Charleston. Yet, like the Delta, Charleston has another identity, an identity that predates cotton by centuries. A single oak that stands on John's Island near Charleston prophetically testifies of that identity.

This *live oak*, a species whose leaves stay green year round, may be 1,400 years old. Named the Angel Oak, it is reportedly the oldest living thing east of the Rockies, predating Columbus and De Soto by centuries. After British settlers arrived, the Angel Oak survived an era when most of the ancient live oaks in South Carolina's Lowcountry were harvested for shipbuilding.

In 1717, the "property where the Angel Oak stands was … part of a land grant to Abraham Waight," says the *Insiders' Guide to Charleston*. "Waight became a prosperous planter with several plantations … The property passed through generations of the Waight family, acquiring the Angel name when Martha Waight married a Justis Angel in 1810."[45] Today the tree that predated planter Waight by centuries now survives him by centuries too.

The Oak is as colossal as it is ancient. Standing in an obscure wooded area, it towers 65 feet tall and has a circumference of 25-and-a-half feet. According to angeloaktree.org, all 19 members of the Charleston Ballet company once hid behind its trunk. Some of its huge limbs rest on the ground. Some limbs run underground for a few feet before emerging again. Its canopy provides an incredible 17,000 square feet of shade.

We may equate Charleston, and indeed all the Deep South, with cotton, plantations, secession, and war. But what's lasted the longest, what's rooted the deepest, is an oak planted by God himself.

Where cotton is king

The true identity of any people reflects the identity of the one true God. The Creator brought forth a universe of astounding variety. Consider the vast varieties of trees alone—and, even more specifically, the numerous types of oaks. This variety in creation displays God's glory.

The variety in peoples and cultures displays God's glory. The Lord created people in his image. Our differences reveal different aspects of his nature. In our fallen nature, we may look radically unlike God. Yet, no aspect of the true identity of any people contradicts the nature of God. No aspect of our true identity dishonors his holy Name.

God is holy. He is love. He is King. Psalm 47 declares, "the Lord Most High is awesome, the great King over all the earth … For God is the King of all the earth … God is seated on his holy throne" (vv. 2, 7, 8).

Where this King rules, righteousness and justice do too.

"But the Lord is king forever; he has set up his throne for judgment. He rules the world with righteousness; he judges the nations with justice" (Ps. 9:7–8 GNT).

"The Lord reigns, let the earth be glad; … righteousness and justice are the foundation of his throne" (Ps. 97:1-2).

When the Lord reigns in our hearts, *we* will reflect his righteousness and justice, his mercy and love. In Proverbs 8:20–21, Wisdom declares, “I walk in the way of righteousness, along the paths of justice, bestowing a rich inheritance on those who love me and making their treasuries full.”

As we’ll see in the next chapter, God took amazing steps to show the Southern people their true identity even as they settled the South. In the early 1800s, many confessed Jesus Christ as Lord and began to embrace who they were in him. At the same time, many began bowing the knee to another king, who bequeathed them a different identity entirely. The more they gave their allegiance to cotton, the more they abandoned love and mercy, the more they aligned with unrighteousness and injustice. Ultimately, that king lured them into needless war.

“Without the South’s obsession with cotton, it is hard to imagine that the Civil War would have occurred at all.”[46]

In March 1858, when Kansas was admitted to the Union as a free state, James Henry Hammond of South Carolina made a speech before the US Senate. In essence, Senator Hammond announced that if the South decided to secede from the Union, no one could stop her. He declared: “Would any sane nation make war on cotton? Without firing a gun, without drawing a sword, should they make war on us we could bring the whole world to our feet … No, you dare not make war on cotton. No power on earth dares to make war upon it. Cotton *is* king.”[47]

In December 1860, South Carolina seceded from the Union, soon followed by 10 other states. In April 1861, the Civil War erupted on South Carolina soil.

Astounding. The people of the South staked everything on following a king their obsession had created. They thought that, if the South seceded, cotton would stave off war. They thought that, if war came, cotton would assure them victory. Yet cotton could not, and did not, do either.

For decades after the war, cotton continued to rule the South. Appeals to diversify crops fell on deaf ears. King Cotton continued to promise riches and success. Instead, it impoverished and bound—blacks and whites, plantation owners and sharecroppers, people and land. In Mississippi today, the Delta soil is some of the richest in the world; the Delta region, one of the most poverty-stricken.

An online article titled, "Mississippi Delta: the land economic recovery never revisits," described a group of young men standing on a street corner in Midnight, Mississippi, early in 2010: "On a weekday morning in the Mississippi Delta, the poorest part of the poorest state in the country, these men in their 20s and 30s had nothing to do. No work. A few had broken their backs picking cotton, when it was cotton season, … until those jobs started to disappear too."

The article continued, "To drive through the Delta now is to traverse a forgotten land in America, a place of big open fields and tumbledown cottages, stitched together by sparsely traveled roads that reach toward a dandelion sun. In town upon town, derelict mills and boarded-up storefronts are emblematic of what some here call a 'permanent recession,' one that began long before the current national crisis and figures to be immune from any national recovery."[48]

The article suggested that the root of the Delta's problem lies in its school system. I'd suggest a deeper root: The Delta has aligned with an identity God never intended.

Hear me now: It's good to appreciate cotton. From its fibers come clothing, fishnets, coffee filters, tents and other products. From its seeds come oil and cattle feed. It's fine to associate the Deep South with cotton, the region's main cash crop for much of its history. Cotton makes a great crop—but a terrible king.

In the 1800s, the good thing Southerners had imported to serve them began to define and rule them. Mesmerized by what King Cotton promised, people repeatedly risked—and routinely lost—everything to serve it. Undaunted, they continued to uproot and cast off whatever stood in the way.

The deadenings

The prophet Zechariah wrote, "Wail, you juniper, for the cedar has fallen; the stately trees are ruined! Wail, oaks of Bashan; the dense forest has been cut down!" (Zech. 11:2). Zechariah wrote about ancient Lebanon, but he might have been writing about the settling of the Mississippi Delta.

There, "Few farmers actually cut down all the trees on their land before planting crops. Instead, they girdled large stands of oaks, hickories, cottonwoods, and other deciduous growth. Trees usually lost most of their leaves within a few weeks of having a ring cut through their bark; branches and trunks fell unpredictably to earth in the 'deadenings' over the subsequent months and years. Farmers commenced planting a first crop of cotton and corn among the bare and crumbling reminders of the great forest and removed deadfalls and stumps as they found the time."[49]

Today, we cannot picture a Delta full of forests. The original identity was uprooted by the settlers' obsession to embrace a new one, filled with white gold. Nor were the forests subdued by people eager to practice God's principles for stewarding the land.

In 1855, Alabama Senator C. C. Clay said to the Chunnemygee Horticultural Society:

> I can show you with sorrow ... the sad memorials of the artless and exhausting culture of cotton. Our smaller planters, after taking the cream off their lands, unable to restore them by rest, manures, or otherwise, are going further west and south, in search of other virgin soils which they may despoil and impoverish in like manner. Our wealthier planters, with greater means and no more skill, are buying out their poorer neighbours, extending their plantations, and adding to their slave force ... In traversing that county, one will discover numerous farmhouses, once the abode of industrious and intelligent freemen, now occupied by slaves, or tenantless, deserted and dilapidated; he will observe fields, once fertile, now unfenced, abandoned, and covered with those evil harbingers, foxtail and broomsedge ... Indeed, a country in its infancy, where fifty years ago scarce a forest tree had been felled by the axe of the pioneer, is already exhibiting the painful signs of senility and decay apparent in Virginia and the Carolinas; ... the spirit of desolation seems brooding over it.[50]

Obsession

So obsessed were the settlers of the South with pursuing white gold that they failed to steward the land wisely. Instead, they despoiled the land and moved, despoiled the land and moved. Further, they did not follow God's pattern of creating variety. They planted little except cotton. They pursued mostly those means of livelihood related in some way to cotton. In a tract published during the Civil War, British abolitionist Emily Shirreff pointed out the dire results:

"The backward state of trade, mining, and industry in general is extraordinary. [Frederick Law] Olmsted says, … quoting from a Southern paper, that the Slave States are 'dependant upon Europe or the North for every yard of cloth, and every coat and boot that we wear; for our axes, scythes, tubs, buckets,—in short for everything, except bread and meat.'"

Shirreff then quoted from *The Impending Crisis of the South*, published in 1857 by Southerner Hinton Rowan Helper:

"'We want Bibles, brooms, buckets, and books,' he says, 'we go to the North; we want pens, ink, paper, and envelopes, and we go to the North; we want shoes, hats, handkerchiefs, umbrellas, pocket-knives, and we go to the North; we want furniture, crockery, glass, ware, and pianos, and we go to the North; we want toys, primers, schoolbooks, fashionable apparel, machinery, modern tombstones, and one thousand other things besides, and we go the North for them all.'

"In the absence of industry they pride themselves on being an agricultural nation," Shirreff continued. Yet, she gave figures that show: "In 1855, the cotton crop of the South was not equal in value by several millions to the crops of hay and fodder, raised in different parts of the Union."[51]

Taproots

Many trees and smaller plants have a *taproot*, a main root that grows directly downward. Some taproots can grow as deep as the tree is high. *Lateral roots* grow out from the taproot. Plants and trees without taproots typically have a network of fine, shallow *fibrous roots.* A taproot system anchors a plant much more securely than a fibrous root system. As a result, a plant with a taproot can be incredibly difficult to uproot. That's frustrating if you need to get rid of a plant, but wonderful if you want it to stand firm.

Cotton plants and most varieties of oaks have taproots. While a cotton taproot goes deep, an oak taproot goes exponentially deeper. In regard to the land, the oak preceded the cotton (in time) and sends down a much deeper root (in space).

The online article, "Acorns to Oaks: How to Grow Your Own Oak Trees" says: Considering how desirable oaks are as landscaping trees, "it is surprising how infrequently they are planted for that purpose. Partly this is because oaks are slow growing and can take as long as two to three decades before they begin to provide significant shade. But mostly it's because the oaks, with their deep penetrating tap roots, do not fit into the current commercial nursery practice of supplying large caliper (trunk diameter) balled and burlaped or container grown trees for planting." Indeed, "oaks can send a tap root down as deep as five feet in the first year of growth. If about 95% of a tree's roots are removed when it's moved from the nursery then oaks do not make good candidates for transplanting. The best and fastest growing oaks are *grown in place*—starting exactly where they'll end up."[52]

Therein lies a picture. Roughly two centuries ago, people settled a land they identified with cotton where, long before, God had created a land with an entirely different root. People did not believe they could prosper in this land apart from one crop. God knows the prosperity of any people is tied, not to what they may sow in the ground, but rather to what is sown in their hearts.

Thus obsessed with sowing one type seed, the people began to equate their own identity with it. Millennia ago, God sowed an extravagant array of seeds in the rich Southern soil, growing forests filled with a variety of trees. Thousands of years before that, he said of the extravagant array of his people: "They will be called mighty oaks, a planting of the Lord for the display of his splendor" (Isa. 61:3).

In this book, *King Cotton* symbolizes far more than the South's obsession with a single crop. King Cotton represents anything or anyone other than the Lord himself that we allow to define us and rule us. When we bow to King Cotton, we *will* assume a false identity. We will act like who we are not.

The Delta's *forgotten forests* and Charleston's *Angel Oak* symbolize our God-given roots. Looking past the identity our ancestors created—the identity we've accepted as "just how we are"—we see our true identity, rooted in the God who declares, "It is I who made the earth and created human beings on it" (Isa. 45:12).

This Lord calls people created in his image to reflect who he is. He commands, "Preserve justice and do righteousness" (Isa. 56:1 NASU). He instructs, "let justice roll on like a river, righteousness like a never-failing stream!" (Amos 5:24).

And he tells us how it's possible. Since the entrance of sin distorted the image and perverted the good creation God had made, the only way we can mirror his attributes is to wed *him*, to enter covenant relationship with him: "I will betroth you to Me forever; Yes, I will betroth you to Me in righteousness and in justice, In lovingkindness and in compassion, And I will betroth you to Me in faithfulness. Then you will know the Lord" (Hos. 2:19–20 NASU). New Living says, "and you will finally know me as the Lord."

God redeems cultures

The contrast of the oak tree and the cotton plant does *not* imply that Southern culture is incompatible with godliness. Every culture has some aspects that are morally good; some, morally neutral; and some, morally corrupt. When God invades any culture, he comes, not to eradicate the culture, but to redeem it. He applauds the things that are morally good and infuses them with his life and power. In regard to the morally neutral things, he gives freedom. Ah, but the things that are morally corrupt, he confronts, uproots, and replaces with what reflects and honors him.

He does not demand that we become who we are not. He reveals to us, as individuals and as a culture, where we've missed the mark we were created to hit. He fills us with desire and power to be, more fully than ever before, who we are. In becoming who he created us to be, we reflect who he is. We bring honor to him.

So when God looks at the culture of the Mississippi Delta, the South Carolina Lowcountry, the Deep South, or the conservative church in the US, he applauds and affirms what is good. He discloses what is morally neutral and gives freedom in regard to it. Ah, but here's the painful part: For his glory and our good, he reveals what needs to be rooted out.

As we cooperate with him, he exposes what has deadened us to him, what has misrepresented him, what holds us perpetually in bondage, what denies our true value and identity, what wars against righteousness and justice, mercy and love. He uproots what promises to enrich us, but only impoverishes us; what repeatedly slams us, yet keeps us clinging obsessively to what we are not.

God does all this in order to return us to the exponentially deeper roots of who we are in Christ. "You received Christ Jesus the Lord, so continue to live as Christ's people. Sink your roots in him and build on him. Be strengthened by the faith that you were taught, and overflow with thanksgiving. Be careful not to let anyone rob you of this faith through a shallow and misleading philosophy. Such a person follows human traditions and the world's way of doing things rather than following Christ" (Col. 2:6–8 *GOD'S WORD*).

Several translations, including the Good News, say that these "shallow and misleading" teachings come from "human beings *and from the ruling spirits of the universe*, and not from Christ" (Col. 2:8 GNT). The Evil One and his cohorts want us to trust in something or someone other than God. They lure us, for example, to make cotton king, because they know: Any part of our loyalty that does not wholly belong to God goes by default to the kingdom of darkness. Satan doesn't care that we didn't mean to give our loyalty to him. He receives it, and controls and destroys us through it.

We in the Southern church culture face a huge challenge here. Just as surely as our society has been connected with cotton, it's also been connected with evangelical Christianity. Thus, we have often assumed the Southern taproot and the Christian taproot to be essentially the same. We've especially assumed that the Southern church mirrors ideal Christianity more nearly than anyone else. Other people, even other Christians, may follow shallow and misleading traditions. They may have accepted the world's way of doing things, but *not* those of us rooted in this conservative church culture. We believe the Bible!

Hear me now: It's good to appreciate the South. Many lovely, delightful, fruitful things flourish here. It's good to affirm ways that genuine Christlikeness is reflected in the region and its people.

Yet no culture is perfect. Every culture needs the purifying work of God. With bulldog tenacity God seeks to accomplish his purifying work in *us*.

Of course, we agree in theory that no culture is perfect. But for generations we've assured one another we're pretty close. Hence the belief during the Civil War that the Confederate cause was righteous and victory inevitable. Hence the phrase that came into vogue after the war's catastrophic loss and humiliating defeat: "our Southern Zion."

Today, we whose church culture has sprung from the Bible Belt desperately need to re-examine our roots. We need to recognize the areas where we and our ancestors have agreed with injustice and unrighteousness. We need to expose the ways we continue to let something shallow and misleading rob us. We need to see where we have deadened our oak taproots to pursue kings of our own making.

The silencing

"'Do not speak out,' so they speak out," wrote a prophet named Micah (Mic. 2:6 NASU).

Historians who've studied the Deep South lament a mindset that grew during the antebellum era and peaked after the Civil War: Collectively, the Southern people agreed to strain out a gnat and swallow a camel, and went to unbelievable lengths to silence anyone who dared suggest that's what they were doing.

"'Do not speak out,' so they speak out."

From the 1830s onward, the church in the South made much ado about personal sins—particularly overt leisure-time behaviors such as drinking, dancing, and card-playing. Yet the elephants in the culture ran amuck while the church folk cooperated in ignoring them. Ministerial voices passionately proclaimed, "All have sinned," and loudly urged personal repentance. Yet they just as loudly insisted that Southern society was as close to "virtue incarnate"[53] as a society could be. The preferred method for dealing with any moral wrongs that the society decided to embrace, or chose to tolerate, was *not* to deal with them. The church colluded in this approach.

If anyone dared to call something "wrong" that the prevailing Southern culture espoused, newspaper editors (including denominational editors) avoided printing it. Polite society avoided discussing it. Politicians avoided debating it. What William W. Freehling observed about South Carolina planters rang true across the Deep South: They "had too great a sense of their society's anxieties and weaknesses—too deep a fear that their institutions could be shattered by words—to tolerate discussion, much less action."[54]

"'Do not speak out,' so they speak out."

In his award-winning book, *Prelude to Civil War*, Freehling describes an event that dramatically illustrates how the silencing looked.

> On July 29, 1835, the steamboat *Columbia*, sailing out of New York, arrived in Charleston and delivered its cargo. The mail from the North was dispatched to Charleston Postmaster Alfred Huger … To his horror, Huger found that the mails were swollen with thousands of antislavery tracts addressed to leading members of the Charleston community, including, as the *Mercury* made a point of reporting, "the clergy of all denominations." The American Anti-Slavery Society had begun its intensive campaign to convince slaveholders that bondage should be abolished.
>
> Huger quickly wrote an express letter to Amos Kendall, President Jackson's postmaster general, requesting instructions for dealing with the crisis. Pending Kendall's reply, Huger determined to keep the "incendiary" propaganda under lock and key. The more hotheaded Charlestonians were not disposed to await federal instructions. By evening an angry mob, three hundred strong, assembled to seize the mails. As the mob marched toward the post office it was met by the city guard and "persuaded" to disperse. Later in the night, a few incorrigible slaveholders broke into the post office and confiscated the heavy sacks of abolitionist tracts. The next evening the antislavery propaganda was burned at an enormous public bonfire on the Charleston parade grounds; effigies of … northern "fanatics" fed the blaze … abolitionist propaganda could not be permitted to circulate in a community full of uneasy planters and restless slaves.[55]

People entrusted with delivering the mail suppressed it. People who considered themselves law-abiding citizens seized the mail and destroyed it. People who did not want anyone to say what their own consciences already knew sighed with relief. Driven by fear, they all colluded in the silencing.

Nor was the Charleston mail-burning an isolated incident: "postmasters censored the mails and mobs roamed the countryside throughout the South in the late summer of 1835."[56]

Reproaches turned back

In the 1830s, slavery was the foremost "incendiary" issue Southerners refused to discuss. With slavery outlawed roughly 150 years ago, we too might sigh with relief and consider the matter closed. Yet bondage still continues wherever people cling to a false identity that wars against their true identity, given by God before the foundation of the world and redeemed with the blood of Jesus Christ.

"'Do not speak out,' so they speak out, *but if they do not speak out concerning these things, reproaches will not be turned back*" (Mic. 2:6 NASU).

The response of Southerners, including the Southern church, to abolitionist mail in 1835 graphically depicts a pattern that has continued until the present. Despite strong appeals from distressed Christians (including Southerners like Hinton Helper), despite legislative rulings and court injunctions, despite war and reconstruction and civil unrest—indeed perhaps because of all those things—the church in the South has historically defended itself and its region as "right," "virtuous," and "misunderstood" and has adamantly refused to admit its flaws.

Further, we have delighted in exporting our way of doing Christianity to the larger American church culture and to the world, convinced that we must help everyone else learn how to do it.

So why would we even *consider* digging and exposing, uprooting and replanting now?

We might be cajoled into confessing flaws of yesteryear that we consider to be behind us. But something within keeps us frightened and defensive at the thought of bringing into the light anything unholy that may still entangle us.

We've so confused the false identity with the true—the two have become so enmeshed in our psyche—that we reject any attempt to separate the precious from the worthless as an assault against *us*. We're proud of our "Southern heritage." We're deathly afraid that exposing the truth will mean losing ourselves. And, well, it will. Ah, but it won't. God will call on us to give up the imposter self to which we've clung, in order that his Bride can emerge.

Together, pride and fear cry, "Do not speak out!" But if we "do not speak out concerning these things, reproaches will not be turned back."

The word translated *reproaches* in Micah 2:6 means "disgrace, reproach, shame, confusion, dishonor, insult, ignominy."[57] The Hebrew root denotes, "the sense of disgrace which attends public humiliation."[58] Could we say the South still carries shame that needs to be removed? Could we say that the US church culture carries reproaches that need to be carried away?

Neither pride nor fear arise from our true identity. Together, they employ silence to suppress shame, pushing it under the surface, so that it festers and grows in secret. For generations, our pride and fear have successfully silenced our speaking out about things we must address in order to send shame packing. It's time to throw off the silencing. But how?

Promised outpouring

In Zechariah 12, God makes a promise to the nation Israel: "I will pour out on the house of David and the inhabitants of Jerusalem a spirit of grace and supplication" (Zech. 12:10).

Reading this verse, we realize God has promised Israel something we also desperately need. Thankfully, the promise belongs to Israel—and to us. "For no matter how many promises God has made, they are 'Yes' in Christ. And so through him the 'Amen' is spoken by us to the glory of God" (2 Cor. 1:20).

The promise, "I will pour out … a spirit of grace and supplication" is Yes to us in Christ! We cry, "Amen! So be it!" *Supplication* denotes an earnest prayer for favor.[59] *Grace* denotes the release of that favor and supply. God promises to trigger something in the spirit realm that will release an outpouring of his grace concurrent with our cry for help.

Isaiah 30:18–19 describes God's strong desire to fulfill this promise, his yearning for the prayer to go up and the grace to flow down: "Yet the Lord longs to be gracious to you; therefore he will rise up to show you compassion. For the Lord is a God of justice. Blessed are all who wait for him! People of Zion, who live in Jerusalem, you will weep no more. How gracious he will be when you cry for help! As soon as he hears, he will answer you."

The Amplified rendering of these verses makes even more clear how much the Lord wants to send this outpouring: "And therefore the Lord [earnestly] waits [expecting, looking, and longing] to be gracious to you; and therefore He lifts Himself up, that He may have mercy on you and show loving-kindness to you. For the Lord is a God of justice. Blessed (happy, fortunate, to be envied) are all those who [earnestly] wait for Him, who expect and look and long for Him [for His victory, His favor, His love, His peace, His joy, and His matchless, unbroken companionship]! O people … you will weep no more. He will surely be gracious to you at the sound of your cry; when He hears it, He will answer you."

Who would *not* want what God offers? Who would *not* want his victory, his favor, his love, his peace, his joy, and his matchless, unbroken companionship? Particularly if we've already identified ourselves with him, would we not immediately, spontaneously cry for that outpouring?

Remarkably, we haven't yet. The deadenings and the silencing have kept us from it. Oh, individuals have cried out. Some entire groups have cried out. But collectively we in the US church culture have not cried out in a way that releases a massive, unrestricted flood of God's grace. We can know we have not sounded this cry because we haven't experienced the results God promises:

"I will pour out … a spirit of grace and supplication. They will look on me, the one they have pierced, and they will mourn for him as one mourns for an only child, and grieve bitterly for him as one grieves for a firstborn son" (Zech. 12:10).

As Christians, we often shake our heads over the state of our country. Yet, when we pray, confessing the sins of "our nation," how often are we mentally pointing away from "us" and toward those we consider "them"? With our lips, we're confessing *our* sins, but with our hearts, we're confessing *theirs.*

When God's Spirit triggers our cry and, simultaneously, releases a flood of his grace, the first result won't be pretty. It won't be fun. We will see where *we* who have identified with Christ have missed him and misrepresented him. No longer will we point fingers or shift blame. We will see how *we*, individually and collectively, have pierced the Lord Jesus. In the moment we see, we will experience the Father's deep, searing grief.

"'On that day a fountain will be opened to the house of David and the inhabitants of Jerusalem, to cleanse them from sin and impurity. On that day, I will banish the names of the idols from the land, and they will be remembered no more,' declares the Lord Almighty" (Zech. 13:1–2).

Praise God, the Father's grief will not swallow us up or beat us down. It will not linger indefinitely, to hold us wallowing in mourning. Rather, on the day we experience godly sorrow, a fountain will burst open to wash us. We'll be clean, clean, clean! In the wake of intense purging, we'll be free, free, free! Anything, everything, that has rivaled the place of Christ in our hearts will be eradicated—utterly gone, completely forgotten.

"On that day living water will flow out from Jerusalem, half of it east to the Dead Sea and half of it west to the Mediterranean Sea, in summer and in winter" (Zech. 14:8).

In our nation, too, Lord? With the eyes of our heart we see the living waters of your Spirit flowing out, half to the east and half to the west, in summer and in winter. We say, "Amen!" to your announcement that sweeping, all-encompassing revival will happen "on that day."

"The Lord will be king over the whole earth. On that day there will be one Lord, and his name the only name" (Zech. 14:9).

The word translated "earth" in Zechariah 14:9 also means "land."[60] Wherever the Lord pours out a spirit of grace and supplication—where people genuinely repent, where the fountain of the Lord cleanses, where wholehearted worship of him arises and where his Spirit flows unhindered—there the Lord will be king. He will rule the whole land.

As Christians, we want that. But we have not wanted it badly enough to look on him whom *we* have pierced. We will not want it badly enough, apart from a spirit of grace and supplication. We will remain stuck until

God unlocks something spiritually that triggers our cry that triggers the flow of his grace.

Just as Elijah waited for a tiny cloud to signal a coming downpour, I'm scanning the heavens, believing our Lord stands ready to pour out a spirit of grace and supplication on us. People who have, all their lives, believed their identity to be tied to something shallow and misleading will pull up that taproot and reestablish their identity as mighty oaks, for the display of God's splendor. Collectively, we will move through the pain of uprooting and into the joy of planting. We'll sink our roots deep in the place they were intended to grow all along—in the God who reveals himself as Father, Son, and Spirit. We'll grow tall and strong in him.

Lord, speak out!

But what about them? As I've talked with people about the concepts in this book, some have immediately begun to magnify the sins of other regions and peoples and to justify what history reveals about the Southern church. Some have, quite emphatically, listed reasons they believe everyone else's wrongs trump (and effectively erase) ours. The fact that this book primarily explores what past events reveal about Southern Christians, especially white Southern Christians, does not mean others are blameless. It means God is cupping our face in his hands and saying, "I want you to see *you*."

After Jesus' resurrection, he appeared to several of his disciples beside the Sea of Galilee. Taking Peter aside, Jesus talked to Peter about Peter.

Some of what Jesus said was not what Peter wanted to hear. Glancing around, Peter saw another disciple. "Lord, what about him?" Peter asked. Jesus' answer included this question: "What is it to you?" (John 21:21, 22 CJB).

Our Lord wants to talk with us about *us*. When we ask him, "What about them?" he answers: "What is it to you?" He has no intention of catering to our desire to compare ourselves with anyone else.

So have we done everything wrong? No. What we *have* done, collectively, generationally, is to insist we've done everything *right*. We've agreed to close our eyes and ears to the ways we've colluded in misrepresenting our Lord. Whether by burning the mail or mobbing the messenger, we've silenced any voices that have spoken up to call us out from our collective sins.

Now, our Lord the King, who created us, who loves us, and who has betrothed himself to us, says what we don't want to hear:

> Do horses run on rock?
> Does one plow there with oxen?
> Yet you have turned justice into poison
> and the fruit of righteousness into bitter wormwood.
> You take pleasure in worthless things.
> You think your power comes from your own strength
> (Amos 6:12–13 CJB).

From the time the South was settled, the region has been identified with Christ. "So he expected justice, but look—bloodshed!—and righteousness, but listen—cries of distress!" (Isa. 5:7 CJB).

Not at all what we want to hear. So how will we respond? Will we close our eyes and cover our ears, as before? Will we deny that it's true? Will we assert, "That's all past"? Will we assume God is talking about "them"? Or will we gather our courage, humble ourselves, and ask,

"How, Lord? How have we and our ancestors done such a thing?"

Now, O Lord, I cry: Pour out a spirit of grace and supplication so powerful that the people most likely to take offense at what you reveal—as well as those most apt to think it has nothing to do with them—will instead lead the way into repentance and awakening, transformation and life. As your Spirit flows and exposes and cleanses and fills, we refuse to silence your voice. Rather, we cry, Speak out! For as you do, reproaches will be turned back. We reject offense and defensiveness. We uproot bitterness and anger. We trample down fear. Though we've aligned with these attitudes for generations, they do not define us. As one, we let go of anything we've thought we had to cling to, anything we've bound ourselves to serve. We embrace our true identity in you as we humble ourselves before you and trust in your unfailing love.

4—The Fast God Has Chosen

Is not this the fast that I choose: to loose the bonds of injustice, to undo the thongs of the yoke, to let the oppressed go free, and to break every yoke?—Isaiah 58:6 NRSV

Repeatedly, we've tried to address the corporate sins of the *nation* without first addressing the corporate sins of the *church*.

Four generations ago, the white church in the Deep South launched the Confederacy with prayer and fasting. Faithful Christians cried out to God, certain their cause was righteous; their war, holy. As the Civil War progressed, Southerners were bombarded with distressing political news, distressing economic news, and tragic news from the battlefields. They prayed and fasted with increasing frequency and fervency.[61] Prostrate before God, they confessed the sins of the *Yankees*—and such things in their own lives as drinking, swearing, and card-playing.

In the end, with the South in ruins and the death toll on both sides numbering well into the hundreds of thousands, the church collectively *still* did not see or uproot the tangle of strongholds that held them. Utterly desolate, they cried,

> "Why have we fasted … and you have not seen it?
> Why have we humbled ourselves, and you have not noticed?"
> (Isa. 58:3)

Today, US Christians in record numbers are crying out to God on behalf of our nation. Bombarded with distressing political news, distressing economic news, and distressing world news, we're praying with increasing frequency and fervency. We've even fasted! Indeed, every time we turn around, someone is calling us to fast and pray for our nation. Already, we too have begun to ask the Lord:

> "Why have we fasted … and you have not seen it?
> Why have we humbled ourselves, and you have not noticed?"

In Isaiah 58, God answered those questions. He said he had not responded because his people were fasting for the wrong reasons and in the wrong way. They had not entered into the fast *he* had chosen.

Today, our Lord who loves us deeply is giving the same answer. Collectively, we've often fasted over *their* sins—confessing the wrongs of people with whom we do not identify or associate, people we consider unrighteous and may even count "the enemy." Repeatedly, we've tried to address the corporate sins of the *nation* without first addressing the corporate sins of the *church*.

Further, we've prayed to "take back our culture." We're quite sure that if Christians who think like us can get into places of influence in all realms of our society, everything will change for good.

For a century after the Civil War, Christians in the South held places of influence in pretty much every area of culture. As already mentioned, they even called the region, "Our Southern Zion."

Certainly, a significant percentage of the population went to church. Many openly acknowledged Jesus as their Savior. More than a few sought to live truly godly lives. But corporately, did the church culture in the South in 1890 and 1920 and 1960 look like Jesus? Did the region my ancestors populated look like God's kingdom on earth? Did their influence produce … widespread awakening? States characterized by justice, mercy, and genuine godliness? Churches filled with God's life and power? Communities known for selfless love?

When we try to "take the land" without first dealing with our corporate sins, we simply transpose our sins into new settings. We may swap "their" sins (the strongholds of the unchurched culture) for "ours" (the strongholds of the church culture). More often, we cross-pollinate and produce new, harder to eradicate sin issues.

If we would cooperate with God in changing cultures and nations, we must first cooperate with him in removing the oppressive yokes from around our own necks.

From Awakening to war

In the mid-1700s (just before the US became a nation), the colonies experienced a massive God-sent Great Awakening. From the 1790s to the 1830s, the new nation experienced an equally powerful Second Great Awakening. The Second Awakening started in New England. In 1801, it hit Kentucky. At the very time pioneers were thronging across the Appalachian Mountains and settling lands that would become the Southern states, awakening swept like wildfire across those lands. The three major denominations—Methodist, Baptist, and Presbyterian—participated together in lively revival meetings filled with visible manifestations of the Holy Spirit and producing radically changed lives. In particular, the Methodist and Baptist denominations—the "holy rollers" of the day—grew exponentially. Spiritual awakening lasted nearly 40 years!

David Goldfield, author of *America Aflame: How the Civil War Created a Nation*, has suggested that the Awakening led to the war: "The Second Great Awakening, a religious revival movement that emerged in the early part of the 19th century, inspired millions of Americans to embrace Jesus Christ as their personal savior," Goldfield wrote. "But it also propelled some to use their faith to wield public policy as a righteous club against those they perceived as a threat to the second coming of Christ—especially slaveholders and Roman Catholics. The mixture of religion and politics eroded the political center and privileged the extremes."

Goldfield added that "compromise and moderation are nearly impossible when each side believes itself righteous and the other damned. For how do you compromise with sin?"[62]

In Goldfield's view, we're better off without awakening. Does that alarm you? Offend you? Before anyone gets all up in arms, let me ask: What is he supposed to think? What will he and many others continue to think, as long as we Bible-believing Christians refuse to see or confess how our behavior has missed and misrepresented Christ?

In the first half of the nineteenth century, the enemy of our souls captured the astounding national good of widespread, long-term spiritual awakening and subverted it to accomplish his own ends. The Evil One—not the Lord—provoked pride, racism, judgmentalism, intractability, and division. The Evil One—not the Lord—sparked condemnation, defensiveness, immorality, and violence. The Evil One—not the Lord—provoked greed and determination to control, gross deception and deep fear.

Tragically, those best equipped to recognize and defeat this enemy instead fell into his traps, right along with the culture around them. God's awakened people justified what they should have denounced and clung to what they should have abandoned. Even more tragic, they dragged the Lord's Name into the melee. They used God's Word to keep from obeying his Spirit. And they who should have had the capacity to marry justice and love instead divorced themselves from both. They who should have offered creative solutions that avoided war, instead led the way into it.

Considering how fractured the US church became after the Second Great Awakening, is it any wonder someone might think awakening itself instigated the Civil War? Is it any wonder that massive moves of God's Spirit have since surged through places and cultures we'd never have dreamed possible, but have fizzled and died in the one nation that has tried the hardest to evangelize the rest of the world?

David Goldfield observed some things accurately. He followed his observations to conclusions that seem logical. We will not disprove his statements by railing against them, but only by confessing together: "It happened as you said, sir. But not because needless bloodshed results when God moves. Rather our ancestors who identified themselves with Christ missed him. They quenched his Spirit and, apart from his Spirit, they could not see sin or righteousness as the Lord sees it. They did not accurately reflect his character. And, frankly, we today have missed him in similar ways."

Revelation from the past

To revert to the vernacular, the shofar is sounding, y'all. As Goldfield intimated, the abolitionists may have been culpable, not for what they tried to do, but for some of the tactics they used. Regardless, the Lord wants to jar *us* from *our* slumber. He wants us to look to him, whom we say we serve, daring to ask, "What turned the Second Great Awakening on its head? What ultimately snuffed that Awakening and has aborted or sabotaged every revival in the US since?"

He wants us to listen, spirit-to-Spirit, to what he reveals.

Part of the church moved away from the bedrock truths of the faith and began to embrace an "anything goes" message. In so doing, that segment of the church corporately quenched and grieved the Spirit. That movement grew out of New England. This is not the place, and I'm not the person, to identify and confess those sins. God is raising strong voices from that region to repent for the strongholds there.

Part of the church held fast to Jesus and to salvation through his blood alone. This movement grew out of the South, where the church prided itself on its dedication to Christ, its faithfulness to Scripture, its love for missions, and its label, "The Bible Belt."

From a Christian perspective, we see the profound implications of abandoning the essentials of the faith. We see the necessity of clinging to Christ and following him. However, we have not seen the profound implications of wedding cultural biases to Christianity's bedrock beliefs. We haven't recognized the error of coupling nonessentials, and even ungodly beliefs and behavior, with essentials of the faith. We have not seen where the church that clung to Jesus missed him.

As already mentioned, every culture has both wonderful qualities and negative qualities. An honest look into the history of the church in the Deep South in no way denies or diminishes the delightful qualities both of the church and the region. Nor does it overlook the fact that individual Christians across the region did and do follow God fully, even when it means standing alone against the culture. But the God who reveals himself as Father, Son, and Spirit is calling the Southern church to go where it has adamantly refused to go. He is calling a church culture that has consistently lifted up the name of Jesus to see and repent for the ways we have not followed Christ fully and have not represented him well.

Suppose someone goes in for a routine checkup and the doctor discovers multiple clogged arteries. That doctor doesn't recount all the ways the person is otherwise healthy. The doctor focuses on exposing a potentially fatal problem and doing the surgery required.

The God who sees our hearts is revealing what we have not recognized and, till now, have refused to see. He commands us, "Look!" His revelations from our past give astounding new insight into our present and hold crucial keys to our future.

"Yes, yes" and "No, no"

In the first three decades of the 1800s, the awakened white Southern church culture said a resounding "yes, yes" to Christ on matters of personal salvation. But by the 1830s, this same church culture—speaking in a concerted, persistent, and increasingly resolute voice—said "no, no" to Christ on issues that reflected their cultural bias. In essence, they said *yes* to awakening—and *no* to reformation. In the words of 1 Kings 18:21, they halted between two opinions.

Strong historical evidence shows that Christians across the South heard the voice of the Spirit on key issues and struggled deeply and at length with the conviction he brought—yet regarding the treatment of whole groups of people, the church ultimately chose to follow the culture, rather than to obey the Spirit of God.[63]

The Indian problem

Awakened by the Spirit, white settlers in "the Great Valley" recognized as wrong the mistreatment of native peoples. *Responding to their culture,* the settlers petitioned the US government for Indian removal from lands they wanted to own. Actively or passively, the settlers abetted the evils leading to and fostered by the Indian Removal Act of 1830—including theft of property, breaking all covenants made with Native American tribes, murder, and wrongful death.

In 1976, Joe W. Burton published a book about the origins of the Southern Baptist Convention that unwittingly captures this grievous halting between opinions.

As throngs of settlers moved into the area that became the Southern states, "There was growing concern for the spiritual welfare of the aborigines. [*However*] Mounting sentiment would lead to the resettlement of Indians in newly assigned Indian Territory in the West. The Cherokees would begin in the fall of 1838 the winter march from Georgia and Carolina, every mile of the devastating journey marked by hunger, disease, bitter cold, and wholesale death ... Mistreatment of one race by another cried out for rectification, as the blood of Cain's brother cried out from the ground. *But* the primary missionary interest of Baptists and of all Christians at that turning time was claimed by the spiritual need of their own kinsmen in newly settled lands."[64]

The slave problem

Awakened by the Spirit, Southerners recognized slavery as "an evil, the curse of which is felt and acknowledged by every enlightened man in the Slave-holding States."[65] In 1827—toward the end of the Second Great Awakening—abolitionist editor Benjamin Lundy estimated that the slave states had 106 antislavery societies with 5,150 members, compared to 24 antislavery societies with 1,475 members in the free states.[66] Thus, though the abolition movement prior to 1830 was small, it was fueled primarily by Southerners.

Responding to their culture, Southern Christians ultimately reversed their stand, declared that slavery was God's plan and insisted that anyone who taught otherwise was both contradicting Scripture and anti-Christian.

The woman problem

Awakened by the Spirit, the Southern church began to recognize women as partners in ministry: "Advocates of the Awakening encouraged women to take an active part in the work of God. Some new groups ... allowed women to lead as well as to support."[67] Women shared in authoritative decision-making in churches. They "were ordained as deaconesses and sometimes as 'eldresses.' There were even women preachers among them."[68]

Responding to their culture, the Christians of the South adopted a beguiling code of "chivalry" drawn from the ancient Greeks and from fictional accounts of the Dark Ages. They promoted as biblical a view of women heavily influenced by Arthurian romance novels and pagan Greek thinking.

Without seeing what they were doing, this segment of the church normalized the cohabitation of what God adores and what he abhors.

While lifting high the name of Christ, the church grieved and quenched the Spirit. While preaching the gospel, the church opened itself to be taken captive by the sin strongholds of the region.

Strongholds and structures

Slavery was the key *presenting* issue, held in place by a tangled web of underlying issues. Dreadful as slavery in this country was, even we white Southerners don't mind too much to confront it today, since we can acknowledge with genuine sincerity that it was wrong and can affirm that we personally did not participate in it.

However, we get frightened, defensive, and downright angry when God uncovers *root sins* that held slavery in place and that continue to produce bad fruit nearly 150 years after slavery itself was cut off. I'd love to hedge here, but it's critical that we do not.

At the root of the inequities in the South lay a determined commitment that one group (in this case, white males) retain the wealth, status, and power in the region. At the root, lay an unshakeable faith in cotton as the means to this end.

Greed saw cotton as white gold, and land and slaves as the necessary ingredients for attaining it. Greed prompted the settlers to deplete the land in one place, then sell their slaves, uproot their families and start again farther south and farther west—repeating the process time and again, despite the pleas and tears of their wives.

Oppressive power had to be wielded to keep slaves (and Native Americans and women and poor whites) "in their place." Control bred uniformity. At times, the oppressed also became oppressors. Those who lacked power to control by force learned to control through such means as manipulation, passive-aggressive behavior, and sabotage.

Pride labeled the South better than the North; its land, richer; its people, more noble; its produce, more important; its Christians, more holy. Pride labeled Southern landowners, "the Chivalry," a new generation of the "aristocratical" knights of King Arthur's courts.

The taproot of greed, pride, and power spawned a tangled mass of other unrighteous roots.

Immorality and violence were rampant in a society where the privileged could get away with both. Slaves were whipped routinely. Slaves who tried to escape were lynched—as, on occasion, were whites who expressed thoughts of freeing their slaves. Slave women were exploited sexually, both for the master's pleasure and to breed more slaves. Children born of slave mothers were slaves. They lived as slaves and were sold away as slaves, regardless of their father's race or status. Angry and humiliated white wives abused the black women from whom their husbands demanded sexual favors. White men fought duels regularly and needlessly. Though the participants called these duels, "affairs of honor,"[69] the most brutal and devious man usually won. Equally vicious and far more common, Southerners brutalized others with words. Church and denominational leaders, newspaper editors and politicians, men and women who disagreed even over minor issues attacked one another with malice and lies. Some verbally dueled to the death.

Division, rejection, and *rebellion* sprang up as some people began to question the rightness of all the above, but the culture as a whole refused reproof. An "us" against "them" mentality flourished. "The world's against us," white Southerners lamented. Over time, *them* became "anyone who doesn't agree with *me*, anyone who in fact doesn't look, speak, and act like a cookie-cutter version of me."

Deception kept up appearances, making it seem impossible that such lovely, hospitable people could acquiesce in such wrongs. Deception intermingled good and evil, confusing the great wrongs in Southern society with all that was truly right, and proclaiming the whole mixture "virtue." Deception convinced Southerners that the Cotton Kingdom equaled the kingdom of God. It convinced Southern Christians that they could close their ears to the Spirit and rightly divide the Word. It convinced Christian leaders that their denomination's seminaries taught truth without any mixture of error.[70] Deception blinded the eyes of the people to the injustice in their midst and the unrighteous roots that had spawned it. Deception disguised and covered up what needed to be exposed and removed.

Fear underlay it all—fear of loss, especially loss of wealth, of status, of power, and of identity; fear of "them" abounded; fear of violence, of rejection, of change. Fear kept people from challenging the status quo. Fear kept people from exposing what deception covered up. Fear kept people from doing what they knew deep inside to be right.

After slavery was abolished, the people committed to this system found other ways to maintain it, including, but not limited to: strict segregation, wide acceptance of Freemasonry, involvement in the Ku Klux Klan, and the passage of "Jim Crow" laws (state laws that effectively undid federal laws giving new rights and voting privileges to blacks.)

Today, a lot has changed. But a lot that needs to change hasn't. In a church culture and a region that boldly lifts up the name of Jesus, a root system opposing his character and ways is still entangled with his name.

White males have the most difficulty seeing and renouncing this system (past and present) because it promises them so much. We won't explore here the emptiness of these promises and the curse that attends its "blessings." But we do need to clarify: White males are not the bad guys. Bashing them is not the answer. Conquering them is not the way to uproot the strongholds. That approach only strengthens and propagates the same corrupt system. The "bad guys" in all this are the "ruling spirits" (Col. 2:8 GNT), the "spiritual forces of evil in the heavenly realms" (Eph. 6:12) that convince people—even sincere Christian people—that one group is supposed to dominate everyone else. This mindset produces race wars, gender wars, generational wars, gang wars, church wars, world wars, civil wars. We enter into it when we decide *our* group must be the one to rule.

Tragically, the growing church culture in the antebellum South not only bought into the system, but also created structures to keep the strongholds in place.

Indeed, the churches of the Bible Belt became so committed to slavery and all the mindsets linked with it that all three main denominations split from their Northern brethren over that issue. Fifteen years before the Southern states seceded from the Union, the Methodists and Baptists of the South left their national denominational organizations and formed regional ones. Ultimately, the Presbyterians also split. Because the church had tried the strategy first, and seemingly so successfully, ministers were among the loudest voices calling for secession in 1860. Thus, the two denominations that had led in embracing the Spirit during the Second Great Awakening led the way into secession only a decade after awakening ended.

The Southern Baptist Convention

Southern Baptists went the furthest in defending and aligning with the "peculiar institution" of the Deep South.

In May 1845, 293 delegates from nine states met in Augusta, GA, to found the Southern Baptist Convention (SBC). The precipitating issue: clashes over whether the Baptist missionary societies in the US should send out missionaries who were slaveholders.[71] Southerners insisted *yes*—and cried loudly that not to allow slaveholders to serve as missionaries violated the rights of all southern Baptists. In reality, the ruling only affected white, male, slaveholding southern Baptists who would not relinquish their slaves in order to go to the mission field.

The real conflict had nothing to do with missions. It had everything to do with a determination clearly stated 44 years later by the editor of the Alabama Baptist newspaper: "The white people of the South mean to rule, and they will rule."[72]

If white southern Baptists acquiesced in the mission boards' decision, they would be tacitly agreeing that slavery might be a sin. If they opened that can of worms, a whole tangle of sin issues would pour out—greed, pride, control, prejudice, immorality, violence, factions, estrangement, deception, fear. If Southerners truly examined these issues—and gave the Holy Spirit permission to speak—a few, many, maybe even a lot might repent. Then pressure from within the South might erupt to free the slaves. The slaves themselves might revolt. Wealth, status, power, all hung in the balance. Thus, by the 1840's, white Southerners had agreed together never to allow any discussion of the topic that even hinted slavery might be sin.

And so it was that, the same year the Methodists split at the Mason-Dixon line, southern Baptist leaders set in motion a similar Baptist split. For more than a decade, the nationwide Baptist mission societies had tried to do the impossible, remain neutral on the hot-button issue of sending slaveholding missionaries. The Triennial Convention, US Baptists' foreign missions organization, had made several uneasy resolutions of neutrality. In 1844, a slaveholder, prompted by Georgia Baptists to apply for home mission service as a test case, was rejected by the Home Mission Society. Then, Alabama Baptists wrote the Acting Board of the Triennial Convention, demanding to know whether that board would send out a slaveholder as a foreign missionary.

Abandoning neutrality, the board responded, "If … any one should offer himself as a missionary, having slaves, and should insist on retaining them as his property, we could not appoint him. One thing is certain; we can never be a party to any arrangement which would imply approbation of slavery."[73]

Incensed, Baptist leaders in the South hastily called a meeting in Augusta. There, they "resolved unanimously" to sever relations with northern Baptists and organize a new convention "*for the peace and harmony*, and in order *to accomplish the greatest amount of good*, and *the maintenance of the Scriptural principles* on which the General Missionary Convention of the Baptist Denomination in the United States was originally formed."[74] Ah, gentlemen, gentlemen.

In *The Southern Baptist Convention: A Sesquicentennial History*, Jesse Fletcher describes this meeting. He writes, "No women registered for these proceedings. Neither were any black members of the churches at the meeting. This is significant because on the rolls of their various congregations both groups probably outnumbered the white males who were there."[75]

A convention with no female and no black delegates reflected the pattern in the typical church gatherings of the antebellum South: The white men led; the white women remained silent; and the black members (male and female) sat in a different section or met at a different time from white members to listen to the preaching of the white pastor. Outside the "sanctuary," white women could teach children and slaves. A few blacks were allowed ministry roles, but their ministry was highly suspect, carefully supervised, and always restricted to the black congregants. For the most part, blacks had to live and minister without benefit of reading Scripture. Laws in most Southern states forbade teaching slaves to read, and most whites were terrified at the thought of a slave reading the whole Bible.

In Augusta, the men organizing the new denomination ironed out the finer points of a constitution already drafted before the meeting. Immediately after the meeting, they released a report explaining why "the organization of the Southern Baptist Convention became necessary." The report reveals astonishing self-deception as to motives, a bold insistence that the founders had acted for the benefit of the very peoples they had driven from the land or continued to enslave on it:

"'One thing *is* certain,' ... 'We can never be a party to any arrangement' for monopolizing the Gospel: any arrangement which ... would first drive us from our beloved colored people ... and from the much-wronged Aborigines of the country ... with the low moan, for spiritual aid, of the four millions of half stifled Red Men, our neighbors; with the sons of Ethiopia among us, stretching forth their hands of supplication for the gospel, to God and all his people."[76]

With great protests of their love for missions and their refusal to "be a party to any arrangement for monopolizing the Gospel," leaders of the newly formed SBC immediately organized Southern foreign and home mission boards. These boards did not exclude white male slaveholders from appointment as missionaries, but did exclude blacks and single women—with the exception of one woman, Harriet Baker, who received a "reluctant appointment" in 1850 and served in China 1851–1853.[77]

More than a century later, Southern Baptist historians still have trouble stating the obvious. In the 150th anniversary history, Jesse Fletcher gives three reasons for formation of the SBC:

- "a growing pride in being a Baptist"—which should rather have motivated the continued support of the national Baptist organizations already in existence.
- "a consuming missionary vision." That certainly is what the founders *said*.
- "entrenched sectionalism."[78]

In his book, *Road to Augusta*, Joe Burton came closer to hitting the nail on the head. Burton wrote, "The widespread notion that slavery provoked the formation of the Southern Baptist Convention has, of course, strong validity in fact."[79]

Covenants with death

One month after the Civil War began, the 16-year-old Southern Baptist Convention met in Savannah, Georgia. May 13, 1861, the messengers prepared a lengthy report with 10 resolutions, delivered four days later to the president of the Confederate Congress meeting in Montgomery, Alabama. Among other things, the Southern Baptist Convention resolved:

> That we most cordially approve of the formation of the Government of the "Confederate States of America," and admire and applaud the noble course of the Government up to the present time.
>
> That we most cordially tender to the President of the "Confederate States," to his Cabinet, and to the members of the Congress now convened at Montgomery the assurances of our sympathy and entire confidence. With them are our hearts and hearty cooperation.[80]

In May 1863, the Southern Baptist Convention meeting in Augusta, Georgia, reiterated its commitment to the Confederacy in a seven-point resolution ironically titled, "Resolution on Peace." The SBC resolved:

> That the events of the past two years have only confirmed the conviction expressed by this Convention at its last session [1861], that the war which has been forced upon us is, on our part, just and necessary, and have only strengthened our opposition to a reunion with the United States on any terms whatever; and while deploring the dreadful evils of the war, and earnestly desiring peace, we have no thought of ever yielding, but will render a hearty support to the Confederate Government in all constitutional measures to secure our independence.[81]

When the church is being conformed to Christ and seeking first his kingdom, it identifies with the surrounding culture in a way that is redemptive and life-giving. The Southern Baptist Convention has, from its inception, identified with the Southern culture in an unhealthy, codependent way. During the Civil War, the SBC formalized this misplaced allegiance.

"We have no thought of ever yielding, but will render a hearty support to the Confederate Government." And so, by two written documents, the denomination pledged undying allegiance to the Confederacy. I have found no record of the SBC ever recanting this commitment.

However, Baptists weren't the only southern church to bind themselves and their generations to Confederate culture. During and especially after the war, preachers of all denominations began glorifying the Confederate war effort, calling it a "baptism of blood" and equating it with the blood sacrifice of Christ: As Jesus' blood provides redemption and sanctification for individuals, they taught, so the blood of Confederate soldiers provided redemption and sanctification for the South.[82]

This trusting in the needless bloodshed of war to accomplish what the blood of Christ alone can accomplish sealed an unholy covenant between the church of the region and the Confederate "lost cause." Thus, the church consummated its marriage to a culture, violated its "covenant of life and peace" with the Lord, and entered what Isaiah calls a "covenant with death."[83]

Unholy covenants made by a culture don't fade away with the passing of time or even the passing of a generation. Such covenants continue until someone takes action decisive enough to annul them.

Thus bound by the covenants of earlier generations, the conservative church culture rooted in the Deep South still today perpetuates a deadly dichotomy, a dual loyalty that produces spiritual schizophrenia. On the one hand, the church seeks to honor the Lord Jesus, to proclaim his gospel, and obey his Word. On the other hand, the church remains hopelessly entangled in the same sin strongholds that King Cotton bequeathed to the nineteenth-century Deep South.

Spiritual father of the SBC

As late as 1830, the church in the South—Methodist, Baptist, Presbyterian—still led the charge of prolonged, dramatic nationwide revival. By 1845, the church in the South was leading the prolonged, dramatic charge to secession and civil war. How could such a thing have happened? We gain crucial insights from the life of one well-known, well-loved, and well-respected Baptist pastor, Richard Furman.

In his history of the SBC, Jesse Fletcher calls Furman, "the spiritual father of the Southern Baptist Convention."[84] Interestingly, Furman died in 1825, 20 years before the forming of the SBC and 35 years before secession and war. But where Furman led, southern Baptists followed.

Born to a slaveholding plantation family in South Carolina, Richard Furman became a Christian and a Baptist in 1771 as a result of the first Great Awakening. In 1787, he became pastor of the most prestigious

Baptist church in the South, First Baptist, Charleston. He pastored there 38 years until his death.

By Furman's day, according to Southern Baptist historian Walter Shurden, Baptists had developed two traditions, the Charleston tradition (Regular Baptists) and the Sandy Creek tradition (Separate Baptists).

Shurden identifies the main characteristic of the Separate (Sandy Creek) Baptists as ARDOR. "Coming out of New England revivalism during the era of the Great Awakening, these fiery frontier folk migrated to the South and settled in Sandy Creek, North Carolina, in 1755."[85] Their worship was fervent and free. They affirmed the role of women in ministry and strongly opposed slavery.

Shurden identifies the main characteristic of the Regular (Charleston tradition) Baptists as ORDER. Their worship, theology, and ecclesiology were hierarchical and systematic.[86] They rejected women in ministry and passionately supported slavery. They led the way in organizing associations, state conventions, and the Southern Baptist Convention.

The Charleston tradition didn't begin with Richard Furman, but according to Shurden, Furman "personified" and "perfected the tradition."[87] He was the quintessential organizer.

- Furman had an unbroken attendance record at meetings of the Charleston Baptist Association for 44 years. He served as moderator of the association for 30 years.[88]
- In 1791, Furman led the Charleston Baptist Association to set up an education fund for young ministers. For the remaining 35 years of his life, he served as the chairman of the General Committee that directed this program.[89]
- In 1814, Furman chaired the meeting in Philadelphia at which the nationwide Baptist foreign mission society was formed. The lengthy name, General Missionary Convention of the Baptist Denomination in the United States of America, for Foreign Missions, was shortened to Triennial Convention because the society met every three years. Furman served as its first president, holding that position for two three-year terms.[90]

- In 1821, Furman led in founding the South Carolina State Convention, the first state Baptist convention. He served as its president for its first four years, until his death in 1825.[91]
- Furman served on numerous other committees, many of them related to public and private education, and apparently chaired every committee on which he served.

The Charleston tradition Baptists were also known as "high church," or "silk stocking," Baptists. In particular, the congregants of First Baptist, Charleston, would have included the elite of the Southern elite—those prestigious families of the South Carolina tidewater who were, not only plantation owners, but the aristocracy among the South's plantation owners. In the government and society, as well as on the plantation, the men of these families *ruled.* Other members of the church made their living selling products and services to these elite or simply enjoyed the elevated status that came from even a minor association with them.

Furman's biographer, James A. Rogers, says that Richard Furman "lived in Charleston too long not to have absorbed the aristocratic character of this chief Southern city."[92] One church member wrote: "I remember the first Sabbath I went to church … in 1804. Never can I forget my astonishment when I saw in a high pulpit Dr. Furman in a black gown and white bands."[93]

How did this "classic southern gentleman"[94] view the role of women? A note written by one of his granddaughters paints a vivid picture. Keep in mind that, in addition to his full-time pastoral duties, Furman continually organized and presided over meetings of one group or another, not only in Charleston, but across South Carolina and in other states. His first wife died in 1787, leaving him with three children. Two years later, 33-year-old Furman married 16-year-old Dorothea Marie (Dolly) Burn. Dolly was born in 1774, the same year Furman married his first wife. Dolly was three years older than Furman's daughter, Rachel. Dolly died at the age of 46, after bearing him 13 children.[95]

A postscript to a letter written by Richard and Dolly's granddaughter reads: "Our grandmother was a little beauty when she married … Every two years grandmother bore a child, until 1819—when Aunt Ann[e] said: 'dear mama died of exhaustion, having borne so many children, and having such a large family to care for.' Of course, grandfather was no doubt thinking of biblical heroes, but my heart has always gone out to the pretty child whose life was one of pain and service until the tired body found rest in God."[96]

Trajectory

Several historians, including Fletcher, have taught that Furman brought together "the best of both the Sandy Creek tradition and the Charleston tradition."[97] But did he?

At the outset of the Second Great Awakening, Furman "received reports" from the revivals at "his citadel of Regular Baptists in Charleston."[98] His responses include some wise, kind remarks. In a letter written in 1802, he termed "'the Revival in the Back and Middle country . . . a blessed visitation from on high' and prayed that it might be extended to the Seacoast: ' . . . that you, that we, and Thousands more may partake of its Blessedness and Joy.'"[99] At about the same time, he stressed the importance of maintaining a balance between wisdom and zeal and avoiding "dangerous and hurtful extremes."[100]

A circular letter of the Charleston Baptist Association in 1803 asked a question Furman considered key: "How may enthusiasm be distinguished from the influence of the spirit and Grace of God on the Heart?"[101]

Furman's answer to that question set the trajectory for the rest of his life, for the Southern Baptist denomination, and the church in the South. Furman came to believe that the key to spiritual discernment lay, not in the people of God helping one another to recognize and obey the voice of God, but in rational thinking, and particularly in a clergy educated in the classics and the sciences.

Furman never seriously entertained the idea that the uneducated and unsophisticated might have something to teach the learned. In an address given in 1824, he said, "These candidates for the ministry may, indeed, be men of God; thoroughly established in the faith of the gospel, and useful, to a certain extent, in winning souls to Christ; but, not being able to wield the weapons of science, they are unable to meet the enemy on his own ground."

Both gracious and pragmatic, Furman followed that statement with a disclaimer: "while we thus argue in favour of literary improvement in the ministry of the Gospel, we would not be understood to consider it as superceding the Grace of God in the heart." Yet, Furman followed his disclaimer with arguments intended to show "the *necessity* of having an *enlightened* Gospel ministry"—ministers enlightened, not by the Holy Spirit, but by "learning, from the improved state of society."[102]

Furman longed for genuine revival, yet tolerated the "fire and fervor" as something that education and civilizing influences would help the people outgrow. A master of diplomacy, he worked diligently to bring together the "backcountry" Baptists and the "silk-stocking" Baptists, but always with the intent of imposing the order of the latter on the ardor of the former. Furman and the other gracious, gentlemanly Charleston tradition leaders wanted an order they would rule.

Exposition of the Views of the Baptists

In 1790—even before the Awakening hit the South—Baptists declared slavery "a violent deprivation of the rights of nature and inconsistent with a republican government."[103] A decade later, young Furman himself called slavery "undoubtedly an evil."[104]

Twenty years passed, during which time Furman himself became a wealthy slave owner. In 1822, Richard Furman wrote a lengthy "Exposition of The Views of the Baptists Relative To The Coloured Population Of The United States In A Communication To The Governor of South Carolina." In his exposition, Furman admitted, "certain writers on politics, morals and religion, and some of them highly respectable, have advanced positions, and inculcated sentiments, very unfriendly to the principle and practice of holding slaves … These sentiments, the [state Baptist] Convention, on whose behalf I address your Excellency, cannot think just, or well founded; for the right of holding slaves is clearly established in the Holy Scriptures, both by precept and example."[105]

Note that Furman did not present the exposition as his personal opinion on the subject. He spoke with authority in behalf of the first state Baptist convention, newly organized just the year before. Further, he presented his rationale as the correct scriptural view. After giving biblical arguments supporting slavery, Furman logically reasoned why "the manner of obtaining slaves from Africa is just" and "purchasing them has been the means of saving human life" and of greatly advancing the slaves' "mental and religious improvement."[106]

He admitted that some people, "by reasoning on abstract principles, are induced to favour the scheme of general emancipation" and that those who oppose slavery often "ascribe their sentiments to Christianity." Yet, Furman wrote that such people, "however benevolent their intentions may be," taught "a perversion of the Scriptural doctrine, through their wrong views of it."[107]

Christian historians have excused Furman as, "like all of us," being captive to his culture. He himself owned slaves. He lived in a plantation society. He wrote his exposition soon after an attempted slave revolt in Charleston was exposed and thwarted. And so, they say, only naturally his reasoning led him to some wrong conclusions.

These same historians laud Furman for his courageous role in the American Revolution, when he stood up to public opinion, risking everything to challenge a system he believed "effectual to the enslaving of Americans."[108]

The Holy Spirit is captive to no culture. He came to guide Christ's followers from all cultures into all truth. He came to convict and convince as to what is sin, what is righteousness, and the reality of judgment.[109] When the Spirit of God finds the people of God going the wrong way, he does not meekly sit by. He calls, he warns, he chides. When he finds us leading others astray, he reprimands even more severely.

To listen to the voice of reason, Furman had to reject the voice of God. What's more, in declaring slavery a biblically sanctioned, positive good, Richard Furman did not follow his culture's lead. He, in fact, led the culture.

In *Prelude to Civil War*, William Freehling wrote, "Before the 1830's southerners often admitted that slavery had no place in a land which assumed that men had a natural right to life, liberty, and the pursuit of happiness."[110] Indeed, "in the 1820's, as earlier, southerners vied with northerners in their condemnation of the peculiar institution."[111] Even those who argued for slavery called it a "necessary evil," admitting, "We abhor, we deplore it ourselves with all the pity of humanity."[112]

During these decades of awakening, the Southern clergy were known, not for defending slavery, but for severely criticizing it. In 1833—11 years after Furman wrote his exposition—a Presbyterian synod of South Carolina and Georgia ministers wrote of slavery: "We are chained to a putrid carcass. It sickens and destroys us. We have a millstone hanging about the neck of our society, to sink us deep in the sea of vice."[113]

Only in the mid-1830's—after the South Carolina nullification crisis and the emancipation of slaves by the British Empire—did the church in the South begin to echo Furman's defense of slavery as a system biblically sanctioned, morally upright, and ordained by God.

Not divinely inspired

In 1822, the leading Baptist of the day and the spiritual father of the Southern Baptist Convention, spoke—and led God's people astray. How could a sincere follower of Christ lead so confidently in the wrong direction? Two years after writing his exposition on slavery and less than a year before his death, Furman gave an address to the churches of South Carolina in behalf of the state Baptist convention.

As already noted, Furman championed higher education for ministers. In this address, he urged that very thing. He countered the argument that the apostles themselves were "uneducated and untrained men" (Acts 4:13 NKJV) by asking several questions and arriving at one startling answer:

> Did [the apostles] not study under the greatest Teacher the world ever knew? Were they not almost constantly with their divine Lord and Master for the space of three years and an half? Besides, were they not inspired by the Holy Ghost and endowed with miraculous power? Will the opponents to a regular course of instruction, for the work of the gospel ministry, say that men are inspired by the Holy Ghost *now*, as the Apostles were?—Or that they *still* have the power of working miracles? Surely they cannot.

Stop and let that sink in. Furman wrote that the Holy Spirit no longer inspires people or works miracles *while a 40-year Great Awakening was still in progress*, an awakening that had radically impacted Baptists across the South. Had years of choosing not to listen to the Spirit deafened his ears? He continued:

> If men are not divinely inspired *now*, and *the age of miracles* has past away, then, surely, it is necessary that attention should be paid to the education of those whom God has been pleased to call to this work without it. We live, beloved Brethren, in an advanced period of the world. The arts and sciences are rapidly progressing.—The human mind is daily acquiring strength and refinement ... Now, who is able to distinguish truth from error? Who stands prepared to strip error of her assumed garments of loveliness, and to make her appear in all her native deformity and vileness? We answer, the man of God; the faithful minister of Jesus Christ; he who believes in his proper Deity, and whose mind, like that of his opponent, has been illuminated by science.[114]

So wrote the faithful minister who, two years earlier, used intellect to reason from Scripture, "proving" slavery both justifiable and moral.

As Furman and other Charleston tradition leaders led in the training of ministers, and those ministers in turn trained their congregations, people struggling with deep conviction over culturally accepted sins now had a reason to ignore the Spirit of Christ. Leaders they admired and trusted had told them the Spirit does not continue to "inspire men." These leaders urged, "Look to us, the trained ministers, if you want to know truth from error." Worship became regimented, women learned they had no place in ministry, and white Southerners found biblical support for rationalizing away their deep guilt over slavery.

In the "backcountry" places where the Spirit had fallen and people had experienced his fire firsthand, churches continued to long for his life, while rejecting his voice. As a result, their love for his Word metamorphosed into a firm conviction that only those who believed as they did had interpreted the Bible correctly. Indeed, within a few years of the forming of the SBC, Baptists across the South embraced the Landmark view that the Baptist church is the only true church. By then, too, the astounding experiences of God's presence had devolved into an unhealthy binge-purge emotionalism that historian Terry Matthews calls "spiritual bulimia."[115] People could eat their fill of culturally acceptable sins all week, disgorge at the altar on Sunday—and then go out to sin some more.

With their ears closed to the Spirit's voice, the Charleston tradition Baptists trusted in ORDER based on human reasoning. With their ears also closed, the Sandy Creek tradition Baptists replaced true spiritual fervor with ARDOR flowing from pumped up emotionalism. The two traditions made an uneasy truce, which Richard Furman worked hard to foster—but the *best* of neither "tradition" survived the quarter-century after the Second Great Awakening.

The church is at its best when the life and power of God are flowing freely and fully in his people, and the Lord himself is ordering our steps.

Sticks and bones

Let me affirm again: In revealing the past, God's purpose is not to point fingers at one denomination or one region, but rather he is seeking to rescue his Bride from all the ways we've compromised our covenant relationship with one another and with him. He is at work to free people who love him—and people who never yet thought of loving him—from attitudes, beliefs, and behaviors they've always associated with Christ, but that produce the opposite of Christ. He is not fostering division, but rather establishing true unity. He is not beating us down, but rather raising us up.

He is inviting us to join him, as Ezekiel joined him, in the two stunning prophetic miracles Ezekiel 37 describes. In Ezekiel's day, Israel had divided, north from south. God told Ezekiel to take two sticks. Then the Lord declared he would do the impossible: make the two sticks into one.

"This is what the Almighty Lord says: … I will form them into one nation in the land … One king will rule all of them. They will no longer be two nations or be divided into two kingdoms. They will no longer dishonor themselves with their idols, with their detestable things, or with their rebellious acts. I will forgive them for all the times they turned away from me and sinned. I will cleanse them so that they will be my people, and I will be their God" (Ezek. 37:21–23 *GOD'S WORD*).

In Ezekiel's day, the people God had destined for wholeness and holiness had divided into two camps. Both camps had dishonored themselves and rebelled against the Lord. Physically, the people still walked around, going through the motions, doing life. Spiritually, they lay, fragmented and defeated. The breath of God in them had been snuffed out. Ezekiel saw them scattered like dry bones across a major battlefield. When God asked him, "Can these bones live?" Ezekiel answered, "Sovereign Lord, you alone know" (Ezek. 37:3).

The Lord exposed all those dry bones, not to trample them and not to bury them, but to raise up *one army* from them. God told Ezekiel, "Speak to the bones": Call out to fractured people, who don't appear to have one bit of life left. Tell them, "The Lord says, 'I will restore you. I will make you whole.'" When Ezekiel obeyed and the miracle happened, God said, "Speak to the breath": Call for the Spirit to enter and mobilize the bodies the dry bones formed (Ezek. 37:4–11).

Remember: the sticks and the bones were God's people. Ezekiel cooperated with God to see his people Israel restored. We cooperate with God to see his church awakened, forgiven, and cleansed; re-formed, filled with the breath, arising as one.

A different kind of fasting

As a critical component, the Lord is calling us to a different kind of fasting than we've known. In Isaiah 58, the Lord took no notice when people abstained from food, yet continued to treat one another terribly. He rejected that kind of fasting then, and he rejects it now.

Entering God's fast, we deny ourselves and humble ourselves in ways we have not since the Second Great Awakening. Entering God's fast, we relinquish self-interest and pride. Entering God's fast, we listen to his voice and treat others the way his Spirit says to treat them, regardless the cost.

> Is not this the fast that I choose:
> to loose the bonds of injustice,
> to undo the thongs of the yoke,
> to let the oppressed go free,
> and to break every yoke?
> Is it not to share your bread with the hungry,

and bring the homeless poor into your house;
when you see the naked, to cover them,
and not to hide yourself from your own kin?
Then your light shall break forth like the dawn,
and your healing shall spring up quickly;
your vindicator shall go before you,
the glory of the Lord shall be your rear guard.
Then you shall call, and the Lord will answer;
you shall cry for help, and he will say, Here I am.
(Isa. 58:6–9 NRSV).

5—Restoring the Foundations

The LORD is initiating a deep work, a foundational shift that must be made correctly and then correctly built upon. In order to re-establish our true root, he is exposing an ungodly root system with a deep taproot that will only grow back if not fully removed.

"Get to work, all you people!"—GOD is speaking. "Yes, get to work! For I am with you." The GOD-of-the-Angel-Armies is speaking! "Put into action the word I covenanted with you when you left Egypt. I'm living and breathing among you right now. Don't be timid. Don't hold back."—Haggai 2:4–6 MSG

Four years before this writing, my husband Jerry and I returned to my home state of Mississippi and moved into a newly built house. Almost immediately, we began to notice issues that, individually, appeared minor, but taken together seemed significant. Doors that closed one day would not close the next. Grouting between tile started cracking. Hairline cracks in the sheetrock began appearing.

Our family room has a vaulted ceiling and imposing two-story walls. Sitting in that room the evening of March 3, Jerry heard a loud pop. Looking up, he saw that one tall, north-south wall had split. A new, ugly crack ran roughly six feet down from the ceiling. Eventually, that crack extended into a 9-foot lightning bolt. At the top, a person's hand could fit sideways into the opening.

A week after that first large crack erupted, I woke to watch another ugly crack forming on one bedroom wall. It ran diagonally upward from a top corner of a door.

For the next three months, major cracking, buckling, and wrinkling continued to appear in the sheetrock in the southeast rooms of the house. Smaller cracks opened in other rooms. During that particularly rainy spring, I spent long nights lying awake, listening to rain fall outside and loud popping sounds inside, as more places separated and buckled. Every day, I saw shouting reminders that action needed to be taken *now.*

Frantic, we hired an engineer to come check our house. On arriving, he walked the interior, surveying the damage. Then, he walked the outside perimeter, carrying a six-foot willowy rod. After he'd completed his initial survey, he called Jerry and me outside to look. As he poked the ground with the rod, the firm ground around three-fourths of the house refused to allow the stick to penetrate at all. But around the entire southeast corner of the house, that six-foot rod went all the way into the ground without ever meeting resistance.

We live on a hill. Suddenly we realized: Our house plan had covered more square feet than the crest of the hill offered, so dirt had been moved in. Yet the dirt had not been compacted properly, not at all. As a result, the southeast portion of our house was sinking.

While most of the visible damage had appeared inside and up, toward the ceiling, the real problem lay below ground, out of sight. While the ugliest issues had to do with sheetrock, doors, and grouting, the most crucial issue by far was a faulty foundation.

A preacher's son, the builder attends church with the realtor who sold us the house. She had described the builder as a person of high integrity who builds homes of high quality. My husband and I had believed her. On discovering our house had foundation problems, we thought the man would apologize profusely and do whatever needed to be done to make things right.

Instead, we encountered denial, lies, and stall tactics that held us and our lawyer at bay until we paid to have the needed foundation work done. It took 11 steel pillars, each of which extended 20 or more feet down to bedrock, to safely anchor the foundation. The day we installed the pillars, the catastrophic damage stopped.

Ultimately, the builder used legal maneuvers to walk away from the responsibility and the repercussions of his poor work. We've paid the costs of repairs. We've not been compensated for the devaluation due to the foundation issues. With no resolution in sight, it looks like injustice and unrighteousness have won.

But the Lord is using the whole sordid mess to say an entirely different thing.

Foundation issues

If you were to lay a giant map of the US atop our floor plan, the part of the house that was sinking would correspond in a startling way to the location of the former Confederacy. The two biggest cracks demarked the Mason-Dixon line. The worst damage was in the southeast sector. Yet, with that section pulling away from the rest of the house, some significant damage showed up in the north and west sectors, in places we'd not have thought would be affected.

When the trauma began, I was already researching the history of the church and the South. I soon realized we were living a prophetic picture, while also walking through a very real, very difficult personal experience.

Like our builder, those who formed the Old South would not admit that they had built on a faulty foundation. They would not take the needed steps to restore the foundation properly. When 11 states seceded from the Union to form the Confederacy, they created a seismic rift within the nation and indeed, a whole slew of rifts in places we wouldn't have dreamed would be affected.

The nation reunited after the Civil War. The rifts were patched, but the South continued to assert that its original foundation was sure.

Fast forward to this century. Before we moved back to Mississippi, the Lord took me through a very traumatic season inside denominational structures I had thought sound. In front of my eyes, fissures popped open. Buckling appeared and enlarged. The damage ran from the top down. Stunned and disbelieving, I watched a lot of cover up—a lot of patching and painting of sheetrock—along with adamant refusal to admit or deal with foundational causes. I watched those who should have shielded the innocent and stopped the wrongdoing, instead, aid and abet the guilty.

Later, stepping back to survey the situation, I saw that the problem extends way beyond one denomination: Similar fissures have erupted across the conservative US church culture in places I never would have dreamed. This plethora of seemingly unrelated "stress fractures" testifies to a common denominator, a major problem that lies below ground and out of sight. The true foundation has been compromised and never properly restored.

The Haggai strategy

About a month into our house crisis, I woke at 2:30 one morning, made my way to my office, knelt on the floor, and cried out to the Lord: "I need to hear from you! It doesn't matter what you say, just please speak."

The day before, I'd read the first chapter of the tiny Old Testament book of Haggai. So I pulled the Amplified Bible from a nearby bookshelf, turned to Haggai, and started reading at chapter two. I got as far as verse 3—and burst out laughing.

"Who is left among you who saw this house in its former glory? And how do you see it now? Is not this in your sight as nothing in comparison to that?"

The Lord God had heard my prayer. He couldn't have answered more specifically. He spoke to me about my house, using words a prophet wrote millennia ago about the Jewish temple. Deeply grateful and deeply intrigued, I continued to read.

> Yet now be strong, alert, and courageous, O Zerubbabel, says the Lord; be strong, alert, and courageous, O Joshua son of Jehozadak, the high priest; and be strong, alert, and courageous, all you people of the land, says the Lord, and work! For I am with you, says the Lord of hosts. According to the promise that I covenanted with you when you came out of Egypt, so My Spirit stands and abides in the midst of you; fear not. For thus says the Lord of hosts: Yet once more, in a little while, I will shake and make tremble the [starry] heavens, the earth, the sea, and the dry land; and I will shake all nations and the desire and the precious things of all nations shall come in, and I will fill this house with splendor, says the Lord of hosts. The silver is Mine and the gold is Mine, says the Lord of hosts. The latter glory of

> this house … shall be greater than the former, says the Lord of hosts; and in this place will I give peace and prosperity, says the Lord of hosts (Hag. 2:3–9 AMP).

Wow. That's pointed. And powerful. And utterly unsettling. And amazing and wonderful and glorious!

While part of our foundation continued to sink, I wrote individual verses from Haggai 2:3–9 in large letters on large sheets of drawing paper and thumb-tacked the sheets onto our cracked and buckling sheetrock. Every time I looked at the broken places, I read God's promises aloud.

Now, a page containing the passage from Haggai 2 still hangs in my kitchen. When I feel betrayed—by the builder, the legal profession, and the state—the Lord says, "I am with you … My Spirit stands and abides in the midst of you." When I feel cheated and robbed, the Lord says, "The silver is Mine and the gold is Mine." When I feel violated and ashamed, the Lord says, "I will fill this house with splendor." When I question our wisdom in buying the house, or in not selling it back as soon as we discovered the foundation problem, the Lord of hosts declares, "In this place will I give peace and prosperity."

Though we haven't yet seen the resolution we've cried to God to bring, we see the Lord in this place. As we've sought him and obeyed what he's said, as we've determined to redeem what we might have cast off, God has manifested his presence here in a remarkable way. One woman who sat in our family room, listening to our story and looking at the wall where the terrible lightning-bolt crack had run, said, "The Lord is here. The Lord is here. The Lord is here."

Yes, the God of the covenant Name is here—here in this house, here in this region, here in his church. Faithfully, he is working to restore the true foundations, both of the land and the people on it. Tenaciously, he chooses to redeem what he might have cast off.

The psalmist sang to the Lord: "The heavens are yours, and yours also the earth; you founded the world and all that is in it … Your arm is endued with power; your hand is strong, your right hand exalted. Righteousness and justice are the foundation of your throne; love and faithfulness go before you. Blessed are those who have learned to acclaim you, who walk in the light of your presence, LORD" (Ps. 89:11, 13–15).

The psalmist sang of the Lord, "The LORD reigns, let the earth be glad … Clouds and thick darkness surround him; righteousness and justice are the foundation of his throne" (Ps. 97:1, 2).

This covenant-keeping LORD will not look the other way when a foundation to which we've attached his name is sinking due to unrighteousness and injustice. He will not agree to our whitewashing the ugly presenting issues, rather than correcting the underlying ones. Further, he will not agree to our bailing out and letting someone else deal with the mess. He created the land and the people on it. He is holy and he is love. He is the just Judge, the righteous King and the resolute Redeemer. He summons us. He entrusts to us the overwhelming task of restoring foundations we did not lay.

"Yet now be strong, alert, and courageous, … be strong, alert, and courageous, … be strong, alert, and courageous, … says the Lord, and work! For I am with you, says the Lord of hosts."

Uproot and tear down, build and plant

God often paints the same process in different metaphors. Each picture reveals different aspects of what he's doing and how we cooperate with him. The same God who restores foundations also uproots and replants.

Notice how the Lord mixes building and planting metaphors in the verses below:

"You received Christ Jesus the Lord, so continue to live as Christ's people. Sink your roots in him and build on him" (Col. 2:6–7 *GOD'S WORD*).

> There! I have put my words in your mouth.
> Today I have placed you over nations and kingdoms
> to uproot and to tear down,
> to destroy and to demolish,
> to build and to plant (Jer. 1:9–10 CJB).

> They will be called Oaks of Righteousness,
> the Plantings of the LORD,
> so that he might display his glory.
> They will rebuild the ancient ruins.
> They will restore the places destroyed long ago (Isa. 61:3–4 *GOD'S WORD*).

God is Redeemer. In his kingdom, uprooting and tearing down are not ends in themselves, but rather a prelude to building and planting. We remove the false and faulty in order to re-establish what is deep and firm, stable and true. To cooperate with the Lord in this process, we must keep remembering: It is a process. Much as we'd like to say a prayer, make a declaration, and consider the matter done, it will not happen that way.

The Lord is initiating a deep work, a foundational shift that must be made correctly and then correctly built upon. In order to re-establish our true root, he is exposing an ungodly root system with a deep taproot that will only grow back if not fully removed.

This book grapples with revelation we must have in order to cooperate with God in this restoring, redeeming work. To accomplish what the Lord intends, we must let his revelation sink deep into our human spirit. We must allow time for his word to gestate and marinate, before we start trying to yank up roots or pour more concrete where it will only do more harm than good.

This chapter helps us begin that marinating process. We'll do what Nehemiah did when the Jerusalem wall lay in ruins, what Haggai and Zechariah did when the temple lay decimated, and what the engineer did when part of our house was sinking: We'll survey the extent of the damage.

We'll look again at the false identity the South embraced and ultimately made covenant with, even as many Southerners also tried to embrace their true identity in Christ. Above ground, we'll see *injustices*, hidden in plain sight. Below the surface, we'll find the *unrighteous roots* that continue to disrupt and destroy. In terms of building and planting, we'll see what shaky foundations, what rotten roots have defiled us and dishonored our Lord for far too long.

Our Father, our Bridegroom, our Redeemer, our Lord, even now pour out a spirit of grace and supplication on us.

Injustice: Slavery and the cotton boll

Since we're exposing a Cotton Kingdom, imagine if you will a cotton plant. Immediately, you notice the *cotton boll.* As the boll is the presenting part of the cotton plant, *slavery* became the presenting issue when a whole region crowned cotton king. The cotton boll is crucial to cotton production. The South considered slavery crucial too. My ancestors saw slavery as a source of status, power, and wealth. Ultimately, they called it "good." Looking back, we see what those who chose to close their eyes could not—the blatant injustice of the slavery system.

Two sisters from Charleston, South Carolina, tell us much. Historians James Oakes, Luther Copeland, John Lee Eighmy, and Terry Matthews help flesh out the picture.

The sisters, Sarah and Angelina Grimké, grew up in a slaveholding family—and grew to detest slavery. Their father, a wealthy planter, served as chief judge of the South Carolina Supreme Court. In early adulthood, first Sarah, then Angelina became Quaker and moved north. In 1837, the antislavery paper, *The Liberator*, published a personal letter Angelina sent to its editor, William Lloyd Garrison. Overnight, the sisters found themselves at the forefront of the abolition movement. Even in the North, they faced strong opposition, both from those who considered emancipation "radical" and from those who insisted women should not speak in public.

In 1838, Angelina married abolitionist Theodore Weld. In 1839, Weld, his wife, and her sister produced the volume that ultimately proved second only to *Uncle Tom's Cabin* in antislavery influence in the US. *American Slavery As It Is: Testimony of a Thousand Witnesses* contains 210 pages of "well-weighed testimony and well-attested facts," most drawn from the writings of slaveholders themselves. A detailed 15-page index completes this authoritative work. Sarah told why she co-edited such a project:

"As I left my native state on account of slavery, and deserted the home of my fathers to escape the sound of the lash and the shrieks of tortured victims, I would gladly bury in oblivion the recollection of those scenes with which I have been familiar; but this may not, cannot be; they come over my memory like gory spectres, and implore me with resistless power, in the name of a God of mercy, in the name of a crucified Savior, in the name of humanity; for the sake of the slaveholder, as well as the slave … to give my testimony respecting the system of American slavery."[116]

Story after story, chart after chart, "a thousand witnesses" expose the gut-wrenching truth of slavery's injustice. Testimonies and facts show "the condition of slaves, in *all respects*."[117]

Slaves were born, lived, and died under "slave codes"—laws dating back to colonial times, created "for the Better Ordering and Governing of Negroes and Other Slaves." The South Carolina Slave Code of 1740 includes 58 sections that systematically stripped blacks (and Indians) of inalienable rights endowed by their Creator. The code made it illegal, for example, for slaves to learn to read and write, to gather without white supervision, or to go out of town or off plantation without a permit.

The code declared: "all Negroes ... and all their issue and offspring, born or to be born, shall be, and they are hereby declared to be, and remain forever hereafter, absolute slaves, and shall follow the condition of the mother, and shall be deemed, held, taken, reputed and adjudged in law, to be chattels personal, in the hands of their owners and possessors."[118]

Chattels means "property." Thus, by law, persons were declared property. James Oakes wrote, "No white person—in any colony, at any time, anywhere in North America—ever suffered such a fate."[119]

Luther Copeland, descendant of a slaveholder, confessed:

The "slavery system which Southern Baptists defended" was "at best ... a benevolent paternalism which treated adult human beings as 'permanent children' whose lives needed constant direction and protection." It was "at worst ... a system of almost unbelievable cruelty which treated persons as nothing more than property that could be violated and destroyed with impunity. Even books which emphasize slavery's benevolence can hardly ignore its brutality, of which the auctions, the kidnappings and the unmerciful and humiliating whippings are examples. More objective studies call attention to the cruelty that 'was endemic in all slaveholding communities,' or to the intrinsic exploitation, brutality and injustice that slavery elicited in the slaveholders ...

"Slaveholders devised a variety of punishments, including selling slaves away from their families and friends. 'But no master denied the propriety of giving a moderate whipping to a disobedient bondsman.' Many lashings were by no means 'moderate'! in some instances, slaves were crippled, maimed or killed as a result of sadistic beatings. Sometimes 'salting' was used as a punishment, that is, washing in brine the cuts which had been produced by the whip. Though some slaveholders were models of moderation and self-restraint and even rebuked their neighbors for their inhumanity, the cruelty of the system was apparent."[120]

Theodore, Angelina, and Sarah compiled mountainous evidence and stunning firsthand testimony showing how the slave codes played out across the South. The law had:

> taken away from the slave his *liberty;* it has robbed him of his right to his own body, of his right to improve his mind, of his right to read the Bible, of his right to worship God according to his conscience, of his right to receive and enjoy what he earns, of his right to live with his wife and children, of his right to better his condition, of his right to eat when he is hungry, to rest when he is tired, to sleep when he needs it, and to cover his nakedness with clothing: this [law] makes the slave a prisoner for life on the plantation, except when his jailor pleases to let him out with a "pass," or sells him, and transfers him in irons to another jail-yard: this [law] traverses the country, buying up men, women, children—chaining them in coffles, and driving them forever from their nearest friends; it sets them on the auction table, to be handled, scrutinized, knocked off to the highest bidder; it proclaims that they shall not have their liberty; and, if their masters give it them, [the law] seizes and throws them back into slavery.[121]

Slaves were sold at a master's whim and a master's death. They were sold when restless masters made the frequent decision to move farther west and south or, even more frequently, when overextended masters needed a quick way to cover their debts.

Elizabeth Keckley described the first time she witnessed "the sale of a human being." Keckley was seven years old and herself a slave when her master "purchased his hogs for the winter, for which he was unable to pay in full. To escape from his embarrassment it was necessary to sell one of the slaves. Little Joe, the son of the cook, was selected … His mother was ordered to dress him up in his Sunday clothes, and send him to the house. He came in with a bright face, was placed in the scales, and was sold, like the hogs, at so much per pound."[122]

Typically ill-clad, sometimes unclothed, and crowded indiscriminately into drafty one-room huts with dirt floors and no beds, slaves suffered in a myriad of ways, catalogued in *American Slavery As It Is.*

"Every body here knows *overdriving* to be one of the most common occurrences, the planters do not deny it, except, perhaps, to northerners," said a theological student in Natchez, Mississippi.[123]

Other eyewitnesses wrote,

"The whip is considered as necessary on a plantation as the plough; and its use is almost as common."[124]

"What is called a moderate flogging at the south is horribly cruel. Should we whip our horses for any offence as they whip their slaves for small offences, we should expose ourselves to the penalty of the law."[125]

"It is the common rule for the slaves to be kept at work *fifteen hours in the day,* and in the time of picking cotton a certain number of pounds is required of each. If this amount is not brought in at night, the slave is whipped, and the number of pounds lacking is added to the next day's job; this course is often repeated from day to day."[126]

Theodore Weld observed, "to furnish men at hard labor from daylight till dark with but 1 7/8 lbs. of *corn* per day, their sole sustenance, is to MURDER THEM BY PIECE-MEAL."[127]

Slave owners knew as much: "at a meeting of planters in South Carolina, the question was seriously discussed whether the slave is more profitable to the owner, if well fed, well clothed, and worked lightly, or if made the most of *at once,* and exhausted in some eight years. The decision was in favor of the last alternative." The "slaveholders generally throughout the far south and south west ... believe it for their interest to wear out the slaves by excessive toil in eight or ten years after they put them into the field."[128]

Angelina Grimké Weld described, in her words, the "utter disregard of the comfort of the slaves, in *little* things":

"Only two meals a day are allowed the house slaves—the *first at twelve* o'clock ... I am sure there must be a good deal of suffering among them from *hunger,* and particularly by children. Besides this, they are often kept from their meals by way of punishment. No table is provided for them to eat from ... I *never* saw slaves seated round a *table* to partake of any meal.

"As the general rule, no lights of any kind, no firewood—no towels, basins, or soap, no tables, chairs, or other furniture, are provided ... when the master's work is done, the slave must find wood for himself if he has a fire."

"Persons who own plantations and yet live in cities, often take children from their parents as soon as they are weaned, and send them into the country; because they do not want the time of the mother taken up by attendance upon her own children, it being too valuable to the mistress. As a *favor,* she is, in some cases, permitted to go to see them once a year. So, on the other hand, if field slaves happen to have children of an age suitable to the convenience of the master, they are taken from their parents and brought to the city."

"Another way in which the feelings of slaves are trifled with and often deeply wounded, is by changing their names; if, at the time they are brought into a family, there is another slave of the same name; or if the owner happens, for some other reason, not to like the name of the new comer. I have known slaves very much grieved at having the names of their children thus changed, when they had been called after a dear relation. Indeed it would be utterly impossible to recount the multitude of ways in which the *heart* of the slave is continually lacerated by the total disregard of his feelings as a social being and a human creature."[129]

Besides exposing the deplorable conditions under which slaves lived, Weld, the Grimké sisters, and others decried the injustice of slavery itself.

William Allan, son of a Presbyterian pastor and slaveholder, said: "The great wrong is *enslaving a man;* all other wrongs are pigmies, compared with that. Facts might be gathered abundantly, to show that it is *slavery itself,* and not cruelties merely, that make slaves unhappy. Even those that are most kindly treated, are generally far from being happy. The slaves in my father's family are almost as kindly treated as *slaves* can be, yet they pant for liberty."[130]

Former slave James Pennington wrote, "My feelings are always outraged when I hear them speak of 'kind masters,'—'Christian masters,'—'the mildest form of slavery,'—'well fed and clothed slaves,' as extenuations of slavery; I am satisfied they either mean to pervert the truth, or they do not know what they say. The being of slavery, its soul and body, lives and moves in the chattel principle, the property principle, the bill of sale principle ...

Talk not then about kind and christian masters. They are not masters of the system. The system is master of them; and the slaves are their vassals.[131]

The Grimké sisters suffered much in order to speak out against the injustices of slavery. They cared deeply about the enslaved. They also cared deeply about the people doing the enslaving.

Angelina wrote, "But it is not alone for the sake of my poor brothers and sisters in bonds, or for the cause of truth, and righteousness, and humanity, that I testify; the deep yearnings of affection for the mother that bore me, who is still a slaveholder, both in fact and in heart; for my brothers and sisters, (a large family circle,) and for my numerous other slaveholding kindred in South Carolina, constrain me to speak: for even were slavery no curse to its victims, the exercise of arbitrary power works such fearful ruin upon the hearts of *slaveholders,* that I should feel impelled to labor and pray for its overthrow with my last energies and latest breath."[132]

According to Terry Matthews: Only one in 11 Southerners owned slaves. Yet this minority wielded great influence, for they included the major molders of public opinion: educators, doctors, politicians, preachers. In South Carolina, 40 percent of Baptist preachers owned slaves.[133]

The wealthy Grimké family owned a plantation. Most slaveholders did not. In *The Ruling Race,* James Oakes described the average slaveholder in 1850 as a white male in his mid-40s, born in the South and master of only a handful of slaves. Oakes remarked:

" … the vast majority of small slaveholders … neither grew up on plantations nor achieved planter status. More typically, their lives were shaped by restlessness, drift, and economic insecurity."[134] Regardless the number of slaves owned, there was a pervasive obsession with owning more.

Said Oakes, "Slaveholding was the symbol of success in the market culture of the Old South. It was an ambition, an achievement, a reward for diligence, hard work, and tenacity. As one Louisiana master wrote, 'A man's merit in this country is estimated according to the number of Negroes he works in the field.'"[135]

Joseph Ingraham told what he had learned during his sojourn in Natchez: "To sell cotton in order to buy negroes—to make more cotton to buy more negroes, 'ad infinitum,' is the aim and direct tendency of all the operations of the thorough-going cotton planter; his whole soul is wrapped up in this pursuit."[136]

That pursuit blinded eyes and hardened hearts. "He who holds human beings as his bona fide property, *regards* them as property, and not as *persons;* this is his permanent state of mind toward them," wrote Weld. "He does not contemplate slaves as human beings, consequently does not *treat* them as such; and with entire indifference sees them suffer privations and writhe under blows, which, if inflicted upon whites, would fill him with horror and indignation."[137]

How tragic when people's "consciences have been seared as with a hot iron" (1 Tim. 4:2)! How exponentially more tragic when those with deadened consciences identify with Christ!

James Oakes attested: "The majority of masters, small slaveholders and large planters alike, were evangelicals." "Slaveholders often remembered the conversion experience as a central event in their lives, one which informed all subsequent thought and actions."[138]

Faithfully, *American Slavery As It Is* recounts eyewitness reports of the seared consciences of Christians.

In a Presbyterian church in Kentucky: "The minister and all the church members held slaves. Some were treated kindly, others harshly. *There was not a shade of difference* between their slaves and those of their *infidel* neighbors, either in their physical, intellectual, or moral state: in some cases they would *suffer* in the comparison."[139]

"Rev. Dr. Staughton, formerly of Philadelphia, often stated, that when he lived at Georgetown, S. C. he could tell the doings of one of the slaveholders of the Baptist church there by his prayers at the prayer meeting. 'If,' said he, 'that man was upon good terms with his slaves, his words were cold and heartless as frost; if he had been whipping a man, he would pray with life; but if he had left a woman whom he had been flogging, tied to a post in his cellar, with a determination to go back and torture her again, O! how he would pray!'"[140]

"Rev. Joseph Hough, ... while traveling in the south, a few years ago, put up one night with a Methodist family, and spent the Sabbath with them. While there, one of the female slaves did something which displeased her mistress. She took a chisel and mallet, and very deliberately cut off one of her toes!"[141]

Sarah Grimké personally witnessed this scene:

> A slave who had been separated from his wife, because it best suited the convenience of his owner, ran away. He was taken up on the plantation where his wife, to whom he was tenderly attached, then lived. His only object in running away was to return to her—no other fault was attributed to him. For this offence he was confined in the stocks *six weeks,* in a miserable hovel, not weather-tight. He received fifty lashes weekly during that time, was allowed food barely sufficient to sustain him, and when released from confinement, was not permitted to return to his wife. His master, although himself a husband and a father, was unmoved by the touching appeals of the slave, who entreated that he might only remain with his wife, promising to discharge his duties faithfully; his master continued inexorable, and he was torn from his wife and family. The owner of this slave was a professing Christian, in full membership with the church, and this circumstance occurred when he was confined to his chamber during his last illness.[142]

In *Churches in Cultural Captivity*, John Lee Eighmy wrote, "Baptists defended slavery through religious journals and at denominational gatherings by expounding on the fanaticism of abolitionism, the scriptural support of slavery, and the need for humane treatment and religious instruction of slaves ... In their rationale, justification of slavery ultimately rested on the opportunity the system provided for the African's salvation from heathenism. To strengthen their case among the more practical-minded slaveholders, Baptist spokesmen were not above promising that religious teaching would make the slave 'more honest, more industrious, and more obedient to his master.'"

"All Baptist periodicals in the South upheld the practice of slavery," Eighmy said.[143]

In the mid-1840s, the defense of this slavery system prompted the split of southern Methodists and southern Baptists from their northern counterparts. A decade-and-a-half later, Mississippi legislators declared "the Immediate Causes which Induce and Justify the Secession of the State of Mississippi from the Federal Union." They began:

"Our position is thoroughly identified with the institution of slavery—the greatest material interest of the world. Its labor supplies the product which constitutes by far the largest and most important portions of commerce of the earth. These products are peculiar to the climate verging on the tropical regions, and by an imperious law of nature, none but the black race can bear exposure to the tropical sun. These products have become necessities of the world, and a blow at slavery is a blow at commerce and civilization."[144]

When we examine the Cotton Kingdom, we see slavery first.

Other injustice issues: Hidden in plain sight

After slavery was abolished, my ancestors, who could not see the contradictions they had embraced, found ways to continue racial injustices against blacks. Segregation forbade social interaction and clearly announced who was superior and who, inferior. Upstanding citizens hiding under robes and hoods kept the old order by violence and intimidation. Many whites publicly protested such tactics, but not with sufficient outrage or singleness of heart to stop the Klan. Lawmakers and police officers created and enforced state laws nullifying rights of blacks that federal laws ensured. Freemasonry promised light and offered power to maintain whatever system the brothers chose. In essence, the defeated South bred a new strain of cotton boll.

Meanwhile, long before abolition, the Cotton Kingdom fostered other injustices. We might compare these injustices to the *branches, stems, and leaves* of the cotton plant. Like the boll, the branches and leaves grow above ground. But while the boll stands out, the rest of the plant often goes unnoticed. So in the antebellum South, injustices other than slavery grew from the same root. These justice issues include the treatment of Native Americans and the view and treatment of women. In comparison with slavery, little notice has been taken of these injustices. Even less have we considered how they contributed to the wholesale bloodshed of the war.

Native Americans

Between 1830 and 1858, most of the Chickasaws, Choctaws, Cherokees, Creeks, Seminoles, and other tribes living east of the Mississippi River were removed to lands in Oklahoma and Kansas. Officially, the tribes relocated voluntarily. In reality, their leaders were often pressured and coerced to sign relocation treaties. As many as 100,000 Native Americans were uprooted from their lands in this way. Tens of thousands died on the journeys west or while attempting to resist relocation.

A PBS article on "Indian Removal" gives a terse description of the most famous of the westward trips. In 1838, 16,000 Cherokee remained on their lands in Georgia, Tennessee, and North Carolina. "The US government sent in 7,000 troops, who forced the Cherokees into stockades at bayonet point. They were not allowed time to gather their belongings, and as they left, whites looted their homes. Then began the march known as the Trail of Tears, in which 4,000 Cherokee people died of cold, hunger, and disease on their way to the western lands."[145]

The settlers who had pressed for Indian Removal didn't grieve the bloodshed and grave injustices it fostered, nor take any steps to right the wrong. Rather, they gave a collective sigh of relief that they no longer had to deal with the "Indian problem."

Yet, technically, the vast majority of displaced Native Americans still lived in the South, for Indian Territory (modern-day Oklahoma) lay below the Missouri Compromise line. Thus, the tribes continued to face strong pressure to affirm and practice black slavery.

When the Civil War broke out, the tribes that had been removed from their Southern homelands became the primary Native American allies of the Confederacy. While some Indians owned slaves, more blamed the US government for passing and enforcing the Indian Removal Act and for continuing to treat the displaced tribes unjustly. Playing on the tribes' distrust of the Union, Confederate leaders wooed the very peoples white Southerners had displaced. In 1861, Albert Pike—a lawyer, Confederate officer, and top-ranking Freemason—negotiated a treaty that promised Native Americans better terms than US treaties offered. The bid by the Five Civilized Tribes for greater justice backfired. After the war, the US nullified all treaties with tribes that had shown Confederate sympathies and punished them severely in other ways, as well.[146]

Women

As the Old South moved farther from awakening and closer to war, white women came to be viewed as decidedly inferior to men—and decidedly superior to them. Thinking influenced by the ancient Greeks denigrated women as helpless, easily deceived, and less mentally astute than men. Thinking influenced by romanticized medieval legends labeled these frail women, "the highest symbol of Southern virtue."[147]

Rollin G. Osterweis called this Greek-medieval view of life, "the Southern cult of chivalry."[148] Its conflicted thinking served two purposes. First, it kept women "in their place": It flattered them as the gender especially virtuous, yet restricted them as the gender specially prone to vice. Second, loud declarations of women's greater virtue served well to excuse less-than-virtuous conduct by men. Most insidious, this mindset was taught as crucial biblical doctrine, in the same way scripture had been co-opted to teach slavery as a positive good.

In her epic saga of the Civil War years, Southern gentlewoman Mary Chesnut recorded this snippet of conversation:

"'Why do we wait and whimper so in our soft Southern speech—we poor women?'

"'Because,' said Mrs. Singleton, in quick and emphatic way, 'you are always excusing yourselves. Men here are masters, and they find fault and bully you. You are afraid of them and take a meek, timid, defensive style.'"[149]

Luther Copeland wrote, "According to the code of chivalry, … women were considered superior to men in purity and were often and in many ways assured their superlative virtue. Actually, however, they were prisoners on their pedestal, the emblem both of 'chastity and powerlessness.' …

"The same system which elevated the white woman to her pedestal consigned the black woman to the fields or kitchen or to the dark corners of the big house where she was expected to be available to the white males of the household and was subject to severe penalties if she refused. In fact, it appears that the more the white man sexually exploited the slave woman, the higher he exalted the white woman as the 'delicate ornament of the parlor.'"[150]

British abolitionist Emily Shirreff published two well-researched tracts on "The Chivalry of the South." Shirreff wrote that the "scenes of licentiousness" in a slaveholder's home "make an Eastern harem seem an abode of purity." Further, the slaveholder "is trained from boyhood to see—for the sake of gain—how far womanhood can be degraded; to see women treated like beasts of burden, and working like them under the lash … "

The slave women were whipped even when pregnant.

" … even in that condition which elsewhere calls for reverent tenderness in all but the most brutalised of men."[151]

South Carolinian Mary Chesnut did not disagree. She wrote, "God forgive us, but ours is a *monstrous* system and wrong and iniquity. Perhaps the rest of the world is as bad—this only I see. Like the patriarchs of old our men live all in one house with their wives and their concubines, and the mulattoes one sees in every family exactly resemble the white children—and every lady tells you who is the father of all the mulatto children in everybody's household, but those in her own she seems to think drop from the clouds, or pretends so to think."[152]

Emily Shirreff wrote, "The Southern gentleman … sells his own son into bondage, his own daughter he sells to bondage and dishonour! … The more children are born on his estate the more dollars will go into his pocket. Whoever the father may be they follow the mother's lot, and go to increase the number of his human chattels. How slight a set-off against these profits are the corruptions tainting his very hearth; the jealousies and heartburnings of the women of his own race, and the misery of the outcasts thus doomed from birth."[153]

Did the Southern view of women guard the region against entering into war? No. Just the opposite. "Ministers identified … 'the purity of our women' with the purity and the virtue of Southern civilization, and by standing between the Yankee invader and their women Southerners could symbolically preserve their civilization's virtue," said Charles Reagan Wilson in *Baptized in Blood*.[154]

Another historian, W. J. Cash, wrote, "She was the South's palladium, this Southern woman … the standard for all its rallying, the mystic symbol of its nationality in the face of the foe … At the last, I verily believe, the ranks of the Confederacy went rolling in battle in the misty conviction that it was wholly for her that they fought."[155]

So in the name of protecting the women of the South from "hosts of ruffians and felons burning with lust and rapine,"[156] the men who had not protected their own wives in their own homes, nor the slave women whom they ruled, led the way to secession and war.

Unrighteousness: Cotton root rot

Cotton is a good plant susceptible to a destructive disease called *cotton root rot.* That's incredibly relevant. When cotton became king, a good root turned rotten. As we've seen, the parts of a diseased cotton plant growing above ground—the boll, stems, and leaves—might represent the injustices of the Cotton Kingdom. Those injustices sprang from ungodly attitudes, commonly held but not admitted or dealt with. Like rotten roots, the unrighteousness below the surface started small and grew into a tangled snarl.

At the center of this root system grew a taproot—a strong, deep, central root formed from an unrighteous triumvirate of *greed, pride,* and *determination to control.* Remember, these rotten roots comprise a *false* identity with which the people of a culture gradually, over time, agreed. No hint of these attitudes is found in our true root in Christ.

W. O. Carver, former missions professor at Southern Baptist Theological Seminary, spoke out against this threefold taproot when he saw it infecting Baptist missions efforts in later generations. He objected to the "rationalized justification of … racial pride … economic greed, and … ambition for power."[157]

Greed

In 1836, Virginian James Davidson traveled across the Midwest and the South. In Vicksburg, Mississippi, Davidson wrote: "The people here are run mad with speculation. They do business in … a kind of phrenzy." The city "is full of Strangers. In fact the South is crowded with strangers; gentlemen adventurers who have dreamed golden dreams of the South, and who think they have nothing more to do than come South and be the Lord of a Cotton Plantation and a hundred slaves."[158]

James Silk Buckingham, from Britain, wrote after touring the South: "this passion for the acquisition of money is much stronger and more universal in this country than in any other under the sun, at least that I have visited."[159]

Historian James Oakes wrote: "The behavior of middle-class slaveholders whose success could well have permitted them the leisurely life so widely associated with the plantation South indicates that such an existence was neither common nor commonly sought. It was the rare master who ceased his quest for more land and slaves, and it was precisely this grasping materialism which stands out in the collective biographies of middle-class slaveholders."[160]

Further, "materialism passed from one generation of slaveholders to the next with all the certainty of a genetic trait. Only a small fraction of masters ever stood aloof from the avid pursuit of wealth … as time went on, most antebellum slaveholders became, if anything, increasingly obsessed with economic prosperity."[161]

"Gain, and the extension of slavery to ensure the gain, are the watchwords," said Emily Shirreff, "a love of gain so intense and so pitiless that to achieve its purposes it tramples on the most sacred rights of humanity and shrinks not from dooming a whole race to every form of misery and degradation."[162]

Colossians 3:5 identifies greed as idolatry. Second Peter 2:14–15 says those "well trained in greed … live under God's curse" (NLT). You cannot determine greed by the amount of money a person has. Ask, rather: What place does money have in the person's heart?

Tragically, after Civil War and Reconstruction left the South's economy in ruins, the people saw nothing but virtue in their pre-war motives. Greed obviously characterized the *North*. But it had *not* characterized the antebellum South! Proud of their agricultural economy, still primarily dependent on cotton, Southerners struggled unsuccessfully to regain their economic footing.

Then, stuck in a seemingly inescapable cycle of poverty and not having admitted or repented for the greed and other wrong attitudes that landed them there, they embraced a bastard child of greed and pride—a poverty spirit. Equating wealth with greed and poverty with godliness, they determined to wear poverty like a badge of honor.

In July 1883, the *Christian Index*, a newspaper published by Georgia Baptists, included these remarks: "God has linked poverty with the whole system of truth. He has ordained it as a perpetual heritage of his people, as a condition of society as inevitable as society itself … We must look at this matter, then, just as we look at any other of the divine enactments, as appealing to our Christian sensibilities. Poverty is not a mere accident, but a law of life … the normal state of society as God has constituted it."[163]

The greed wasn't gone. Just denied.

Power

Mary Chesnut observed, "How men can go blustering around—making everybody uncomfortable simply to show that they are masters—and we only women and children at their mercy … The master is kind and amiable when not crossed. Given to hospitality on a grand scale. Jovial, genial, friendly, courtly in his politeness. As absolute a tyrant as the czar of Russia, the khan of Tartary—or the sultan of Turkey."[164]

Chesnut didn't let Southern women off the hook, either. She described a wartime "aid association" meeting in these words: "The ladies were old ones and all wanted their own way … Fierce dames some of them—august, severe matrons—who evidently had not been accustomed to hear the other side of any argument from anybody, just old enough to find the last pleasure in life in power—and the power to make their claws felt."[165]

After the war, the Virginia Baptist newspaper advised, "Conciliation, firmness and justice, are the elements by which we are to control the negro … and when this is done, there is no nation of people so well suited to our purposes as the African."[166]

The *Alabama Baptist* asserted, "The white people of the South mean to rule, and they will rule."[167]

"Arbitrary power is to the mind what alcohol is to the body; it intoxicates," said Theodore Weld.[168]

Jesus said, "You've observed how godless rulers throw their weight around, how quickly a little power goes to their heads. It's not going to be that way with you. Whoever wants to be great must become a servant. Whoever wants to be first among you must be your slave" (Matt. 20:25–27 MSG).

Notice he did not say, "Make others your slaves, and then quote verses to them about serving and submission."

Pride

In the antebellum South, a people seeking an identity refused to give up what God required them to give up in order to step fully into their true identity in Christ. Instead, they found what seemed a far easier way to create a society of "virtue" and "honor." They read romanticized novels of medieval knights and maidens—and decided, "That's us." Proudly, obsessively, the South tried to live out the wildly popular novels of Sir Walter Scott.

Rollin G. Osterweis, author of *Romanticism and Nationalism in the Old South*, described the "cult of chivalry" this obsession produced.

" … the planters of the South delighted to refer to themselves, in the late antebellum years, as 'The Chivalry.' The term appears over and over again in the pages of the Southern periodicals. It was borrowed from Sir Walter, to whom 'The Chivalry' connoted the knightly class, with emphasis on the gallantry, honor, and courtesy associated with that class … The Southerners became obsessed with the word."[169]

Antebellum Southerners looked down on the slaveless society of the North. Long before the war, they came to consider Yankees a different race altogether, and a decidedly inferior one.

An English traveler who visited Columbia, South Carolina, in 1835 wrote of the Southern men he met 25 years before the war: "here are fine elements for future dissension; for imbibing from their infancy the notion that they are born to command, it will be intolerable to them to submit to be, in their own estimation, the drudges of the Northern manufacturers, whom they despise as an inferior race of men. Even now there is nothing a Southern man resents so much as to be called a Yankee."[170]

In June 1860, the *Southern Literary Messenger* of Richmond published an article entitled, "The Difference of Race Between the Northern People and the Southern People." The author, "a distinguished gentleman of Alabama," wrote that the white population of the North was descended from "the common people of England," the ancient Saxons, and "have severe traits of religious fanaticism." By contrast, white Southerners were "directly descended from the Norman Barons of William the Conqueror, a race distinguished in its earliest history for its warlike and fearless character, a race in all times since renowned for its gallantry; chivalry, honor, gentleness, and intellect."[171]

"We think every Southerner equal to three Yankees at least," Mary Chesnut wrote.[172]

American Slavery As It Is includes this excerpt from a sermon preached in 1791: "Slavery has a most direct tendency to haughtiness, and a *domineering spirit* and conduct in the proprietors of the slaves, in their children, and in all who have the control of them. A man who has been bred up in domineering over negroes, can scarcely avoid contracting such a habit of haughtiness and domination as will express itself in his general treatment of mankind, whether in his private capacity, or in any office, civil or military, with which he may be invested."[173]

In a sermon preached after the Civil War, Episcopal Bishop Stephen Elliott "chastened his people for their pride. 'I am afraid that many of us have said: "Men may despoil us of our property, of our homes, of our rights, of our privileges; but they shall not deprive us of our pride, or our associations, or our memories. We will make these our idols, and will cherish and worship these in our inmost hearts!"'"[174]

Philippians 2:3–4 says, "Do nothing out of selfish ambition or vain conceit. Rather, in humility value others above yourselves, not looking to your own interests but each of you to the interests of the others."

Other unrighteous roots

Very quickly, the threefold King Cotton taproot spawned other roots, all of them becoming so entangled and enmeshed that it's often difficult to separate one from the other.

Immorality and Violence

"All varieties of sources for the antebellum South are redolent with violence," wrote David Grimsted in his book, *American Mobbing, 1828–1861.* "Public murder and intimidation took on added vigor from a society where status and character were tied to mastery, to the numbers of people over whom one wielded unquestioned domination."[175]

Emily Shirreff wrote:

"A gentleman of veracity, now living in the South, told me that among his friends he had once numbered two young men who were themselves intimate friends, till one of them, taking offence at some foolish words uttered by the other, challenged him. A large crowd assembled to see the duel, which took place on a piece of prairie ground. The combatants came armed with rifles, and at the first interchange of shots the challenged man fell, disabled by a ball in his thigh. The other, throwing down his rifle, walked towards him, and kneeling by his side drew a bowie-knife and deliberately murdered him. The crowd of bystanders not only permitted this, but the assassin still lives in the community, has since married, and, as far as my informant could judge, his social position has been rather advanced than otherwise from thus dealing with his enemy."[176]

"The killing of a slave was almost never regarded as murder, and the rape of slave women was treated as a form of trespassing," says the PBS Online article on antebellum slavery.[177]

Gloria Browne-Marshall wrote, "Indians and Blacks, as well as their children, were prohibited by law from defending themselves against abuse, sexual and otherwise, at the hands of Whites. A slave who defended herself against the attack of a White person was subject to cruel beatings by either the master or mistress … The life of sexual debasement and cruelty which was the reality of female slaves was largely ignored by White Christian society in America."[178]

Thomas Jefferson, himself a slaveholder, wrote, "The WHOLE COMMERCE between master and slave, is a PERPETUAL EXERCISE of the most *boisterous passions,* the most unremitting DESPOTISM on the one part, and degrading submission on the other … The parent *storms,* the child looks on, catches the lineaments of *wrath,* puts on the same airs in the circle of smaller slaves, GIVES LOOSE TO THE WORST OF

PASSIONS; and thus *nursed, educated, and daily exercised in tyranny,* cannot but be stamped by it with odious peculiarities."[179]

In a culture that looked the other way when those in power committed immorality and violence, several slave revolts erupted. August 1831, Nat Turner's Rebellion broke out near Jerusalem, Virginia. Believing God had sanctioned him, Turner, with six other slaves, entered his master's chamber in the middle of the night and began to kill. Before the insurrection ended, at least 40 slaves had joined Turner. At least 55 whites were bludgeoned, stabbed, and hacked to death. The state executed Turner and 54 other people and banished many more. In the hysteria that followed the rebellion, white mobs murdered closed to 200 blacks.[180]

Fear

Understandably, Southerners were consumed with fear: settlers feared Indians, whites feared blacks, blacks feared the whip, the sexual demands, and being sold away from their families.

"FEAR is the only motive with which the slave is plied during his whole existence," said the authors of *American Slavery As It Is*.[181]

Slaveholders feared judgment. One slaveholder wrote, "In this state of slavery I *almost feel* that every *apparent blessing* is attended with *a curse*."[182]

"The more slaveholders glorified success, the more they feared failure," James Oakes observed.[183]

Women feared abusive and unfaithful men. White women also feared falling from their pedestals, and thus losing the only status they had. Ever admonished not to become like Yankee women (aggressive and unsubmissive), Southern women acquiesced with choices they knew in their hearts to be terribly wrong.

In the wake of the Civil War, men feared women's uprisings almost as much as they had previously feared slave uprisings. They "feared those women who desired to be 'a competitor of man in the struggle of life, in the affairs of business.'"[184] They feared "their women" would "forsake their homes and occupy the pulpits."[185]

Indeed, the people who wielded the most power in Southern society were often the most afraid. Journalist and political strategist Duff Green saw that. In 1835, Green said the South had "most to fear" from the "consciences and fears of the slave-holders themselves." He urged, "We must satisfy the consciences, we must allay the fears of our people. We must satisfy them that slavery is of itself right; that it is not a sin against God; that it is not an evil, moral or political."[186]

Ultimately, white Southerners feared *anyone* who spoke out to identify *any* of the unrighteousness and injustice with which they'd aligned. Goaded to panic by the few among them who had everything to lose, they agreed in silencing anyone who even mildly hinted at the society's wrongs. They colluded in devising ways never to let such "incendiary" voices speak.

"If subjected to a barrage of criticism, conscience-stricken planters might become covert abolitionists who would fight half-heartedly for slavery's perpetuation and relax the discipline which kept their slaves in order," observed historian William Freehling. "Moreover, public debate might increase the restlessness of Negro slaves and would certainly magnify the apprehensions of the white community."[187]

"Hence, no free press, no free pulpit, no free politics can be permitted in the South," Frederick Olmsted wrote.[188]

Division, Rejection, Rebellion

Greed, pride, and control—and the incessant fear they prompted—caused strife.

In the 1830s, as soon as awakening floundered, the denominations that had stood together in the revival tents, worshiping, taking communion, and watching the Spirit fall, fell themselves into rancorous division, not over slavery, but over all manner of theological differences not foundational to the faith. This wasn't just true of the South. When Alexis de Toqueville visited the US in the early 1830s, he "found remarkable the seemingly endless number of sects into which American Christianity was divided."[189] Thus, more than a decade before denominations began to split over the slavery issue, the church split and split and split again on the basis of "denominational distinctives."

The most rancorous rifts occurred in the region where the different "sects" actually had the most in common—and the greatest commitment to the bedrock beliefs of the faith—the evangelical South. Joe Burton described Tennessee in 1835 in these words: "Religious views of the widest difference ... were expressed with utmost candor. Debate was the order of the day. To these debates between popular champions the people flocked ... Lines of the sharpest distinction were thus drawn between the denominations."[190]

By "religious views of the widest difference," Burton meant that evangelical denominations unequivocally committed to salvation by grace, through the shed blood of the Lord Jesus Christ, fueled strong denominational loyalties based on every possible finer point of church polity or doctrine. By "utmost candor," he meant those debating the issues went for the jugular, and their audiences loved it. "Lines of sharpest distinction" required people to choose sides: "Here are the bullet points to which you must agree if you're to be counted one of *us*. If you disagree on a single point, you, my friend, have stepped across the line. You've become one of *them*. And their doctrines we believe to be a slippery slope to heresy and hell."

Tragically, we who identify ourselves with Christ set ourselves up to embrace error:

- when we look to reason or emotion to guide us, even as we close our ears to the Spirit;
- when we divide over matters on which Scripture gives latitude;
- when we consider ourselves right, and everyone else wrong, on every single point.

And so, instead of choosing by love to serve one another, instead of helping each other in the unity of the Spirit to balance the paradoxes of the faith, the denominations bred division and isolation.

As pastors and leaders of Southern churches fought one another over points of doctrine and church government, they stopped confronting the unjust practices and unrighteous attitudes of their culture that had permeated the church. They had very practical reasons for doing so. The wealthiest and most powerful church members, if not the pastors themselves, had significant investment in slaves.

Eventually, the same voices that vilified each other over denominational issues banded together to vilify anyone who dared call any of the South's cultural practices "sin." By 1860, these voices insisted as one that the Southern church was *right*; their society, *virtuous*; and they could prove it *biblically*. Anyone who disagreed had—not a different view of Scripture—but an unscriptural, unchristian view. Further, anyone who disagreed had insulted the South's honor, proving themselves "against us." Any voice that pled for repentance was labeled "incendiary" and counted as a gauntlet thrown down, inviting a duel to the death.

Taking up the gauntlet, the South prepared for war. Even before the first shots were fired, Mary Chesnut observed: "We are divorced, North from South, because we hated each other so."[191] But also: "We are abusing one another as fiercely as ever we abused Yankees. It is disheartening."[192]

Later, as battle after battle raged, she wrote:

"Old Mr. Chesnut tramped about and said: … 'I always knew that the world was against us.'"[193]

"Soon I made the unpleasant discovery that we had forgotten Yankees and were fighting each other."[194]

"Small war in the Ladies Aid Society. Harriet president, Sue Bonney V.P.—and already secession in the air—a row all the time in full blast. At first there were nearly a hundred members—eighty or ninety always present at a meeting—now ten or twenty are all that they can show."[195]

"We are a frantic, dissatisfied, leveling republic." "We crippled ourselves—blew ourselves up by intestine strife."[196]

Toward the war's end, with the death toll mounting exponentially and all hope for a Confederate victory squashed, Chesnut kept hearing young soldiers sing this refrain, 'We will never give it up—no never.'"[197]

Historian Rufus Spain summarized and quoted comments by the editor of the Georgia Baptist paper, written just months after the Confederate defeat: "If reunion with the North—either religious or political—were contingent upon the South's humbling herself, … then 'there can be neither union nor communion between us this side of eternity.'"[198]

Deception

Throughout the antebellum years, a significant percentage of Southerners looked to Jesus for salvation, had high regard for the Bible, and genuinely sought to live by its precepts. Only a small percentage owned slaves, yet the influence of that minority and the deception of King Cotton so permeated the region that, by 1860, the white culture as a whole had come to defend slavery and to see their identity in terms of it. What they did not see did hurt them.

They did not see the spiritual schizophrenia this produced, the confusing entanglement of a godly identity and an ungodly one.

"I have undergone no change on the righteousness of slavery, nor can I change until convinced that our Bible is not the book of God," wrote a contributor to the Georgia *Christian Index*, April 9, 1868.[199]

They did not see the profound contradictions their conflicting allegiances led them to embrace.

"Freedom is not possible without slavery," said the Richmond *Enquirer.*[200]

They did not see how far afield their pride led them.

In 1857, John Winston of Alabama proclaimed, "So great has become the necessities of the world for cotton alone—which can only be produced, to any considerable extent, by slave labor, and in Southern climes, that the suspension of involuntary servitude for a single year only, would cause convulsions in all the governments of the civilized world, the disastrous results of which, it would be beyond human ken to foresee."[201]

They didn't see how often appearances belied the truth. Mary Chesnut recorded this overheard conversation:

"'What a perfect gentleman—so fine-looking, highbred, distinguished. Easy, free and, above all, graceful in his bearing—so high-toned! He is always indignant at any symptoms of wrongdoing. He is charming, the man of all others I like to have strangers see—a noble representative of our country.'

"'Yes. Every word true. He is all that. And then the other side of the picture is true, too. You can always find him—you know where to find him!—wherever there is a looking glass, a bottle, or a woman. There will he be also.'"[202]

The authors of *American Slavery As It Is* explained, "The declarations of slaveholders, that they treat their slaves well, will put no man in a quandary, who keeps in mind this simple principle, that the state of mind towards others, which leads one to inflict cruelties on them, *blinds the inflicter to the real nature of his own acts.*"[203]

They did not see what they didn't want to see. Chesnut wrote of her mother-in-law, a plantation matriarch whose 90-year-old husband still consorted with the slave women:

"Mrs. Chesnut set her face resolutely to see only the pleasant things of life and shut her eyes to wrong and said it was not there ... She sat like a canary bird in her nest ... and made her atmosphere a roseate-hued mist for her own private delusion."[204]

The deception continued after the war. In 1929, Wilbur J. Cash described "The Mind of the South" in these words: "Its salient characteristic is a magnificent incapacity for the real ... The very legend of the Old South, for example, is warp and woof of the Southern mind. The 'plantation' which prevailed outside the tidewater and delta regions was actually no more than a farm; its owner was, properly, neither a planter nor an aristocrat, but a backwoods farmer; yet the pretension to aristocracy was universal ... Their pride and their legend, handed down to their descendants, are today the basis of all social life in the South."[205]

"Yet, he is never—consciously, at least—a hypocrite," Cash wrote. "Whatever pleases him he counts as real. Whatever does not please him he holds as non-existent."[206]

Sincere Christian people fell for the deception that Southern culture was virtue incarnate, and that anyone who challenged the South on any point opposed God himself.

"The pulpits of the South offered the 'dark suggestion that the God of the Yankees was not God at all but the Antichrist loosed at last from the pit.'"[207]

Contradiction and confusion

Today, as in previous generations, Southerners are characteristically friendly, eminently likable, courteous, and fun-loving. Most still live by the watchword, "Be nice." Those who meet us, interact with us, or live among us may sometimes find it almost impossible to believe that the other face exists.

Some Southerners *have* followed the Lord Jesus into freedom from every aspect of this deadly root. But many—perhaps most—who genuinely want to follow Christ are building partly on the rock and partly on sinking sand. They're still tied somewhere to unrighteous roots that continue to sabotage their lives, their health, their generations, their relationships, and their witness to the character of God. To add to the confusion, folk who do not know Christ often sparkle with Southern charm. They too have a side that is genuinely winsome. They smile, do good deeds, and may go out of their way to help a stranger. That's the side we've all been taught always to show, even to ourselves.

Sadly, the hidden face does exist. We in the Southern church culture still practice injustice without even seeing it. We still insist we're doing "what's right" when, in fact, we're driven by unrighteous attitudes we can't begin to fathom or overcome. Trying to be good Christians, we present the "good" face and hide the other, even from ourselves. If we do admit how desperately out of order a situation has become, we often blame the persons flailing most wildly against the hypocrisy. We look for a way of escape from *them*. The enemy of our souls loves to misdirect us that way. Even when we do rightly assess the issues, we may think ours is the only life, the only family, the only church gripped by such evils. Isolated, we continue in bondage when, together, we could run free.

Before the rest of the church folds its arms and shakes its head, may I ask: Hasn't much of this false identity also taken root in the larger conservative US church culture? Can't we see it across the world in places where we've sown the gospel and, with it, planted replicas of ourselves?

Southerners past and present, who grew up confusing a false identity with their true one, have relocated, geographically and denominationally. Preachers, publishers, and missionaries from the South have broadcast the gospel far and wide—along with all that southern culture has attached to it. Not in the Deep South alone do we see:

- Deep division in families and churches—rifts that often lead to splits.
- Lines drawn where God has not drawn them and people required to take sides.
- Whole groups of people treated as second-class citizens.
- Vicious power struggles among Christian leaders.
- Venomous verbal attacks leveled at persons or groups that someone with clout wants to discredit—malicious meanness done purportedly to defend the Word, protect the mission, or guard the "sheep."
- Immorality—done in secret.
- Abuse—physical, sexual, emotional, and verbal—also done in secret and often extremely well hidden. In fact, churches and good Christian families often actively collude in hiding it.
- Greed—prompting all manner of decisions made ostensibly for far more noble motives, or perhaps simply deemed expedient. One denominational leader, who chose not to risk the economic repercussions of doing the right thing, wrote the whole matter off with these words: "Politics are just a fact of life."
- A poverty spirit—systemic poverty that may or may not be economic; a pervasive mindset Graham Cooke describes as "the acceptance of meager possibility ... accepting a limitation and being governed by lack."[208]
- Deep and pervasive fear—though we often don't call it fear. We're worried, stressed, or anxious. We aim to please ... everyone. We fret over the state of the nation and the world. We pray and act, not out of a deep desire to see God's kingdom come, but from exactly the same fear that gripped the South before the Civil War: a gnawing fear of loss. Meanwhile, all kinds of chronic and incurable illnesses beset us, and we don't realize we're literally "sick with fear."
- Exceeding pride—pride in "us," compared to "them"; especially pride in our righteousness, compared with everyone else's; pride in our level of Christianity, compared to others.
- A culture of rejection, including deadly self-rejection. Dishonor, often disguised as honor. Disrespect masquerading as respect.

- An incredible capacity for denial and deception, including utter self-deception. We see clear evidence that we and those around us are operating out of conflicting identities. Instead of admitting it and letting God show us what to do about it, we embrace the face we want to see and pretend the other doesn't exist.
- All-out wars in the Body of Christ. And concurrently: culture wars in which we, who have not yet taken seriously Christ's command to love one another as he loved us, cast ourselves as the knights in shining armor who must save our nation and the world.

We are like Jesus

"In this world we are like Jesus," says 1 John 4:17. Let that truth reverberate in your inmost being. Let it go deep. Let it gestate and marinate until it impacts you, spirit, soul, and body: *"In this world we are like Jesus."*

If we're settling for less, something is terribly wrong. God is terribly grieved.

"Like Jesus" does not mean having the Christian appearance down pat. Jesus never did approve of cleaning only the outside of the cup. If the reality behind the appearance often looks radically unlike Jesus, we may think we're doing a good job of covering it, but he knows. And, odds are, so do some of the people we think we've fooled. If we're vacillating between two identities—one, we parade; and one, we camouflage—one of two things is true. Either we don't know Jesus at all. Or we've been double-minded in seeking to follow him. We haven't realized it because generations before us did it, and we've grown up in the midst of it. But in order to deliver us, God the Spirit is showing us the truth.

Certainly, Christians are human. Ah, but we're not "only human." We're new at the core of our being, and the Spirit of God lives within.

Certainly we still sin, even when we want to follow Christ fully. Yet when Jesus is Lord of our lives, the Spirit pinpoints the sin and gives us desire and power to confess and turn from it.

Certainly, growth in Christ is a messy, lengthy process. But it is also an inexorable process: The God who began it will complete it. The Spirit joyfully coaches us to maturity in our new, true identity.

When we continue to practice any of the above attitudes, without seeing them, or without having the desire or power to break free, that's a huge red flag. It signals that we (and often our ancestors before us) have chosen to resist the Spirit to the point that he is quenched and grieved. The Spirit's life, grace, and power are continually flowing—yet, like water in a kinked hose, much that's available to us cannot reach us. The sins we continue to entertain have become strongholds in our lives.

The unconfessed strongholds, or iniquities, of one generation plague succeeding generations—becoming harder to see, harder to conquer as each generation allows the unrighteous roots to grow a little larger, a little deeper, a little more entangled. That does not mean we're "fated" to follow in our parents' footsteps. In Exodus, the children who grew up in the wilderness demonstrated that a generation can choose to reverse the choices of the previous one. But if we do not make the reversal, if instead we continue in our fathers' choices, the strongholds become more deeply entrenched; the false identity, more ingrained. Like our ancestors before us, we spend our lives repeating destructive cycles, because we don't know who we are.

What doesn't work

That's grievous. It needs to be grieved. The whole rotten root needs to be uprooted; the righteous foundation, restored. Ah, but exposing such wretched stuff unleashes strong emotions—bitterness, anger, shame, fear. Know this: Seeing the truth does not create the emotions, but rather brings to the surface what we've deeply repressed. Unless we choose to act from our spirit and to humble our soul, the strong emotions that rise up will trigger again the default responses we and our ancestors have made for so long. Trouble is, the default responses keep us in the same cycles. They don't work to set us free.

Denial and blame

We do not "uproot and tear down … build and plant" by denying or by blaming.

But it's so tempting to try.

God is exposing a root system we do not want to see. It's appalling to realize we've agreed with such rottenness. It's agonizing to see how much we've lost as a result. Not knowing how to begin to deal with such a snarl, not wanting to know how pervasive and deadly it is, we may try to keep doing what we've been doing, hoping that if we ignore the ugliness, it will just go away.

Then, when the situation gets messy enough that we cannot deny it, we may resort to blaming: The fault lies with *that* race, *that* region, *that* generation, *that* gender, *that* political party, *that* denomination, *that* church, *that* person.

Stop it! Please, please stop it! Stop denying. Stop blaming. Begin this minute to cooperate with the God who has dragged the mess out into the open for this one reason: He has foundations to restore.

When the sheetrock in our new house began cracking and buckling, the builder kept denying the structure had any foundation problems. He offered to come patch the presenting issues. If we had believed his words and pursued that course, the damage would have continued to worsen. Part of our house would have continued to sink.

When the builder could not deny the foundation issues any longer, he began blaming others. Ultimately, he blamed practically every subcontractor who worked on the house. He even blamed us! In turn, we could have sat back, pointing fingers and refusing to act.

Instead, God told us to work. He showed us what to do. Regardless who had caused the problem, our priority had to be: clearly identify the key issue and fix it correctly. Our priority had to be to restore.

Running or resenting

We in the Southern church culture desperately need to give God permission to show us where this tangled system of injustice and unrighteousness has affected and continues to affect our lives, our families, and our generations, both physical and spiritual.

Further, as already suggested, many who are not white Southerners and many who have never have been church-goers may also find deep-rooted issues in their lives and families that can be traced back to the Cotton Kingdom. For one thing, deep-seated sin attitudes that were never addressed continue to manifest in generation after generation, regardless where those generations have gone and what they've done to "get away." How many have left the structure, not knowing they were taking along the strongholds! Whether they moved to another region, changed denominations, ran away from home, or left the church, they continued to build on faulty foundations.

But also, the people most abused by rotten King Cotton have often unwittingly perpetuated the system. Ironically, neither they nor their ancestors may have ever bowed the knee to cotton. Instead, ravaged by centuries of injustice, they became bitter. Bitterness does not free us. It does not re-establish a righteous foundation. It does not bring justice. Rather, bitterness creates a mirror image of the system that has treated us so cruelly. Bitterness opens us to become what we hate.

Consider Nat Turner. Trying to escape a violent, oppressive, fear-based slave system, he embraced practically every aspect of its unrighteous root. He employed exactly the same tactics that had been used to hold his people in bondage. He initiated injustice. He mirrored those he hated. So in the generations since: Many who have fought against an ungodly system have ultimately, through bitterness, planted the same iniquities in their own lives and families. They may be black, white, Native American, or another race. They may be Southerners, Northerners, or neither of the above. They may be women or men. Regardless, someone in their lineage let a root of bitterness creep in. Because no one has repented and renounced the bitterness, it has continued to grow—but often to hide—and so to decimate each generation.

We do not "uproot and tear down … build and plant" by running away or by letting bitterness grow up.

Our Father is pointing out what we haven't wanted to see "so that we might share in his holiness." Hebrews 12 says, "No discipline is enjoyable while it is happening—it's painful! But afterward there will be a peaceful harvest of right living for those who are trained in this way. So take a new grip with your tired hands and strengthen your weak knees. Mark out a straight path for your feet so that those who are weak and lame will not fall but become strong ... Look after each other so that none of you fails to receive the grace of God. Watch out that no poisonous root of bitterness grows up to trouble you, corrupting many" (vv. 10–16 NLT).

Do all this, says the Amplified Bible, "in order that no root of resentment (rancor, bitterness, or hatred) shoots forth and causes trouble and bitter torment, and the many become contaminated and defiled by it."

Our Bridegroom is purifying his Bride. He's dragging our past into the open, not to stir up old resentments, but to get rid of them once and for all. He's making us face the music because he loves us, he hates what sin does to us—and he knows who we really are.

"In this world we are like Jesus."

When we realize how radically unlike Jesus we've looked, it undoes us. But he does not intend that it destroy us. In fact, just the opposite: He shows us the truth in order to turn us back from our destructive path, in order to restore at the source what's cracking and buckling all around us. Our Father, our Bridegroom, our Redeemer, our Lord, calls to us, "Don't deny or blame. Don't run or resent. Return to me."

He teaches us, Spirit-to-spirit, what we previously knew only with our minds: "God is love. Whoever lives in love lives in God, and God in them. This is how love is made complete among us so that we will have confidence on the day of judgment: In this world we are like Jesus. There is no fear in love. But perfect love drives out fear, because fear has to do with punishment. The one who fears is not made perfect in love. We love because he first loved us" (1 John 4:16–19).

Contrary to what we may have believed, we don't *sort of* follow Jesus all our lives and then suddenly become like him when the last trumpet sounds. Rather, *this* is how we have confidence on the day of judgment: Wooed by his love, we begin today to cooperate with him, out of a heart fully yielded to him. Unafraid, we confess the truth as our Lord reveals it to us. In union and communion with him, we abandon whatever doesn't look like him. In the process, his love works so miraculously in us that, long before the final trumpet, our resemblance to our Bridegroom is unmistakable. In this world, we are like him.

Confess and wait

If any part of our lives, our generations, our culture, or our church culture is built on a faulty foundation, it affects the whole. As we begin to see the extent of the damage, we grieve. As we grieve, we humble ourselves before the God of righteousness and justice, the LORD of covenant love. As we seek him, he shows us how to cooperate with him to restore godly foundations and reestablish the righteous root. Little by little, he identifies the key foundational issues. As he does, he gives us grace and power to confess, to repent, and to restore.

To begin, we confess who he is. By the Spirit, we declare his justice and righteousness, his love for every people and land. We announce the righteous root and godly fruit of his kingdom. We confess, with the prophet Isaiah,

> The LORD is exalted, for he dwells on high;
> he will fill Zion with his justice and righteousness.
> He will be the sure foundation for your times,
> a rich store of salvation and wisdom and knowledge;
> the fear of the LORD is the key to this treasure (Isa. 33:5–6).

We receive what our God says of himself:

> Watch closely. I'm laying a foundation in Zion,
> a solid granite foundation, squared and true.
> And this is the meaning of the stone:
> A TRUSTING LIFE WON'T TOPPLE (Isa. 28:16 MSG).

The more clearly we see him, the more clearly we see who we are in him, and the more clearly we see the ways we and the generations before us have misrepresented him. We hear his voice announcing:

> If you get rid of unfair practices,
> quit blaming victims,
> quit gossiping about other people's sins,
> If you are generous with the hungry
> and start giving yourselves to the down-and-out,

> Your lives will begin to glow in the darkness,
> your shadowed lives will be bathed in sunlight.
> I will always show you where to go.
> I'll give you a full life in the emptiest of places—
> firm muscles, strong bones.
> You'll be like a well-watered garden,
> a gurgling spring that never runs dry.
> You'll use the old rubble of past lives to build anew,
> rebuild the foundations from out of your past.
> You'll be known as those who can fix anything,
> restore old ruins, rebuild and renovate,
> make the community livable again (Isa. 58:9–12 MSG).

Grieving our sin and loss, deeply moved by our Lord's grief and love, and energized by his promises, we may want to jump right in, plucking up every rotten root in sight. But he tells us, "Wait! Desist. Be still."

How often have we tried in vain to uproot the tangle of ungodly attitudes plaguing our church culture? We've chopped at one root, tugged on another, with minimal results for all our efforts. Certainly, we can confess that we and our ancestors have agreed, passively and actively, with injustice and the underlying unrighteousness that spawned it. We can determine by God's grace, through his Spirit, to cooperate fully to uproot and tear down, build and plant.

But before we set to work pulling up specific roots, our Lord has more to reveal: He wants to make clear how unholy covenants made by generations before us continue to hold our false identity in place.

To be free to become who we are, we must cooperate with him to annul those covenants. To be solid, squared, and true, our restored foundation must be anchored to the right cornerstone, an unrivaled covenant with the Lord Jesus Christ.

Prepare to work

In Ephesians 2:20–22, the apostle Paul cried, "You, too, are built upon the foundation laid by the apostles and prophets, the cornerstone being Christ Jesus himself. He is the one who holds the whole building together and makes it grow into a sacred temple dedicated to the Lord. In union with him you too are being built together with all the others into a place where God lives through his Spirit" (GNT).

Paul declared what is already true in the spiritual realm. Our job is to cooperate with God to usher it into the earth realm.

"Is there anyone here who saw the Temple the way it used to be, all glorious? And what do you see now? Not much, right?" (Hag. 2:3 MSG).

Today, God is echoing the questions he asked Haggai: "Is there anyone here who has seen the awakened church, all glorious?" It's out there, you know, in some of the most unlikely places in the world. "And what do you see now in the conservative US church culture as a whole? Not much, right?"

"*Not much*?" we protest, "What do you mean, 'Not much'?" We start to recount all the good things we've done for God, all the buildings we've built, all the souls we've won. But we don't need to waste our breath. Our Lord has never forgotten one thing his people have done that is truly good. Yet, he also sees what has kept us from doing and being much, much more.

As he unveils grave foundational issues that have resulted in generations of strife and destruction, lifelessness and loss, we throw down the last remnants of defensiveness. We agree with what he says, much as we wish it were not true. We confess!

Expectantly, we *wait* for him to reveal all we need to know in order to realign fully with the true Cornerstone. Then, we will hear him say,

"'Get to work, all you people!'—God is speaking. 'Yes, get to work! For I am with you.' The God-of-the-Angel-Armies is speaking! 'Put into action the word I covenanted with you when you left Egypt. I'm living and breathing among you right now. Don't be timid. Don't hold back … I own the silver, I own the gold.' Decree of God-of-the-Angel-Armies. 'This Temple is going to end up far better than it started out, a glorious beginning but an even more glorious finish: a place in which I will hand out wholeness and holiness.' Decree of God-of-the-Angel-Armies" (Hag. 2:4–9 MSG).

By the Spirit who works mightily within us, we will *work*. We'll cooperate as he raises us up into a sacred temple dedicated to the Lord. We won't be timid. We won't hold back. Building on a firm foundation anchored in Jesus Christ, we will together become a place where God lives and where he makes people holy and whole.

6—The Blood of the Covenant

Receive rivers of the grace of God. He is Ancient of Days. He is the covenant-keeping God of Abraham, Isaac, and Jacob. He made a covenant of grace with you. You have been wounded by covenant-breakers, but God cannot break his covenant. Be blessed with an infusion of the faithfulness of the heart of covenant-keeping God.—Sylvia Gunter[209]

I was reading Nehemiah tonight and was struck by Chapter 9, verse 38, "We make a sure covenant and write it: our leaders, our Levites, and our priests seal it." I thought ... that is what we will be doing—sealing the covenant once again with God.—Marion Neill[210]

A friend whom I love entered an ill-advised covenant.

She married a man she thought she knew but who, immediately after the wedding, revealed himself to be someone entirely different. While they dated, he presented himself as kind, gentle, considerate, and consummately Christian. He even read his Bible every morning. As soon as the two had uttered their vows, he showed himself a bully with a narcissistic personality disorder and a violent temper.

He had married to secure a servant he could manipulate and intimidate into doing whatever he pleased. He wanted to rule her every action, down to the way she arranged the cups in the kitchen cabinet. Any time she even inadvertently did a task "wrong," he used profound contempt or rage to "correct" her.

My friend has a servant spirit. She would gladly, tirelessly, have met the needs of someone who cherished and honored her. Indeed, for decades prior to this marriage, she had loved and served people who could not or did not show her appropriate appreciation. But this man who altered so radically after she had married him terrified her.

Overwhelmed by fear and torment, coupled with the shame of having made such a foolish choice, she became physically sick. In a matter of weeks, her body began to shut down. In fact, she became so ill so quickly that her doctor asked, "*What* is going on?" Alarmed at my friend's condition, the doctor advised her to leave her husband. But my friend considered the marriage covenant sacred, not to be broken. Didn't she have to remain until death?

Deception!

My friend entered an ill-advised covenant because she was deceived. She was deceived by a *deceptive* man, who reinvented himself to get what he wanted. While they dated, he hunted her the same way he hunted game. With astonishing perseverance and self-control, he acted the ways he needed to act in order to "catch" her.

She was deceived by a *deceived* man. He had played the part of the committed Christian so long that he himself believed the lie. People who saw him weekly at church, as well as those casually acquainted with him through his work or community involvement, thought highly of him. Only the people closest to him knew his real character, and they helped him keep it hidden.

My friend was deceived because her own strong *desires* kept her from seeing what she was seeing. Looking back later, she could count numerous red flags she had ignored or rationalized away. Even while he acted kind and thoughtful, he controlled and manipulated, pressuring her to agree to a marriage that something deep within her warned against. When she tried to express her reservations, he made her feel foolish and confused.

Multiple times, she tried to end the relationship. Each time, he returned with more kindness and thoughtfulness. Each time, he held out to her the promise of a very different relationship from what he truly wanted or had the capacity to provide, a relationship in which she could love and be loved.

How she longed for such a relationship! Every time she agreed again to get back together with him, the warning bell deep inside her seemed a little more muffled, a little more ridiculous. Why was she hesitating? Shouldn't she leap at this opportunity?

Finally, one day, she did.

The covenant Name

My friend rightly understood: Covenant is not to be taken lightly.

Nelson's Illustrated Bible Dictionary explains *covenant* as "an agreement between two people or two groups that involves promises on the part of each to the other." Ah, but "a covenant, in the biblical sense, implies much more than a contract or simple agreement. A contract always has an end date, while a covenant is a permanent arrangement … a contract generally involves only one part of a person, such as a skill, while a covenant covers a person's total being."

Covenant is both lasting and all-encompassing. It binds two parties together more completely and more permanently than anything else. Thus, "the concept of covenant between God and His people is one of the most important theological truths of the Bible."[211]

In our society, promises are often made to be broken. In God's kingdom, promises are made to be kept—especially promises made in context of covenant.

By his own initiative, the Lord entered covenants with Noah, with Abraham, with the nation Israel, with the tribe of Levi, and with David. Eternally faithful, God has kept every covenant he's made. So intent is he on keeping covenant that he made covenant with Israel in order to honor his covenant with Abraham made hundreds of years earlier.

Preparing to make covenant with the Israelites, the Lord appeared to Moses in a burning bush and announced that he had come to deliver the nation from enslavement in Egypt. "God also said to Moses, 'Say to the Israelites, "The Lord, the God of your fathers—the God of Abraham, the God of Isaac and the God of Jacob—has sent me to you."'" (Ex. 3:15).

Where we read an impersonal title, "the Lord," God revealed his personal Name—the Name no one today knows how to pronounce. The Jews considered that Name so sacred they would write only the consonants, transliterated **JHVH**. Instead of speaking the Name aloud, they would substitute *Adonai* ("my Lord") or *HaShem* ("the Name"), or sometimes they would say the four consonants, "*Yud-Heh-Vav-Heh*" (pronounced yude-heh-vahv-heh), as we might say a person's initials. Today, this inscrutable Name is sometimes rendered *Jehovah* or *Yahweh*. In most English Bible translations, it's rendered "the Lord" (all caps).[212] But it is not a title. It is the *Name* that most profoundly reveals who God is.

All God's names reveal his nature. But this unpronounceable Name is the one by which God most emphatically seeks to be known. Again and again throughout the Old Testament, he repeats the refrain first introduced in Exodus (insert your pronunciation of choice): "Then you will know that I am **JHVH**" (Ex. 6:7). "The Egyptians will know that I am **JHVH**" (Ex. 7:5). "They will know that I am **JHVH**" (Ex. 29:46).

This is the Name God himself has linked in the strongest way possible to his covenant relationship with his people.

When Pharaoh at first would not let the Israelites go but instead made their work harder, Moses complained to the Lord. In answer, as previously noted, God identified himself three times by the Name: "I am **JHVH**." "I am **JHVH**." "I am **JHVH**" (Ex. 6:2, 6, 8). In the midst of that threefold proclamation, *Adonai* emphasized the connection between the Name, the covenant, deliverance from bondage, and intimate relationship with him:

"*I have remembered my covenant* [the one made hundreds of years earlier with Abraham]. Therefore, say to the Israelites: 'I am the Lord, and *I will bring you out* from under the yoke of the Egyptians. *I will free you* from being slaves to them, and *I will redeem you* with an outstretched arm and with mighty acts of judgment. *I will take you as my own people, and I will be your God*'" (Ex. 6:5–7).

With our minds, we can only guess at how to pronounce this intimate, covenant Name of God. Yet in our inmost being we can know his Name.

Yahweh has determined to present himself so clearly that anyone from any nation can know his covenant nature: "And so I will show my greatness and my holiness, and I will make myself known in the sight of many nations. Then they will know that I am the Lord" (Ezek. 38:23).

What's more, *HaShem* stands ready to breathe his Name, Spirit to spirit, to those with whom he has entered covenant. He delights in showing his Bride aspects of his nature that he reveals to no one else. In Isaiah 52:6, he says, "Therefore My people shall know what My name is and what it means; therefore they shall know in that day that I am He who speaks; behold, I AM!" (AMP).

After God delivered the Israelites from Egypt, he met with them at Mt. Sinai and invited them to enter a covenant of blood with him. When the people agreed, he guided the process through his servant Moses. Notice the repeated identification of God by his covenant Name.

> When Moses went and told the people all the Lord's words and laws, they responded with one voice, "Everything the Lord has said we will do." Moses then wrote down everything the Lord had said.
>
> He got up early the next morning and built an altar at the foot of the mountain and set up twelve stone pillars representing the twelve tribes of Israel. Then he sent young Israelite men, and they offered burnt offerings and sacrificed young bulls as fellowship offerings to the Lord. Moses took half of the blood and put it in bowls, and the other half he splashed against the altar. Then he took the Book of the Covenant and read it to the people. They responded, "We will do everything the Lord has said; we will obey."
>
> Moses then took the blood, sprinkled it on the people and said, "This is the blood of the covenant that the Lord has made with you in accordance with all these words" (Ex. 24:3–8).

Most sacred of compacts

Twenty years after the Civil War ended, Henry Clay Trumbull published a book titled, *Blood Covenant: A Primitive Rite and Its Bearing on Scripture.*

In his book, Trumbull remarked that the Christians of his day had failed to recognize the significance of blood covenant.

He described *blood covenant* as "a form of mutual covenanting, by which two persons enter into the closest, the most enduring, and the most sacred of compacts."[213] Such a covenant "has been understood as equivalent to an inter-commingling of natures."[214] "It forms a tie, or a union, which cannot be dissolved. In marriage, divorce is a possibility: not so in the covenant of blood."[215]

At Mt. Sinai, the Israelites entered a blood covenant with the Lord God, confident they could keep it. They could not. Within weeks, they had broken the first two agreements of the covenant: They worshiped another god. They bowed before an idol they themselves had made.

Even before making covenant with Israel, the Lord knew the people would not, could not, keep it. Yet he pledged himself to them and, even when they failed, he continued in that covenant relationship. As the Lord established and persevered in keeping the Mosaic covenant, he paved the way for a new, better one, sealed, not with the blood of sacrificed animals, but with the blood of the Lord Jesus Christ.

Centuries after Moses declared to Israel, "This is the blood of the covenant that the Lord has made with you," Jesus sat at the last meal he would eat with his disciples before his crucifixion. "This is my blood of the covenant, which is poured out for many for the forgiveness of sins," Jesus said. Passing a cup of wine, he invited his followers into this new covenant: "Drink from it, all of you" (Matt. 26:28, 27).

Hebrews 9 says:

> For this reason Christ is the mediator of a new covenant, that those who are called may receive the promised eternal inheritance—now that he has died as a ransom to set them free from the sins committed under the first covenant … even the first covenant was not put into effect without blood. When Moses had proclaimed every command of the law to all the people, he took the blood of calves, together with water, scarlet wool and branches of hyssop, and sprinkled the scroll and all the people. He said, "This is the blood of the covenant, which God has commanded you to keep." In the same way, he sprinkled

> with the blood both the tabernacle and everything used in its ceremonies. In fact, the law requires that nearly everything be cleansed with blood, and without the shedding of blood there is no forgiveness (vv. 15, 18–22).

We have in Christ this priceless treasure: a blood covenant with the living God that we can keep. An eternal agreement through which we enjoy intimate, lasting, all-encompassing relationship with *Jehovah*. He forgives us. He writes his laws on our hearts. He becomes our God; we, his people. He knows us; and we, him. He loves us; and we, him. He lives in us, and we in him.

Trumbull said that blood covenant accomplishes the "inter-commingling of natures." Notice how Jesus described this "inter-commingling" at the same time he instituted the covenant meal we call the Lord's Supper: "I will ask the Father, and he will give you another advocate to help you and be with you forever—the Spirit of truth. The world cannot accept him, because it neither sees him nor knows him. But you know him, for he lives with you and will be in you. I will not leave you as orphans; I will come to you. Before long, the world will not see me anymore, but you will see me. Because I live, you also will live. On that day you will realize that I am in my Father, and you are in me, and I am in you" (John 14:16–20).

Peter drank the covenant cup. He heard Jesus' covenant promises and shortly afterward experienced their fulfillment. Later, Peter described what this covenant relationship with Christ includes: "By his divine power, God has given us everything we need for living a godly life. We have received all of this by coming to know him, the one who called us to himself by means of his marvelous glory and excellence. And because of his glory and excellence, he has given us great and precious promises. These are the promises that *enable you to share his divine nature* and escape the world's corruption caused by human desires" (2 Peter 1:3–4 NLT).

We stand amazed: God in Christ has given us everything we need for life and godliness. We have received his great and precious promises, promises made to be kept. Most astonishing of all, because of the blood covenant with Jesus that we have entered, we share his divine nature. As a result, we're able to "escape the world's corruption caused by human desires." We cannot celebrate this closest, most enduring, and most sacred of compacts enough.

And we dare not treat it lightly. By the sacrificial death and bodily resurrection of the Son, by the power of the Spirit, the Father has created the highest and holiest, strongest and best blood covenant. After centuries of history showed it impossible for humans to keep covenant with God, he made the way!

Hebrews 10:10, 14–18 describes the astonishing sufficiency of this covenant:

> We have been made holy through the sacrifice of the body of Jesus Christ once for all … For by one sacrifice he has made perfect forever those who are being made holy. The Holy Spirit also testifies to us about this. First he says: "This is the covenant I will make with them after that time, says the Lord. I will put my laws in their hearts, and I will write them on their minds." Then he adds: "Their sins and lawless acts I will remember no more." And where these have been forgiven, sacrifice for sin is no longer necessary.

Immediately after these magnificent declarations, Hebrews describes the stunning paradox: the sacrifice of Jesus is complete, yet by our own willful acts, we can thwart the fullness of what it has accomplished. Hebrews 10:26–31 issues one of the strongest warnings of Scripture:

> If *we* deliberately keep on sinning after *we* have received the knowledge of the truth, no sacrifice for sins is left, but only a fearful expectation of judgment and of raging fire that will consume the enemies of God. Anyone who rejected the law of Moses died without mercy on the testimony of two or three witnesses. How much more severely do you think those deserve to be punished who have trampled the Son of God underfoot, who have treated as an unholy thing the blood of the covenant that sanctified them, and who have insulted the Spirit of grace? For *we know him* who said, "It is mine to avenge; I will repay," and again, "The Lord will judge *his people*." It is a dreadful thing to fall into the hands of the living God.

Distinctly, decidedly, emphatically

We could spend hours debating the theological implications of that last passage. But what if, instead, we simply receive the warning? What if we recognize the perilous position of those who treat as a cheap thing the blood of God's covenant that sanctified them?

Only as we begin to grasp the force of blood covenant and the holiness of our blood covenant with Christ, can we begin to grasp what took place with regard to covenant in the Southern church culture during the decades surrounding the Civil War. With our new understanding of covenant, let's look more closely at some historic events mentioned briefly in previous chapters.

Remember the setting: In the early decades of the 1800s, the Second Great Awakening profoundly impacted the church in the South. The awakened church exuberantly received the Lord Jesus Christ—and yet, over time, chose to refuse the voice of his Spirit regarding the treatment of whole groups of people.

When challenged—particularly by Northerners, whom white Southerners considered far less righteous—the South in general and the Southern church in particular grew increasingly defensive and deceived. The presenting issue was slavery. In the first light of awakening, people across the South widely agreed that slavery was an evil, unconscionable system. Preachers in the South loudly denounced it. By the 1820s, however, people across the South spoke of slavery as a "necessary" evil. Far fewer preachers mentioned it. By the 1840s, preachers and people agreed in calling slavery a positive good, designed by God and advocated in his Word.

In October, 1858, secessionist James Henry Hammond, of South Carolina, described the startling turn-around that had occurred: "And what then [in 1833] was the state of opinion in the South? Washington had emancipated his slaves. Jefferson had bitterly denounced the system, and had done all he could to destroy it … The inevitable effect in the South was, that she believed slavery to be an evil—weakness—disgraceful—nay, a sin. She shrank from the discussion of it … and in fear and trembling she awaited a doom that she deemed inevitable. But a few bold spirits took the question up; they compelled the South to investigate it anew and thoroughly, and what is the result? Why, it would be difficult now to find a southern man who feels the system to be the slightest burthen on his conscience."[216]

In the mid-1840s, the Methodists and Baptists of the South—the two groups that had experienced the Spirit of God most powerfully and had grown the most numerically as a result of the Second Great Awakening—withdrew from association with their Northern brethren and created new, regional denominations. Southern Baptists declared they were forced to make the move because the northern Baptists had broken covenant with them (by deciding slaveholders could not be appointed as missionaries).

As other denominations followed suit, the Southern church chose to separate and the Northern church let them go, in spite of their covenant relationship with one another in Christ and their agreement on the bedrock beliefs of the faith, because both sides considered it too hard to go forward together. Thus unhindered by the dissenting voices of their brothers and sisters in Christ, the Southern church collectively persisted in aligning with those things in the Southern culture that did not line up with God, instead of challenging the culture to reconsider its choices.

In December 1860, Southern states began withdrawing from the Union. April 12, 1861, Southerners fired on Union troops stationed at Ft. Sumter, South Carolina, starting Civil War. One month later, on May 13, the Southern Baptist Convention meeting at Savannah, Georgia, passed a report and resolutions declaring in no uncertain terms the denomination's allegiance to the Confederacy. Four days later, the Congress of the Confederate States, meeting in Montgomery, Alabama, received the report and wrote it into their minutes.

Some may protest that a declaration made by the few who attended the 1861 SBC meeting does not speak for the denomination as a whole. Yet, the SBC constitution itself states that the few who convene in annual meeting *are* the whole. In his article, "Your SBC Executive Committee," long-term SBC attorney James P. Guenther wrote, "What many don't realize is that the Convention is not made up of churches, but actually 'consists of messengers who are members of Baptist churches cooperating with the Convention.' Those messengers enjoy messenger status only during the two-day annual session and any special session that might be convened."[217]

That's astonishing. Churches and church members at large do not make up the SBC, but only have the option of "cooperating" with it—and thus (knowingly or unknowingly) aligning with whatever has already been decided during the two days annually that the Southern Baptist Convention officially, "corporeally," exists.

The 1861 report of the Southern Baptist Convention began with words reminiscent of the Declaration of Independence: "We hold this truth to be self-evident." The report then launched into a vivid description of Northerners as fanatical aggressors, eager to wage a war of "savage barbarity" against the South, with even the Northern churches and pastors "breathing out slaughter." The report described the Southern people as innocent victims who had done everything in their power to avoid the rift and, even now, "will pray for our enemies in the spirit of that Divine Master, who, when he was reviled, reviled not again." The first resolution declared "that impartial history can not charge upon the South the dissolution of the Union."

The report continued: "In view of such premises this convention can not keep silence … it is bound to utter its voice distinctly, decidedly, emphatically." And thus the Southern Baptist Convention did. Let's look again at the heart of the 1861 resolutions:

> That we most cordially approve of the formation of the Government of the "Confederate States of America," and admire and applaud the noble course of that Government up to the present time.
>
> That we most cordially tender to the President of the "Confederate States," to his Cabinet, and to the members of the Congress now convened at Montgomery the assurances of our sympathy and entire confidence. With them are our hearts and hearty cooperation.[218]

Two years later, the SBC met again in Augusta, Georgia, reiterating and strengthening its commitment to the Confederacy in a "Resolution on Peace." Here again is the heart of that resolution:

> RESOLVED, 1st. That the events of the past two years have only confirmed the conviction expressed by this Convention at its last session, that the war which has been forced upon us is, on our part, just and necessary, and have only strengthened our opposition to a reunion with the United States on any terms whatever; and while deploring the dreadful evils of the war, and

> earnestly desiring peace, we have no thought of ever yielding, but will render a hearty support to the Confederate Government in all constitutional measures to secure our independence.[219]

In 1861 and 1863, the Southern Baptist Convention distinctly, decidedly, emphatically pledged allegiance to the Confederate government. Delegates vested with the full authority of the convention made written commitments that they themselves declared permanent and all-encompassing. "We have no thought of ever yielding," they vowed.

The Confederacy was birthed from broken covenant. It was never recognized as a nation by any foreign government.[220] It did not survive the war. Thus by a permanent compact, the SBC had bound itself to a corpse.

Baptism of blood

Historian Charles Reagan Wilson has chronicled another, more inclusive, aspect of the covenant between the Southern church and the Confederacy in his book, *Baptized in Blood: The Religion of the Lost Cause 1865–1920.* Throughout the Civil War and for decades afterward, "a recurring phrase in the Confederate religious lexicon was 'baptism of blood,'" wrote Wilson.[221] Ministers of all denominations sang this refrain. For example:

November 1860. Presbyterian James H. Thornwell "called for secession, even though 'our path to victory may be through a baptism of blood.'"[222]

1863. Episcopal rector B. T. Lacy declared, "A grand responsibility rests upon our young republic, and a mighty work lies before it. Baptized in its infancy in blood, may it receive the baptism of the Holy Ghost, and be consecrated to its high and holy mission among the nations of the earth."[223]

1890. Presbyterian minister James H. McNeilly wrote of Confederates "who poured their blood like festal wine, a libation to liberty." Wilson summarized McNeilly's articles by saying: the Confederates "were not necessarily wrong in fighting the war." "Nor was Pilate just and Christ a failure."[224] Thus McNeilly, like many other church leaders, compared the Yankees to the man who gave the crucifixion order; and the Confederacy, to Christ.

1901. "The Mississippi minister George C. Harris admitted in a sermon that while the Confederates, like all men, had been sinners, those sins were 'washed away under the baptism of blood.'"[225]

1910. "El Dorado, Arkansas, erected a marble drinking fountain to the Confederacy; its publicity statement said—in a phrase culled from countless hymns and sermons on the sacrificial Jesus—that the water in it symbolized 'the loving stream of blood' shed by the Southern soldiers. Drinkers from the fount were thus symbolically baptized in Confederate blood."[226]

1918. More than 50 years after the Civil War, minister Warren A. Candler said this of the Confederate soldiers: "The blood of our slain on a thousand fields is the cement which holds the living together in bonds too dear to be easily forgotten or heedlessly broken."[227] Cement, indeed.

"Clergymen compared the sacrificial, redemptive deaths of the Confederates to the passion of Christ. Carter Helm Jones of Louisville reminded his audience of war veterans of 'the memories of your Gethsemane' and 'the agonies of your Golgotha.' The Reverend H. M. Wharton, through the voice of a fictional clergyman in his novel *White Blood*, made the same point, likening the fate of the South near the war's end to 'the blessed Saviour who passed from gloomy Gethsemane to the judgment hall, through the fearful ordeal of being forsaken by His friends, and then on to the bloody Cross.'"[228]

"This evocative, powerful terminology suggested the role of war in bringing a redemption from past sins, an atonement, and a sanctification for the future."[229]

Redemption. Sanctification. Atonement. What sins had all that bloodshed atoned for? "Instead of seeing the nation's baptism of blood as a divine act sweeping away slavery," said Terry Matthews, "religious leaders in the region … began to argue that defeat had really been an effort on the part of God to get the South's attention, and to bring it to its collective knees in repentance for the drunkenness, card-playing, and swearing that had gone on during the war years."[230]

People who trust the shed blood of Jesus to redeem and sanctify them enter into the new covenant in his blood. They receive the Holy Spirit, and their sins "are washed away." They declare the covenant by baptism and by partaking the covenant meal of bread and wine. Southerners who trusted the bloodshed of war to redeem and sanctify their society entered a different covenant. They described that covenant, as well, in terms of physical baptism and Holy Ghost baptism, sins washed away, and symbolically drinking the blood.

The SBC put its vows to the Confederacy in writing. The Southern church culture across denominational lines entered covenant by the blood. The blood of Confederate soldiers. The people in the churches would have told you that Jesus' blood alone saves. Yet another loyalty at once competed against and enmeshed with their allegiance to Christ. A belief pervaded the region that "the shedding of [Confederate] blood cleansed all of Southern society, as well as its individual soldiers."[231]

The blood of hundreds of thousands of soldiers from both sides was shed during the war. The South saw no redemptive role for the Yankees' blood. Yet, desperate to make sense of the war and still deeply deceived, the Southern church used the term "baptism of blood" in such a way as to bind themselves to the dead Confederacy by a covenant act.

They covenanted to resurrect their pre-war "Southern identity"—not the true God-given identity of the land and people, but the false identity King Cotton had bequeathed them. They lashed themselves permanently to what they themselves now called the Lost Cause. Likening the war to the cross, they cried, "The South will rise again!"

Absolute surrender of one's separate self

Henry Clay Trumbull wrote in 1885, "A covenant of blood, a covenant made by the inter-commingling of blood, has been recognized as the closest, the holiest, and the most indissoluble, compact conceivable. Such a covenant clearly involves an absolute surrender of one's separate self, and an irrevocable merging of one's individual nature" with the nature of the other party in the compact.[232]

By virtue of their covenant with Christ, my Southern ancestors opened themselves to "share his divine nature"—his righteousness and justice, his mercy and love. Sometimes they did look startlingly like Jesus. Individually and collectively, they showed glimpses of his character and his ways. But sometimes, what appeared godly proved to be a religious act, a pretense so well-rehearsed that the characters themselves believed it real.

For they had also made covenant with a kingdom ruled by another king. They'd sealed the bond they had been gravitating toward for decades, the "wedding" of the Southern culture and the Southern church. At first mention, such a bond might sound like a good thing. Isn't the church supposed to impact the culture? It is indeed. Yet the Bride of Christ never wins a culture by making covenant with it. Such a covenant prostitutes us collectively, for the Bride is to be in covenant solely with the Bridegroom.

By virtue of this competing covenant, the church in the South absolutely surrendered any measure of separateness from the culture. People who identified themselves with Christ opened themselves and their generations to every sin stronghold in King Cotton's realm.

They embraced a dual loyalty, like a woman trying to be married to two husbands at the same time. They moved from double-mindedness to a full-blown dual identity, a split personality, spiritual schizophrenia.

Imagine a woman with two husbands. When she's with one husband, she's one person. When with the other, she's an entirely different person. And thus she lives two separate lives, neither true, until the first husband finds out about the second. He's stunned and incensed!

She's stunningly deceived and arrogant. "Don't worry," she says. "I'll stay married to you. You'll always be my *first* husband. Now I have another husband too. That's all."

Speechless, he cries, "That's illegal!"

"Regardless what the law says, I'm going to do it," she retorts. "I love you—and I love him. It'll work just fine."

At that, the husband looks her in the eye and says, "I'm walking out. I love you. But I will not live here with you unless and until you choose me alone."

Halting between two opinions, the church culture of the South deeply grieved their Bridegroom. Choosing a dual loyalty, people identified with Christ embraced—and then became enslaved by—a tangled web of attitudes that directly contradict who he is. By their own choices, they distanced themselves from the One who has power and authority both to demolish the sin strongholds and to deliver the people held by them. Thus powerless to address the most entrenched sins in the region, the church turned its collective attention to controlling, hiding, and even redefining sin.

"The posture of the church in the South was to support and defend, to shore up and bolster,"[233] said Wake Forest University professor Terry Matthews.

Southern Baptist authors reveal what this meant within that denomination.

In his 150-year history of the SBC, Jesse Fletcher wrote, "While the institution of slavery no longer existed ... sectional bitterness and division had, if anything, deepened." The future of Southern Baptists "was being constrained by a past that included a lost cause and a persistent southern culture."[234]

In *The Southern Baptist Convention and the Judgment of History*, Luther Copeland wrote, "Southern Baptists not only defended slavery. They also came to sanction secession, the Confederacy and the Civil War ... So they became united with the Confederacy in origin and support, and also in defeat."[235]

After the war, "The SBC became for all intents and purposes the 'Established Church of the south,'" said Copeland. "Southern Baptists conformed to the standards of Southern culture rather than acted prophetically to challenge and change those standards."[236]

In seven extended chapters, Copeland described how that cultural conforming looked and its effects even today. Toward the end of chapter 1, he wrote, "This profound identification of Southern Baptists with the South, with its memory of the defense of slavery, its deeply entrenched racism, its Messianic sense of chosenness and of a defeat requiring vindication, was to plague Southern Baptists throughout their history. Hardly any aspect of Southern Baptist life was unaffected by it."[237]

Another Southern Baptist, John Lee Eighmy, titled his book on the post-war social attitudes of Southern Baptists, *Churches in Cultural Captivity*. In the Epilogue to the book written after Eighmy's death, Samuel S. Hill,

Jr., wrote, "'Churches in cultural captivity' is a strong accusation, but it is borne out by the facts."[238]

Dueling covenants

You don't have to read far in scripture to find that God detests any covenant that counterfeits and competes with our blood covenant with his Son. He detests such covenants because they demean the cross: Christ alone died a sacrificial death that atoned for sins, and Christ alone rose again to give us resurrection life. God detests such covenants because they rob, kill, and destroy people Jesus came to save. All God's covenants, both Old Testament and New, are covenants of love, life, and peace.

Moses declared, "Know therefore that the Lord your God is God; he is the faithful God, keeping his covenant of love to a thousand generations of those who love him and keep his commandments" (Deut. 7:9). Solomon, Nehemiah, and Daniel all echoed the refrain that *Jehovah*, the God who makes himself known by his personal covenant Name, keeps his covenant of love.

Isaiah wrote, "'Though the mountains be shaken and the hills be removed, yet my unfailing love for you will not be shaken nor my covenant of peace be removed,' says the Lord, who has compassion on you" (Isa. 54:10). Ezekiel too rejoiced in God's everlasting covenant of peace.

In Numbers 25, God made a covenant of peace with the tribe of Levi because one priest, Phinehas, was zealous for God's honor.

The wandering Israelites had "yoked themselves to the Baal of Peor," first by committing sexual immorality with Baal worshipers, then by sacrificing to and bowing before idols. "And the Lord's anger burned against them" (Num. 25:3). *HaShem* had made with them a covenant of love and life. Deceived by their desires, they bound themselves to other gods, yet still tried to worship the Lord in the way he had prescribed.

In so doing, they treated as an unholy thing their blood covenant with *Adonai*.

Some covenants are openly anti-Christ. They bind us to something or someone that requires our choosing, up front, between them and him.

More insidious are those covenants that both compete with Christ and counterfeit him. Such covenants entangle themselves in our minds and hearts with our true covenant with Christ. We begin to believe that the one complements, and even equals, the other and so deceive ourselves into thinking we can align with both. We cannot. The trying tears us apart.

Knowing the Lord, yet yoked to a counterfeit covenant, we live like the Israelites in the wilderness. God is with us, as he was with those bickering, grumbling, wandering Israelites. He provides for us, as he did them. God has promised us, as he did them, a land of milk and honey, of peace and rest and abundance. Yet we've settled for an existence that doesn't even come close to what he intends us to know.

With our Lord in our midst, offering us relationship, identity, purpose, and inheritance, we live yoked to what can only counterfeit it all. We spend our days in a barren place, near God yet profoundly separated from him and never really knowing him, making do with manna, squabbling and complaining, wandering in circles, convinced that this is as good as it gets.

The Exodus, the meeting with God at Sinai, the tabernacle, indeed the entire Old Covenant pointed to the coming of Jesus Christ. He alone died in our behalf and rose again. He alone can offer us a covenant of life. Any bond, any allegiance, that competes with our blood covenant with him begets bloodguilt and produces only death.

When the wandering Israelites bound themselves by blood sacrifices to false gods, plague broke out, and 24,000 people died (Num. 25:1–9).

Psalm 106:30–31 says, "But Phinehas stood up and intervened, and the plague was checked. This was credited to him as righteousness for endless generations to come."

Centuries later, God sent a strong warning through the prophet Malachi to Phinehas' descendants, the Levitical priests:

> "And now, you priests, this warning is for you. If you do not listen, and if you do not resolve to honor my name," says the Lord Almighty, "I will send a curse on you, and I will curse your blessings. Yes, I have already cursed them, because you have not resolved to honor me. Because of you I will rebuke

> your descendants; I will smear on your faces the dung from your festival sacrifices, and you will be carried off with it. And you will know that I have sent you this warning so that my covenant with Levi may continue," says the LORD Almighty. "My covenant was with him, a covenant of life and peace, and I gave them to him; this called for reverence and he revered me and stood in awe of my name" (Mal. 2:1–5).

We invite curses instead of blessings when we disdain God's covenant of life and peace. We invite curses instead of blessings when we dishonor his Name.

Don't miss the phrase, "Because of you I will rebuke your descendants." Don't miss the promise to Phinehas in Psalm 106 that his concern for God's honor would affect "endless generations to come." What one generation does with regard to covenant invariably ripples down through succeeding generations, visiting life and blessings, or death and curses on those who come after.

Notice too that God sent his warning to the priests of Malachi's day "so that my covenant with Levi may continue." God wanted deeply, passionately, for generation after generation to enjoy the blessings of love, peace, and life that his covenant brings.

Today, he still wants deeply, passionately, for generation after generation to enjoy the blessings that flow from his covenant. He wants to avoid generations of tragedy that accrue when we yoke ourselves to covenants with death.

Annulling covenants with death

Consider the word of *Yud-Heh-Vav-Heh* in Isaiah 28:15–18 in light of the "baptism of blood" to which the Southern church clung:

> *You boast,* "We have entered into a covenant with death,
> with the realm of the dead we have made an agreement.
> When an overwhelming scourge sweeps by,
> it cannot touch us,
> for we have made a lie our refuge
> and falsehood our hiding place."

So this is what the Sovereign Lord says:
"See, I lay a stone in Zion, a tested stone,
a precious cornerstone for a sure foundation;
the one who relies on it
will never be stricken with panic.
I will make justice the measuring line
and righteousness the plumb line;
hail will sweep away your refuge, the lie,
and water will overflow your hiding place.
Your covenant with death will be annulled;
your agreement with the realm of the dead will not stand."

Sometimes people deliberately make covenants with death. More often, people enter such covenants because they're deceived. They think the agreement they've entered will somehow protect them: "When an overwhelming scourge sweeps by, it cannot touch us," they cry. Such covenants may indeed offer a measure of protection, as might a pact with a mob boss. But like agreements with the mob, covenants with death always destroy.

My friend found that out. A wonderful lady who knows and loves the Lord, she would never decide, "I'll make a covenant with death." Yet deceived by strong desires, she made a series of choices that led her into an abusive marriage. She made a covenant that immediately began to crush the life out of her. How unspeakably grateful, humbled, and overwhelmed she was to find that the God who hates divorce still loves her and, in his grace and mercy, granted her a release from a covenant she never should have made.

In the Southern church culture of the past, many people knew and loved the Lord. Yet, deceived by strong cultural biases, my ancestors collectively made a series of choices that led them to covenant with death. Thinking such a covenant necessary to maintain their identity, they took refuge in a lie. Though the agreement immediately turned aggressive and abusive, they could not evict what they had wed. As long as their unholy covenants remain in force, neither can we.

And thus, countless individuals and families, communities and churches remain captive to the strongholds that yoked the Southern culture and the Southern church of another era. Even now, we have a strong propensity to repeat the same destructive cycles and incredible difficulty breaking out of them. Thankfully, we do see some significant positive change. Sadly, the changes are often fragile and sometimes superficial.

Tenacious iniquities—greed, pride, manipulation and control, immorality and violence, division, rejection and rebellion, deception and fear—continue to conquer us, each held in place by a lasting, all-encompassing blood covenant that is not a covenant of love, peace, or life. How then, can anyone break free?

Know this: God is far more committed than we are to overturning covenants with death that bind his people. He will go to astonishing lengths to do the impossible. When he arises to act, it's at once wonderful and terrible. It takes our breath away.

First, our holy and jealous God routes deception. In Isaiah 28, *Yahweh* sends hail and flood to sweep away the lies we've believed. Suddenly, we *see* the truth. Then he deals a deathblow to unholy binding agreements: "Your covenant with death will be annulled; your agreement with the realm of the dead will not stand."

Remember: A blood covenant is the most indissoluble compact conceivable. It doesn't have an expiration date. It cannot be revoked. Covenants of life bless endless generations. Covenants with death oppress successive generations, in a family, a region or nation, and in a church culture.

The only thing that can annul a blood covenant is a higher covenant. Praise the Lord—*Jehovah*, *Adonai*, *HaShem*, *Yud-Heh-Vav-Heh*! The covenant of life accomplished through the blood of the Lord Jesus Christ trumps every other covenant.

"See, I lay a stone in Zion, a tested stone, a precious cornerstone for a sure foundation; the one who relies on it will never be stricken with panic." The Amplified Version says: "he who believes (trusts in, relies on, and adheres to that Stone) will not be ashamed or give way or hasten away [in sudden panic]" (Isa. 28:16).

Yet notice what God says will happen when he annuls a covenant with death: "When the overwhelming scourge sweeps by, you will be beaten down by it. As often as it comes it will carry you away; morning after morning, by day and by night, it will sweep through" (Isa. 28:18–19).

When the Sovereign Lord rises to sweep away deadly covenants that his people have entered, he first rips away the deception so people can see the corpse to which they're bound. Those who let go of every false covenant and rely on Jesus alone "will not be ashamed or give way." Yet those who cling to a covenant God is annulling will be swept away with it.

What does that look like? What does Isaiah 28 imply? I'll leave you to grapple before the Lord with those questions. Remember, though: God deals with individuals and with peoples. He acts in time and in eternity. His ways are past finding out. And we will never grasp his goodness or his severity if we try to do so soul first.

So tell your mental reasonings and your emotional churnings to stand down, and listen as *Adonai* speaks Spirit-to-spirit: "The Lord will judge his own people." "For the time has come for judgment, and it must begin with God's household. And if judgment begins with us, what terrible fate awaits those who have never obeyed God's Good News?" (Heb. 10:30; 1 Peter 4:17 NLT).

Listen as he warns of grave consequences in a matter we might consider trivial:

"Whoever eats the Lord's bread or drinks the Lord's cup in an unworthy manner will be guilty of desecrating the body and blood of the Lord! So let a person examine himself first, and then he may eat of the bread and drink from the cup; for a person who eats and drinks without recognizing the body eats and drinks judgment upon himself. This is why many among you are weak and sick, and some have died! If we would examine ourselves, we would not come under judgment. But when we are judged by the Lord, we are being disciplined, so that we will not be condemned along with the world" (1 Cor. 11:27–32 CJB).

Why is taking the Lord's Supper such a weighty issue? Because it's a covenant act. It's an inter-commingling-of-natures act: "Is not the cup of thanksgiving for which we give thanks a participation in the blood of Christ? And is not the bread that we break a participation in the body of Christ?" (1 Cor. 10:16).

When we take the meal carelessly, or take it as if we were fully aligned with our blood covenant in Christ when, in fact, we are not, we treat as something common the blood of the covenant that made us holy. We sin against the blood by which we're atoned.

Repeatedly God shows us mercy. Repeatedly, he extends grace. At the same time, he continually convicts us of sin and of righteousness and of judgment. If we refuse to hear and turn, the Lord will act to clear his Name from the muck with which we've smeared it. He will act as strongly as needed to purify his Bride and to call us back to wholehearted devotion to him.

Why in the world would we want to force his hand? Why hold our ground until the Lord has to judge? Why not let his *kindness* lead us to repentance? Why not now let Holy Spirit uncover and remove any loyalties that compete with our commitment to Christ? Why not gladly cooperate with our Father in decisively annulling covenants with death?

The Phinehas legacy

If we want to walk free from bloodguilt, to restore righteous foundations and replant righteous roots, the key to it all, the critical first step, is to seal again our covenant with the Lord, to return to that place of faithfulness and intimacy where our Bridegroom can teach us his Name. To do so requires that we convene the court of heaven. Standing before the righteous Judge, with the Son as our Advocate and Holy Spirit on the witness stand, we plead guilty to the unthinkable, echoing the confession of Psalm 106:[239]

> Both we and our ancestors have sinned;
> we have committed iniquity, have done wickedly …
> They served their idols,
> which became a snare to them.
> They sacrificed their sons
> and their daughters to the demons;
> they poured out innocent blood,
> the blood of their sons and daughters,
> whom they sacrificed to the idols of Canaan;
> and the land was polluted with blood.
> Thus they became unclean by their acts,
> and prostituted themselves in their doings.

We confess the goodness and severity of God:

> Then the anger of the Lord was kindled against his people, …
> Their enemies oppressed them,
> and they were brought into subjection under their power.
> Many times he delivered them,
> but they were rebellious in their purposes,
> and were brought low through their iniquity.
> Nevertheless he regarded their distress
> when he heard their cry.
> For their sake he remembered his covenant,
> and showed compassion according to the abundance of his steadfast love.

We cry as one:

> Save us, O Lord our God, …
> that we may give thanks to your holy name
> and glory in your praise.

The resetting of covenant can be done individually, with astounding results. Remember Phinehas. *Yahweh* himself said of that one courageous priest, "he did not tolerate any rivals to me and brought about forgiveness for the people's sin" (Num. 25:13 GNT). Thus, one man who treated as holy God's Name and his covenant with his people impacted an entire nation and "endless generations" afterwards.

How much deeper and broader and wider and higher the results when whole groups of believers renounce unholy covenants that we and our ancestors have made, when we stand together to reaffirm our covenant with Christ alone!

Such acts of re-covenanting have no effect if done in word only, waving around the appropriate phrases like a magic wand. God knows our hearts. He knows when we're outwardly saying the right words but, like the priests of Malachi's day, inwardly "have not resolved to honor" him. And he knows when, suddenly seeing the truth, we cry out for the honor of our God.

Bride of Christ, I urge you to seal again your covenant with the God of the covenant Name.

Yeshua, Lord Jesus, you alone are Lord. By your sacrificial death and resurrection, you alone provide redemption, sanctification, and atonement. I confess as sin my ancestors' binding themselves, by the shed blood of Confederate soldiers, to an identity not from you. I confess as sin my ancestors' trust in Confederate blood to sanctify Southern society. I renounce their determination to glorify and cling to the Lost Cause. I renounce the covenants they made with death. Please show me any allegiances in my life that have competed against and entangled with my allegiance to you. I confess that every such allegiance tramples the Son of God underfoot, treats as an unholy thing the blood of the covenant that sanctified me, and insults the Spirit of grace. Spirit-to-Spirit, I will listen as you identify anything that has hindered me from being wholly devoted to you. By your grace, I will name and turn from every competing loyalty you show me. Even now, I confess: Jesus, you alone are Lord. Thank you for the eternal covenant of life, love, and peace that I have entered by your blood. And now, I trust your shed blood and your resurrection power to annul every covenant with death that has bound my life and my generations. Thank you for forgiving me. Thank you for cancelling the power of those unholy covenants, delivering me and my generations from their destruction, and restoring our true identity in you.

"Now may the God of peace, who through the blood of the eternal covenant brought back from the dead our Lord Jesus, that great Shepherd of the sheep, equip you with everything good for doing his will, and may he work in us what is pleasing to him, through Jesus Christ, to whom be glory for ever and ever. Amen" (Heb. 13:20–21).

Especially, may our Lord say of you and me, as he did of Phinehas: They have "stopped my anger against the People … Because [they were] as zealous for my honor as I myself am."[240]

7—An Undivided Heart

There appears to be no limit to which some of us will go to save our idol, while at the same time telling ourselves eagerly that we are trusting in Christ alone. It takes a violent act of renunciation to deliver us from the hidden idol; and since very few modern Christians understand that such an act is necessary, and only a small number of those who know are willing to do, it follows that relatively few professors of the Christian faith these days have ever experienced the painful act of renunciation that frees the heart from idolatry.—A. W. Tozer[241]

God, your God, is testing you to find out if you totally love him with everything you have in you. You are to follow only God, your God, hold him in deep reverence, keep his commandments, listen obediently to what he says, serve him—hold on to him for dear life!—Deuteronomy 13:3–4 MSG

This is a story—a parable, if you will—of a woman and a preacher. To my knowledge the woman didn't know the preacher; nor he, her. Dressed in suit and tie, he stood weekly before a congregation of thousands. Bedridden, she watched him preach on TV. Who knows how much of his sermons she understood. She had long since been diagnosed with an illness doctors didn't call schizophrenia, but treated with schizophrenia meds.

One Sunday morning, the preacher preached from this text:

"If a prophet, or one who foretells by dreams, appears among you and announces to you a sign or wonder, and if the sign or wonder spoken of takes place, and the prophet says, 'Let us follow other gods' (gods you have not known) 'and let us worship them,' you must not listen to the words of that prophet or dreamer. The Lord your God is testing you to find out whether you love him with all your heart and with all your soul. It is the Lord your God you must follow, and him you must revere. Keep his commands and obey him; serve him and hold fast to him" (Deut. 13:1–4).

The woman who watched the TV preacher loved God. She had taught her children to love God. She had served God faithfully in church roles that fit her passion and her gifts. She had read, studied, and freely marked her Bible. Among the many passages she had underlined is this one from Psalm 9:

"I will praise thee, O Lord, with my whole heart; I will shew forth all thy marvelous works. I will be glad and rejoice in thee: I will sing praise to thy name, O thou most High" (vv. 1–2 KJV).

The woman had praised, loved, and believed the Lord. She had also believed a prophet named Rejection. The prophet had hammered his message home through her father, a faithful church member, deacon, and Freemason. The prophet spoke also through other personal relationships and through the people with whom she served at church. Some didn't value her or treat her with respect. Some didn't take her seriously because she was a woman, given more to expressing her emotions than to calm, rational thought. Some saw her as a threat to their status. Filled with jealousy, they talked about her, isolated and scorned her.

The woman began to swing between believing what God said about who she was, and what Rejection said. In her Bible, she had underlined and highlighted 2 Corinthians 10:3–5: "For though we walk in the flesh, we do not war after the flesh; (For the weapons of our warfare are not carnal, but mighty through God to the pulling down of strong holds;) Casting down imaginations, and every high thing that exalteth itself against the knowledge of God, and bringing into captivity every thought to the obedience of Christ" (KJV).

Tragically, the woman did not use the mighty weapons available to her to pull down the stronghold of Rejection. She did not cast down the lies Rejection told. Rather, she decided they must be true. After all, the prophet had come with very convincing signs and wonders: Her own father had soundly rejected her time and again; others echoed the same refrain. How could she believe herself "accepted in the Beloved" (Eph. 1:6 NKJV), when a host of voices in chorus proclaimed an entirely different word?

For years, the woman halted between believing the truth and believing the oh-so-convincing lies. She did not rest in her heavenly Father's lavish love and, from that place, war to fulfill the birthright redeemed with her Bridegroom's blood.

Granted, it takes war to cast "down imaginations, and every high thing" that exalts itself against the knowledge of God. It takes war to bring "into captivity every thought to the obedience of Christ." It's impossible to wage that war in our own strength, much less win it. But God doesn't expect us to conquer such strongholds alone. He has provided mighty weapons. And he himself has entered the battle in our behalf.

The woman knew that. She had underlined, highlighted, and starred 2 Corinthians 12:9: "And he said unto me, My grace is sufficient for thee: for my strength is made perfect in weakness" (KJV).

Praise God, she didn't have to be superwoman in order to send Rejection packing every time he knocked. The one thing she did need? Singleness of heart. Rejection could not have toppled her if she had stood in her Father's strength, choosing to believe *him* regardless how things looked. The Evil One got to her—he gained the upper hand in her life—because he was able to keep her swinging like a pendulum between truth and lies. In particular, she swung between her God-given identity and the false labels the enemy had attached.

The more she believed herself *inVALid*, the more she became an *INvalid.*

The more she let herself be victimized by Rejection, the greater the bond with that abusive false prophet. Desperate to escape Rejection, she began to pursue it. She saw it where it did not exist. She created it where it had not been. Eventually, her mind scripted stories in which everyone was against her. She firmly believed the stories true. Ultimately, she believed that those who most loved her and most wanted to help her were all in conspiracy against her.

The TV preacher stood before thousands. Quoting from Scripture, he challenged those gathered and those watching from home, "Love the Lord your God with all your heart and with all your soul."

What a contrast from the woman! He looked successful. She looked broken. He appeared popular. She had few friends. He spoke from an influential pulpit. She had no voice.

Yet they were alike in this: Both had declared their love for God. Both had sought to follow God. And both had done exactly what the preacher's text warned against. Instead of following God fully, both had also followed a believable, wooing voice that left them with a deeply divided heart. She had believed Rejection. He had believed Religion.

For a time, the woman had successfully hidden her double-mindedness. Then, the truth had become painfully obvious. If at any point she had quit halting between two opinions, if she had sought the Lord with all her heart, she would have found him. He himself promises it! And she would have found herself fully validated in him. Seeking the Lord and validation, she never fully knew either.

The preacher carefully cultivated a public image of devotion to Jesus alone. Yet in and out of the pulpit, he revealed a mixed allegiance—loyalty to God entwined with loyalty to a system that has promised him power and status. Yes, he too sought the Lord and validation.

As he preached that day, his words included truth, but they were singularly devoid of life. Indeed, words that should have offered listeners a deep, fresh breath of air instead seemed to suck the oxygen right out of the atmosphere.

The preacher urged people to love the Lord with all their hearts. Yet, tragically, he himself *did not know* how to do it. He *did not know* what wholehearted devotion to God looked like. He could only offer a checklist: pray, read your Bible, witness, do not forsake the assembling of yourselves together (on Sundays in a church building), serve God (in a church-sanctioned role). "You cannot love God if you don't do these things," he said.

The checklist method

You can't explain wholehearted love for God in terms of checklists. You cannot cultivate such a love by keeping rules, even seemingly pious rules.

The Galatians tried it. Paul wrote to stop them. In Galatians 3, he said, "Rule-keeping does not naturally evolve into living by faith, but only perpetuates itself in more and more rule-keeping, a fact observed in Scripture: 'The one who does these things [rule-keeping] continues to live by them.' Christ redeemed us from that self-defeating, cursed life by absorbing it completely into himself ... For if any kind of rule-keeping had power to create life in us, we would certainly have gotten it by this time" (Gal. 3:12–13, 22 MSG).

Paul knew from his own experience the hopelessness of the checklist method:

> I tried keeping rules and working my head off to please God, and it didn't work. So I quit being a "law man" so that I could be God's man. Christ's life showed me how, and enabled me to do it. I identified myself completely with him. Indeed, I have been crucified with Christ. My ego is no longer central. It is no longer important that I appear righteous before you or have your good opinion, and I am no longer driven to impress God. Christ lives in me. The life you see me living is not "mine," but it is lived by faith in the Son of God, who loved me and gave himself for me. I am not going to go back on that.
>
> Is it not clear to you that to go back to that old rule-keeping, peer-pleasing religion would be an abandonment of everything personal and free in my relationship with God? I refuse to do that, to repudiate God's grace. If a living relationship with God could come by rule-keeping, then Christ died unnecessarily (Gal. 2:19–21 MSG).

When you love the Lord wholeheartedly, you will pursue him in all the ways the preacher listed. You will converse with your Lord often. You'll walk in authentic relationship with his Body. You'll hunger for his Word. You'll delight in serving him. Your lips and your life will tell who he is. And yet your choices may look far different from what your church-culture thinking demands. Indeed, the more you pursue God, the more often he will put you in a position where, to follow him fully, you must do the opposite of what your particular church culture approves.

Herein lies a huge challenge. If generations of doing things a certain way have in your mind become enmeshed with Christ and his Word, you will be tempted to think God's voice is counseling rebellion, and the voice of Religion is God's. You will feel guilty for obeying the Lord! You'll find it incredibly hard to do so.

He who loves you is exposing your divided heart.

As you bring your confusion to him, he will reveal his Word, that you thought you already knew. He will teach you his character; he'll make you know his Name. As you set your heart to seek him, he will show you, moment by moment, how it looks to love him wholeheartedly. In the process, he will uncover every allegiance that competes for his place in your heart. He'll insist that you forsake them all. To uproot any attachment that reaches that deep within will require, as Tozer said, "a violent act of renunciation." You cannot do it, except by the Spirit of Christ. You will not do it, unless impelled by his love.

If you think the preacher's checklist method sounds safer and infinitely easier, know this: No matter how biblical, no matter how orthodox, checklists do not produce wholly devoted followers of Christ. Rather, checklists lull you into a dangerous place.

Making your list and checking it twice, you climb into your "rule-keeping, peer-pleasing" box of choice. Floating downstream with the current, you adjust course as needed to remain in the safe middle. To your shock, you and your box plunge right over the cliff.

Paul cried out to the Galatian believers, desperate to keep them from making the plunge:

"Let me put this question to you: How did your new life begin? Was it by working your heads off to please God? Or was it by responding to God's Message to you? Are you going to continue this craziness? For only crazy people would think they could complete by their own efforts what was begun by God. If you weren't smart enough or strong enough to begin it, how do you suppose you could perfect it? Did you go through this whole painful learning process for nothing? It is not yet a total loss, but it certainly will be if you keep this up!" (Gal. 3:2–4 MSG).

Wholly devoted

Paul's frantic cry echoes the fervor of God himself. He has paid the ultimate price to offer us covenant relationship. He calls for wholehearted devotion from his covenant Bride. He will settle for nothing less. Throughout Scripture, he sounds this refrain. Especially in Deuteronomy, we hear time and again: "Love the LORD your God with all your heart and with all your soul and with all your strength" (Deut. 6:5).

Requiring the impossible, our Lord makes it possible: "The LORD your God will circumcise your hearts and the hearts of your descendants, so that you may love him with all your heart and with all your soul, and live." Requiring an undivided heart, the Lord explains why: "For I command you today to love the LORD your God, to walk in obedience to him, and to keep his commands, decrees and laws; then you will live and increase, and the LORD your God will bless you in the land you are entering to possess" (Deut. 30:6, 16).

In the New Testament, Jesus announced this as "the first and greatest commandment": "Love the Lord your God with all your heart and with all your soul and with all your mind" (Matt. 22:38, 37). The beloved disciple John wrote: "Everyone who loves has been born of God and knows God. Whoever does not love does not know God, because God is love" (1 John 4:7–8).

The God *who is love* loves us, pours his love into us, and then calls forth that love from us. He commands us to do what he himself has designed us to do: love him with a pure, uncontested love. Responding in love to his love, we open ourselves fully to the flow of his life. We increase. We live.

When we give to another any of the adoration, trust, service, or honor that rightfully belongs to our LORD, he uses a strong term to describe what has divided our heart. He calls it *idolatry.*

The key to life

The day God came down on Mt. Sinai, the day all Israel saw his glory and heard his voice, he spoke the Ten Words. The Israelites had not yet entered covenant with the Lord. Before they took such a momentous step, *HaShem* announced who he is and what covenant with him requires.

He began: "I am the Lord your God, who brought you out of Egypt, out of the land of slavery. You shall have no other gods before me." He continued: "You shall not make for yourself an image in the form of anything in heaven above or on the earth beneath or in the waters below. You shall not bow down to them or worship them; for I, the Lord your God, am a jealous God, punishing the children for the sin of the parents to the third and fourth generation of those who hate me, but showing love to a thousand generations of those who love me and keep my commandments" (Ex. 20:2–6).

The command, "You shall have no other gods before me," can also be translated, "You shall have no other gods in addition to me." The phrase "before me" might literally be rendered, "in my face."[242]

The nation Israel entered covenant with God, and then broke the first two covenant commandments time and again. Typically, the people didn't quit God entirely. Rather, they tried to worship him *and* something else. Sometimes they even called their false gods by the name of the Lord. Often, they bowed before *idols*—tangible, man-made images of something God had created, which people had perverted into objects of worship. Ah, but as they bowed before the visible idols made by their own hands, they also bowed before invisible *gods*—malevolent spirit beings.

Deuteronomy 10:12 asks, "What does the Lord your God ask of you but to fear the Lord your God, to walk in obedience to him, to love him, to serve the Lord your God with all your heart and with all your soul?" In a nutshell: What does the Lord your God ask of you but to worship him alone? To *worship* is to do all of the above—to fear with reverential awe, to love, to obey and serve, bowing down in homage before.

Always, worship is a *voluntary* act. It's a choice. And yet, when it comes to worship, we may not always make the choices we think we're making. We may think worship is all about singing songs and lifting hands when, at the core, it's a heart issue. We may think we're worshiping the true God when, instead, we're bowing before something lesser that we connect with him. We may think our worship acceptable based on the feelings it stirs in us. Yet while our soul is soaring, the Spirit may be grieved.

We may love and serve, reverence and bow before the works of our hands. Yet, fooled by denial or deception, we may not recognize that as worshiping an idol. We may do what God has said out of deep love for him, giving selfless service that delights and honors him. Yet, because it doesn't happen in a corporate "worship" setting, we may not recognize that as worshiping the Lord.

Worship is a *spiritual* act. In worship, people subject themselves to a spiritual kingdom. There are many earthly kingdoms, and they come and go. There are two spiritual kingdoms—only two—opposing each other through all of time. The two kingdoms are not equal, and they are not alike. One kingdom is an eternal kingdom ruled by the one true God. The second kingdom was formed in rebellion against the first.

This rebellious kingdom is ruled by a hierarchy of fallen angels Scripture calls "evil spirits" and "demons." They long for the worship due solely to God. Indeed, these unseen spirit beings lay claim to any worship not acceptable to the one true God. They receive every form of illegitimate worship, regardless whether a person means to worship them.

When we allow anything or anyone to threaten the place of Christ in our hearts, we give worship to the rebellious kingdom. The evil spirits who inhabit that kingdom crave worship, yet utterly disdain the people duped into giving it. Filled with hatred and rage, demons rob, terrorize, and destroy anyone who, knowingly or unknowingly, bows to them.

In 1 Corinthians 10:19–20, the apostle Paul distinguished between man-made idols and the gods behind them. He said, "Do I mean then that food sacrificed to an idol is anything, or that an idol is anything? No, but the sacrifices of pagans are offered to demons, not to God, and I do not want you to be participants with demons."

Consider that Paul said to *Christians*, "I do not want you to be participants with demons." Earlier in the same chapter, he urged *Christians*, "Do not be idolaters" (v. 7), and, "Therefore, my dear friends, flee from idolatry" (v. 14). John the beloved disciple echoed the same warning: "Dear children, keep yourselves from idols" (1 John 5:21).

Our Lord commands us to love and worship him alone *because he alone is the true God*—the Creator, the Redeemer, the King, our Father, our true Bridegroom, the Lord of the covenant Name. He alone is righteous, holy, merciful, almighty, and just. He alone is eternal. He alone has all authority in heaven and on earth. He alone is love. *Yud-Heh-Vav-Heh* alone is worthy of worship.

Further, our Lord commands us to worship him alone *in order to protect us*. When we give even some of our worship to anything or anyone other than him, we prostrate ourselves before powerful spirit beings that hate us with violent hatred. We subject ourselves to those obsessed with doing us harm. Far worse, when we enter covenant with God through the shed blood of Jesus Christ and then try to commingle worship of God with worship of another, we sin against the blood by which we were atoned. We bring on ourselves a staggering burden of bloodguilt. If we do not repent, we bequeath the same propensity, with escalating results, to the generations to come.

The God who loves us commands us to love and fear him alone *because that is the key to life*. Indeed, wholehearted love for the Lord is the fountainhead, the cornerstone, the taproot of our true identity. It's the core, the essence, of the *you* God created you to be. It's the wellspring of blessing to your offspring for a thousand generations.

Once you enter covenant relationship with the one Lord—once the Son redeems you, the Father receives you, and the Spirit baptizes you—it's your true nature to love him with all your heart and mind and soul and strength. You're like the very happily married woman whom someone reminds about all the available men in the world. She doesn't care. She's not tempted. And if at any point temptation does momentarily rear its head, her love for her husband and his love for her immediately draw her back.

Spiritual schizophrenia

"GOD spoke all these words: I am GOD, your God … No other gods, only me" (Ex. 20:1–3 MSG).

Joshua cried, "Fear the LORD, and serve him with integrity and faithfulness. Get rid of the gods your ancestors served … and serve only the LORD" (Josh. 24:14 *GOD'S WORD*).

Elijah asked, "How long will you waver between two opinions? If the LORD is God, follow him; but if Baal is God, follow him" (1 Kings 18:21).

Jesus said, "No one can serve two masters; for either he will hate the one and love the other, or he will stand by and be devoted to the one and despise and be against the other. You *cannot* serve God and mammon (deceitful riches, money, possessions, or whatever is trusted in)" (Matt. 6:24 AMP).

When we defy or even dilute our uncontested love for God, we break the first two commandments. We bring illicit lovers into our Bridegroom's chambers. We slap our Lord in the face.

In so doing, we invite spiritual schizophrenia. Halting between two opinions, we become divided in heart. That's why James warned so strongly against double-mindedness. A little vacillating may seem innocuous at first, even steadying, but it's like trying to stand with each foot in a different boat, as the boats go opposite ways: " … be sure that your faith is in God alone. Do not waver, for a person with divided loyalty is as unsettled as a wave of the sea that is blown and tossed by the wind. Such people should not expect to receive anything from the Lord. Their loyalty is divided between God and the world, and they are unstable in everything they do" (James 1:6–8 NLT).

What can divide our hearts that way? Anything or anyone we trust as much as our Lord. Anything or anyone we believe instead of him. Anyone or anything we value as highly as him. Anyone or anything that becomes a rival to him. Any master that receives our homage, then pins us to the floor and demands our loyalty—even if that master insists that serving him equals serving Jesus. Any passion that promises to satisfy us more fully than *Yeshua*. Any lover that sidles up and whispers, "I can coexist with, and even complement, your worship of God."

"Lord, it's easy to see pagan idols of other cultures," I prayed one day. "What do *we* worship in addition to you?" I sat stunned when he answered, "Just about everything."

Double-mindedness and the spiritual schizophrenia it produces may manifest in an individual or a whole group of people, including a family and a church culture. Here are some ways it may look:

Some of the time, people believe what God says—about who he is and who they are—but sometimes they believe the opposite.

Regarding who God is: Publicly, they sing his praises. Privately, they often feel he can't be trusted and isn't fair. In difficult times, they may inwardly accuse God of abandoning them, while outwardly trying to say the faith-words other Christians expect to hear.

Regarding who they are: They hear the oft-repeated refrain, "We're all just sinners, saved by grace." They think that means the sinful self is their truest self; and the godly self, something always out of reach that they must ever strive toward. They weigh such teachings, along with the negative words others have said about them and the evidence of their own lives, against the Scripture's proclamation that anyone in Christ "is a new creation (a new creature altogether)" (2 Cor. 5:17 AMP). They swing between believing the truth and the so-very-convincing lie. Desperately, often obsessively, they seek validation, because they cannot believe they have already received it in Christ. If faith does not win the battle with unbelief, they become like waves of the sea, driven and tossed by the wind.[243]

People obey some of what God tells them, but not all.

Typically, they refuse obediences that appear to cost too much. In so doing, they choose to value whatever they're afraid of losing more than they value the Lord. If they do not repent, they will try to rationalize away what they know in their spirit is rebellion.

People want to please God—and they want very much to please people.

They have no idea how often their choices are motivated by a desire for approval by parents, family, co-workers, cultural community (including church community), or people of status in their world. Paul asked, "Am I now trying to win human approval, or God's approval? Or am I trying to please people? If I were still trying to please people, I would not be a servant of Christ" (Gal. 1:10).

Trying to please people is a different thing entirely from loving people. Paul urged, "Be devoted to one another in love. Honor one another above yourselves" (Rom. 12:10–11). Jesus said the second most important commandment is: "Love your neighbor as yourself" (Mark 12:31). Ah, but we cannot obey the commandment second in importance apart from obeying the first: "Love the Lord your God with all your heart and with all your soul and with all your mind and with all your strength" (Mark 12:30).

Genuine love and honor toward people flow out of single-hearted, undiluted worship of the Lord. By contrast, people-pleasing flows from a yearning for validation and affirmation. People-pleasing poses as love. It serves from a desire to curry favor. It appears to give honor, while grabbing for honor instead.

When we try to please people and to please God, we're attempting to serve two masters. Any time we're torn between doing what we know in our deepest being that God is telling us to do and doing what we think will earn the approval of others, our hearts are divided by a counterfeit of love. Any time we're torn between doing what we know in our deepest being that God is telling us to do and doing what we think is required to submit to a person or structure, our hearts are divided by a counterfeit of honor. True love, real honor, often look quite different from what we've thought. If we have to disobey God to do it, we've fallen for the counterfeit.

Know this: We love each other warmly and well, we excel in honoring others above ourselves, only as we obey God out of a heart wholly devoted to him.

People confuse loyalty to Christ with loyalty to something they link with Christ.

Over time, they may come to see whatever they've connected with Christ as inseparable from him. When that happens, they will disobey the Lord in order to obey the person or structure they've connected with him. They will seek above all else to protect and defend what they've linked with Christ (their church or denomination; their political party; their region or nation; the leader they've chosen to follow, etc.), thinking that in so doing, they are defending God.

And thus, over time, a person or group hesitating between faith and unbelief, obedience and rebellion, genuine love and a people-pleasing spirit, the true Lord and a counterfeit loyalty, will begin to show two radically different sides, sometimes swinging wildly between them.

Even when the spiritual schizophrenia has become full-blown, it may be astonishingly hard to spot, especially for those in closest proximity to it. For, typically, such double-mindedness is accompanied by strong deception.

We tend to see what we expect to see. And we in the conservative US church culture tend to see *our* words, attitudes, and behaviors as pretty close to right. Especially, we may expect the most active church members and the leaders of our organizations, congregations, and ministries to believe, think, say, and do what is godly. After all, the "committed Christians" in our churches have a long history of checking the right boxes. We've assumed they/we must be in right standing with God.

Happily, many who name the name of Christ truly believe, think, say, and do what is godly. The Lord knows who they are! He does not consult any checklist to find them, and we who use the checklist method may not even recognize them. Still, *Yeshua* honors and delights in them.

Sadly, in our church culture the appearance of godliness often belies the reality. For the "most active" church members, as well as the leaders who have moved up the ranks in our structures, are often the most susceptible to confusing loyalty to *Christ* with loyalty to *things connected with Christ.* They're especially susceptible to making a hidden idol of the organizations, ministries, and titles which offer them significance and power. Refusing to admit the truth even to themselves, they may descend into double-mindedness, all the while showing a winsome, squeaky-clean image to the world. I confess! I was among them!

But God uncovers us. He confronts our denial. He exposes our divided hearts.

Twice in the last decade, he has confronted me about significant double-mindedness in my heart. Once, he showed me I was trying to be married to him and to please a religious system I'd always associated with him. He replayed in my mind what that had looked like through the years. The realization utterly undid me.

About four years later, he showed me I was double-minded about my identity.

A Christian since childhood, I could rattle off—and thought I believed—all the ways we're made new in Christ. What's more, the Lord Jesus had taken me through an intense time of stripping away the old. He had catapulted me into a remarkable season of becoming the new, true me. Still, I swung between believing what he said and believing the lying labels attached to me by people whose approval I valued. Not to believe God is to call him a liar. It's to fall for the oldest trick in the book, to entertain the serpent's question: "Did God really say?" (Gen. 3:1). Again, the Lord utterly exposed me.

Both times, he first showed me the dire consequences of not uprooting double-mindedness and then revealed the sin in me. He did it gently, but firmly, not shaming me, but rather pinpointing what needed to go. Both times, I threw myself at his feet, confessing and repenting.

Even a hint of a divided heart should put us on high alert: We have put ourselves in deadly danger! We have compromised our most precious relationship! We have dishonored our Lord and God!

The pride factor

What makes us susceptible to a divided heart? Any wound or trauma. Any cherished sin—greed, violence, immorality, deception, fear, desire to control, to name a few. What makes us *most* susceptible to a divided heart and most resistant to seeing or confessing it? May I suggest: *pride*. Pride cohabits with denial. The two together rob us of the ability to see where our real loyalties lie.

I confess: The structure my spiritual forebears created, and to which I gave allegiance, was conceived in pride—and promotes a divided heart.

In *The Southern Baptist Convention: A Sesquicentennial History*, Jesse Fletcher said of the SBC's founding: "the nearest thing to a taproot was a growing pride in being a Baptist."[244]

Early on, this denominational pride led to a very public, very bitter "duel" between perhaps the two most influential Southern Baptists of the day. Not only did each of the two men wield great influence, but also each represented one of the two camps that have fought for control of the SBC ever since. Ironically, the two began as allies.[245]

In July 1845, two months after the founding of the SBC, a young man named James R. Graves moved to Nashville and joined First Baptist Church. The pastor, R. B. C. Howell, already had commanding stature in the new denomination.

Howell had himself moved to Nashville in 1835. For a decade, he had published the influential newspaper, the Tennessee *Baptist.* Although he did not attend the meeting in Augusta at which the SBC was formed, Howell did accept a position as one of the new denomination's vice-presidents. Every year of his life afterward, Howell served as a vice-president or president of the SBC. Indeed, according to Joe Burton, Howell "was elected to office in every Baptist body of which he was ever a member, and to every level of official responsibility."[246]

Reminiscent of Richard Furman and the Charleston tradition, R. B. C. Howell delighted in order. "He was a thorough Baptist, always jealous of the fair fame and name of his denomination," wrote J. J. Burnett in 1919.[247] Howell wanted the SBC mission boards and other denominational entities to flourish. He enjoyed linking his name with them and wielding power through them.

J. R. Graves, by contrast, had the fervor of the Sandy Creek tradition. A Bible-thumping preacher, Graves could hold a crowd "spellbound" for hours. Ah, but Graves inflamed the soul while quenching the spirit. He said he taught Baptists to "accept and practice the teachings of Christ and his apostles."[248] Yet an honest appraisal reveals: J. R. Graves did not rightly divide the word of truth. Rather, he interposed views from his own imagination and from Freemasonry, then used reasoning, sarcasm, and ridicule to attack and destroy anyone who disagreed on any point.

R. B. C. Howell apparently did not at first see Graves' vicious side. In 1845, when the two met, Howell was impressed with the young teacher. Shortly afterward, Howell helped Graves become pastor of Nashville's Second Baptist Church. Next, Howell invited Graves to serve as assistant editor of the *Baptist.* When Howell resigned as the paper's editor, Graves succeeded him.

In 1850, Howell left First Baptist, Nashville, to pastor a church in Richmond, Virginia. The following year, James R. Graves held a meeting in Cotton Grove Baptist Church, near Jackson, Tennessee. There, Graves launched the Landmark Movement.

Most Southern Baptists today haven't ever heard of the Landmark Movement. Few would say they hold to Landmark beliefs. Yet the denomination continues to be profoundly affected by the Landmark spirit.

Southern Baptist historians acknowledge as much. "It is impossible to understand Southern Baptists apart from Landmarkism," said historian Leon McBeth. Another, James Tull, wrote that Landmarkism began as a "self-conscious and separable element" in Southern Baptist life, standing "over against denominational traditionalism as an irritant and a challenger." But then "it quietly entered into the bloodstream of the denomination as a chronic element."[249]

The "rise of Landmarkism ... coincided with the controversy over slavery, the separation of Northern and Southern Baptists, and the Civil War," wrote Timothy George.[250] Northern Baptists paid little attention to Landmark doctrine. Southern Baptists, on the other hand, widely embraced it. For the teaching fed their growing defensiveness, their growing pride in their own conservative Christianity (as opposed to the North's liberalism), and their growing certainty that they were right and the rest of the world was wrong.

Passionately, proudly, James R. Graves offered them an exclusivist doctrine of the church. Vigorously, tenaciously, he labeled all other teaching "unscriptural." He declared:

- The local church is the only church. The "universal church" does not exist.
- The Baptist church is the only legitimate local church. The Baptist church alone can trace its existence all the way back to the Jerusalem church. All other supposed churches are mere human "societies" or apostate deviations from the Baptist norm.
- Only Baptist churches are authorized to baptize and to serve the Lord's Supper.
- Only Baptist preachers may stand in a Baptist pulpit.
- Only Baptist churches can send out missionaries. Mission boards and denominational agencies, even SBC ones, violate the authority of local churches.[251]

Graves railed against denominational entities, yet "held numerous denominational offices."[252] He tried to use the very system he called unbiblical to ensure that his teachings prevailed. Ultimately, his political clout fell short, for the Southern Baptist Convention could not officially sanction the Landmark Movement without disavowing its own structures. Yet Graves' powers of persuasion carried the day.

I confess: What my Southern Baptist ancestors would not write into their official documents, they absorbed into their very bloodstream.

From that first meeting in Cotton Grove Baptist Church in 1851, the success of Graves' movement was immediate; Graves' popularity, profound.

In 1857, R. B. C. Howell was asked to return as pastor of First Baptist, Nashville, where Graves was again a member. Burton wrote, "Like the king in the fable who returned home to find another occupying his throne, Howell returned to find another entrenched in favor."[253]

When Howell began to oppose the Landmarkers' agenda, Graves began to attack Howell in the pages of the newspaper Howell himself had begun. In 1858, Howell led the Nashville church to "try" J.R. Graves on multiple counts of character assassination of Howell and other ministers.[254] According to Joe Burton, the trial was aimed at a "deep-seated spirit of dogmatic assertiveness which could never be tolerated in a spiritual democracy." At the same time, Howell had a personal agenda: Zealously, he sought to defeat the "self-aggrandized arrogance of a man who always claimed that he was right and everyone else was wrong."[255]

Graves walked out mid-trial, taking 23 church members with him and declaring his group the true First Baptist Church. The original First Baptist continued the trial, pronouncing Graves guilty as charged. But the trial did not exorcise arrogance or Landmarkism from the SBC. Graves refused to accept the guilty verdict. Indeed, he declared a mistrial.

Ah, yes, the man who taught that the local church alone had authority to discipline one of its members now asserted that any church that conducted such a trial was no longer a church! Intent on destroying those who had confronted him, Graves went after Howell and First Baptist, Nashville, with a vengeance, all the while declaring *them* the aggressors and himself, the victim.

"A consummate propagandist by nature and talent, Graves swayed the Baptist masses of the Southwest [the Southern states not on the East coast] by both tongue and pen. He exploited fully the 'persecutions' against himself and other Landmarkers, gaining sympathy for his cause. For many months after the trial, he spread the account of its proceedings upon the pages of the Tennessee Baptist," said James Tull.[256]

"The humiliation of Howell must have been extraordinarily acute, for he was at this time in his third term as president of the Southern Baptist Convention. In a period of one year, approximately, after the expulsion of Graves, Howell was confronted with the anomalous situation of being the pastor of a church which had been excluded from every associative body with which it had been affiliated, except the Southern Baptist Convention."[257] In 1859, Howell responded to Graves' near-successful campaign to unseat him as SBC president by waiting until the votes were counted and his reelection secured—and then resigning.

Graves continued to teach Landmark doctrines and draw large audiences. Howell continued to serve as an SBC *vice*-president. Even with the outbreak of war, the two continued to feud.

Howell was right when he wrote about Landmarkism in 1862, "Those who receive its principles are inflated by them into pride and selfishness."[258] But what Howell saw so clearly in Graves, others clearly saw in Howell.

Burton, Howell's biographer, described the man as very "dominant ... proud ... opinionated, self-assured." A contemporary of Howell's told of his air of "self-appreciation," his "seemingly ostentatious manners," his "swelled and pompous vanity which made him forbidding and unapproachable"—and his "cordially warm and generous nature."[259]

Howell's own son Morton exposed fraudulent ancestral claims that his father's pride produced. R. B. C. wrote that he was "descended from the Tudor house of Wales." Morton "went to great lengths to disprove this proud claim." R. B. C. claimed to be son of an upper-class planter. Morton showed that his father's father was rather a backwoods farmer who may never even have owned land.[260]

Toward the end of his life, R. B. C. Howell penned a summary of his ministry career, a significant portion of which is included in *Road to Augusta*. The summary lists in detail churches Howell pastored, number of people he baptized at each, number of churches he organized, number of ministers he ordained, number of couples he married, and number of sermons he preached. According to his reckoning, for example, he had delivered 9,308 sermons, 780 as a licentiate and 8,428 as a pastor. Howell also listed his publishing credits, honors received, and offices held within the SBC.[261]

The proud, opinionated Howell, who made false claims of exclusive lineage and counted every sermon he ever preached, died in 1868, having dueled J. R. Graves to the death. Howell never realized he could not uproot from the denomination or from another leader in it what had become deeply rooted within himself.

After the Civil War, Graves moved to a new headquarters in Memphis and, for the next 30 years, continued propagating his Landmark doctrines among a deeply humiliated people who wanted to believe, "We're the only ones getting it right."

'Southern' and 'Christian': one and the same?

The year after the Civil War ended, Richmond editor Edward A. Pollard wrote a book, *The Lost Cause,* calling "for a 'war of ideas' to retain the Southern identity."[262] Across denominational lines, Southern ministers rose up to answer Pollard's call. With their preachers leading the way, the church pledged, by the blood of the fallen Confederate soldiers, to build a Southern Zion—a newer, better re-creation of their antebellum society—where they would show everyone else what it looked like to worship the God of the Bible aright.

Charles Reagan Wilson and Terry Matthews describe the confused identity that resulted:

"The years from 1865 to 1880 were ones of poverty, confusion, and disorganization in Southern life … during this period the Lost Cause myth emerged. In these years many Southerners, especially military leaders, bickered over defeat and lambasted allegedly disloyal Southerners. Southern ministers, who had been perhaps the most unswervingly loyal of all Confederates, did not generally participate in this bickering, instead maintaining that the Confederacy was a glorious fight for virtue and liberty. Eventually their view triumphed throughout the South."[263]

"The South's cause was not just its own; it was God's, hence it was a righteous one. The teachings of the Bible, the preservation of the Southern way of life, and the region's convictions about the good society were closely linked. It was God's will that the South and the Southern way of life survive."[264]

"The South quickly came to see itself as the new children of Israel—God's chosen people—a righteous remnant—who had been charged with the task of saving the nation from the immorality of the North … The saints of this variant of Christianity were those who fought and died for the Cause, as well as such living figures as Robert E. Lee, who came to be the Christ figure for this new faith."[265]

"'Southern' and 'Christian' came to be seen as one and the same. The religion that resulted was [an] interesting mixture of Southern nationalism and evangelicalism, and most resembled a revivalistic movement whose aim was to restore a golden age that was believed to have existed in the society's past."[266]

"Southern ministers … supervised and institutionalized the teaching of a 'correct' interpretation of Southern history."[267]

"Southern ministers and other rhetoricians portrayed Robert E. Lee, Stonewall Jackson, Jefferson Davis, and many other wartime heroes as religious saints and martyrs. They were said to epitomize the best of Christian and Southern values."[268]

"Clergymen alluded to the Arthurian tales, visualizing the Confederates 'on a field of chivalry more glorious than any since the Round Table.' … After considering the ancients, the Baptist preacher S. A. Goodwin, at the time of Jefferson Davis's funeral in 1889, insisted that 'In all the galaxy of fame there is no brighter constellation than that of the "Heroes of the Lost Cause."'"[269]

A frenzy of monument-building began in the mid-1870s and continued well into the twentieth century. In Richmond, the former Confederate capital, the first statue in the South dedicated to Stonewall Jackson was unveiled, October 26, 1875. Moses Drury Hoge, pastor of Richmond's Second Presbyterian Church, gave the featured address. *"We lay the corner-stone of a new Pantheon in commemoration of our country's fame,"* Hoge declared. By "our country," he meant, not the US, but the Confederacy. The Pantheon was the temple to all the gods of ancient Rome.[270]

Pride? Denial? According to Lost Cause teachings, a "pantheon of Southern heroes ... had emerged during the Civil War to battle the forces of evil, as symbolized by the Yankee. The myth enacted the Christian story of Christ's suffering and death, with the Confederacy at the sacred center." As Christ had risen again, surely the South would too.[271]

"There were any number of schools that developed for the sole purpose of educating children in the traditions of the Lost Cause. Many denominational colleges were centers of the Lost Cause Religion. Preachers who taught there promoted the link between the Confederacy and Christianity ... Leadership in this movement belonged to the Southern Baptists."[272]

"Each Lost Cause ritual and organization was tangible evidence that Southerners had made a religion out of their history."[273]

How long will you waver?

In the days when Ahab and Jezebel ruled Israel, a famine devastated the land for three years. Before the famine started, God sent Elijah to Ahab to prophesy that it would come. As the famine neared its end, God sent Elijah back to Ahab.

Elijah called for a power encounter on Mt. Carmel. The prophets of Baal and Asherah, 850 in all, would erect an altar to their gods. Elijah would erect an altar to *HaShem*, the God of the covenant Name. Each would prepare a sacrificial bull and lay it on their altar. "Then you call on the name of your god, and I will call on the name of the Lord. The god who answers by fire—he is God" (1 Kings 18:24).

As the people assembled, Elijah went before them and said, "How long will you waver between two opinions? If the Lord is God, follow him; but if Baal is God, follow him" (1 Kings 18:21). In answer, the people said nothing, for they had deeply divided hearts.

'Christian' and 'Mason': a truthful testimony?

The awakened church frowned on Freemasonry throughout the first half of the nineteenth century. In his 1887 report on "The Early Baptist Churches of Kentucky," William Pratt wrote, "Another matter troubled the churches at the opening of the present century, viz., *secret societies*. The first lodge of Free-masons in Kentucky was formed November 17, 1788, at Lexington." Pratt told of four occasions between 1805 and 1818 when a Baptist Association or church condemned participation in secret societies, specifically Freemasonry.[274]

One of the primary figures associated with the Second Great Awakening, Charles Finney, described the good things that resulted when churches took such a stand:

"The facts were such, the revelations were so clear, that the Baptist denomination ... took the lead in renouncing and denouncing the institution ... Now, it is worthy of all consideration and remembrance, that God set the seal of His approbation upon the action taken by those churches at that time, by pouring out His Spirit upon them. Great revivals immediately followed over that whole region. The discussion of the subject, and the action of the churches took place in 1827-'8 and '9, and in 1830 the greatest revival spread over this region that had ever been known in this or any other country."[275]

Himself a former Mason who repudiated the Lodge after his conversion, Finney wrote extensively to expose the truth about Masonic teachings, rituals, and practices. He called Freemasonry "an enormous falsehood" and "an anti-Christian institution."[276] He urged Christians to have no connection with it. Thorough in his research and bold in his presentation, Finney based his assessment of Freemasonry on the authoritative writings of Masonic leaders themselves. Several of his printed articles were republished in 1869 as a book titled, *The Character, Claims, and Practical Workings of Freemasonry.*

Like others who've spoken out since, Finney saw that Freemasonry promises status and "light," but in reality blinds and binds. Those who take its oaths and accept its curses bind themselves to their Masonic brothers above every other relationship—including fellow Christians, including family and wife. Helping a fellow Mason outranks doing what is legal, supersedes doing what is morally right. Further, Freemasons enslave themselves and the generations that follow to a cruel taskmaster who assures his subjects he can be any god they choose.

After exploring the matter for 10 chapters, Finney wrote:

> Freemasonry is now revealed. It is no longer a secret to any who wish to be informed. Its nature, character, aims, oaths, principles, doctrines, usages, are in print, and the books in which they are revealed are scattered broadcast over the land … Now, since these revelations are made, and both the church and the world are aware of what Masonry really is, God demands, and the world has a right to expect, that the church will take due action and bear a truthful testimony in respect to this institution. She can not now innocently hold her peace. The light has come. Fidelity to God, and to the souls of men, require that the church, which is the light of the world, should speak out … As God's witnesses, as the pillar and ground of the truth, the church is bound to give the trumpet no uncertain sound …[277]

So great was the outcry against Freemasonry among Christians in the first half of the nineteenth century that the bulk of ministers and church leaders either avoided the Lodge entirely or kept their participation well hidden.

In the South, however, the Civil War changed all that. After the war, Freemasonry offered an effective means for recreating a society in which white males maintained a superior, set-apart status. Freemasonry promised identity. It whispered, "Your cause is *not* lost."

Finney the revivalist lived in Ohio and held his revival meetings in the North. An abolitionist, he also promoted freedom for women to speak (or at least pray) in the public assembly and to be educated alongside men. When Finney's book was published in 1869—while the South still suffered under the excesses of Reconstruction—few white Southerners had any interest in listening to a Yankee preacher's call to the church to separate itself from Freemasonry. Rather, Southern men in droves—and most notably pastors and deacons—joined the Lodge or announced their membership in it. All across Dixie, Freemasonry came out of the closet.

Christian leaders who joined secret societies continued to proclaim the Gospel. They continued to preach, "Jesus alone saves." Yet they bound themselves by blasphemous oaths and potent curses to structures that use much symbolism from the Bible, but so mix and distort it as to produce worship, not of the God of Scripture, but the god Scripture identifies as Baal.

Old Landmarkism: What Is It?

R. B. C. Howell was a forerunner of sorts. Howell was a Mason, and apparently so even before the Civil War and thus before Freemasonry was considered acceptable by Southern church leaders.

James R. Graves was a forerunner too. He led the way into Landmarkism, proclaiming Baptists alone had "organized according to the pattern of the Jerusalem Church." In 1880, Graves published his teachings in a book titled, *Old Landmarkism: What Is It?*

In his own words, Graves identified this bedrock belief of the Landmark Movement: "that Baptist churches are the churches of Christ, and ... they alone hold, and have *alone* ever held, and preserved the doctrine of the gospel in all ages since the ascension of Christ." Graves defined the Old Landmarks as "those principles which all true Baptists, in all ages, have professed to believe."[278]

Identifying 10 "principles" that comprise "the mission of Landmark Baptists," Graves named this as No. 1: "As Baptists, we are to stand for the supreme authority of the New Testament as our only and sufficient rule of faith and practice. The New Testament, and that alone, as opposed to all human tradition in matters, both of faith and practice, we must claim as containing *the* distinguishing doctrine of our denomination—a doctrine for which we are called earnestly to contend."[279]

Notice: Graves insisted that all his teachings came directly from Scripture and, specifically, from the New Testament. He further insisted that "*the* distinguishing doctrine of our denomination"—what sets Baptists apart from everyone else—is commitment to the New Testament, not human tradition, in matters of faith and practice.

Yet, Graves' enigmatic use of the term, "landmarks," a word that appears nowhere in the New Testament, and his founding of Baptist Landmarkism came on the heels of profound interest in Freemasonry "landmarks."

In 1845 (the same year the SBC was founded), Albert G. Mackey published the first edition of *A Lexicon of Freemasonry*. As Grand Secretary and Grand Lecturer of the Grand Lodge of South Carolina and as Secretary General of the Supreme Council for the Southern Jurisdiction of the United States, Mackey was extremely influential and well-connected. According to the

Encyclopedia of Freemasonry, "Mackey was in active correspondence with almost every Grand Master, Grand Lodge, and other Grand Bodies and Officers for nearly half a century."[280]

In an era when Freemasonry was on the rise, especially in the South, Mackey's works were enormously popular and carried enormous weight. *The* most influential topic that Mackey's *Lexicon* introduced was that of Masonic Landmarks. Between 1845 and 1860, five editions of his *Lexicon* were published. All five included this much-discussed entry:

> LANDMARKS. In ancient times, it was the custom to mark the boundaries of lands by means of stone pillars, the removal of which, by malicious persons, would be the occasion of much confusion, men having no other guide than these pillars by which to distinguish the limits of their property. To remove them, therefore, was considered a heinous crime. "Thou shalt not," says the Jewish law, "remove thy neighbour's landmark, which they of old time have set in thine inheritance." Hence those peculiar marks of distinction by which we are separated from the profane world, and by which we are enabled to designate our inheritance as the "sons of light," are called the landmarks of the order.[281]

In 1851, six years after Mackey's *Lexicon* was first published, J. R. Graves launched the Landmark Movement. Nearly 30 years later, Graves put his teachings into book form.

In defining Masonic Landmarks, Mackey quoted the first part of Deuteronomy 19:14: "Thou shalt not remove thy neighbour's landmark, which they of old time have set in thine inheritance" (KJV). When Graves wrote his book on Baptist Landmarks, he placed on the title page slightly misquoted versions of two very similar verses:[282]

"Remove not the ancient landmarks which thy fathers have set."—Solomon.

"Some remove the old landmarks."—Job.

From that point, Graves began to expound a set of principles that he claimed to be both biblical and unchangeable. Again, he followed Mackey's lead. In 1858, thirteen years after declaring that Masonic Landmarks existed, Mackey had itemized them. Though others have since changed Mackey's list, he himself emphasized again and again in his writings that the landmarks were both ancient and unchangeable.

Mackey wrote in 1856: "The first great duty, not only of every lodge, but of every Mason, is to see that the landmarks of the Order shall never be impaired ... As its members have received the ritual from their predecessors, so are they bound to transmit it, unchanged, in the slightest degree, to their successors."[283]

Graves wrote in 1880: "I understand these Scriptures to teach that this organization [the local Baptist church], called here 'kingdom' and 'church' is ... the "stone cut out without hands;" it is a perfect product of infinite wisdom. For man or angel to presume to modify it in the least, by additions, changes, or repeals, is to profane it and offer an insult to its divine Founder."[284]

Mackey's Landmarks decided issues of the "regularity" of a Masonic Lodge, Grand Lodge, or Grand Orient. Graves' Landmarks supposedly decided the issue of authenticity of a church—that is, whether it actually *was* a church or rather a "human society."

Lest you think I'm imagining the parallels between Baptist Landmarks and Masonic Landmarks, J. R. Graves himself connects the two. Indeed, the man who emphatically declared that all his teachings came from the New Testament and none from human tradition, reasons from Masonic principles and Masonic order to prove his thesis statement, that Baptists alone are the true church.

Consider these five excerpts from *Old Landmarkism: What Is It?*, by J. R. Graves. Comments in brackets are my parentheses:

> The sense in which any existing Baptist church is the successor of the First Church of Judea—the model and pattern of all—is the same as that existing between any regular Masonic Lodge and the first Lodge that was ever instituted. Ten thousand local Lodges may have existed and passed away, but this fact in nowise affects the continuity of Masonry. From the day it was organized as symbolic Masonry, it has stood; and, though it may have decayed in some places, it has flourished in others, and never has had but *one beginning*. Thus it has been with that institution

called the Kingdom of Christ; it has had a continuous existence, or the words of Christ have failed.[285]

> *The* [local Baptist] *church is alone authorized to receive, to discipline, and to exclude her own members* [unless, of course, the member she is disciplining and excluding is Graves himself, in which case the church that tries to do so is no longer a church] ... She [the local Baptist church] can not authorize her *ministers* to examine and baptize members into her fellowship without her personal presence and action upon each case ... What would an intelligent Mason think should a Master Mason claim the right to administer the initial rite of masonry to whom he pleased without the knowledge or consent of the lodge, or to advance one in a Masonic degree by virtue of his being an officer? What Masonic Lodge on earth would receive his members or recognize his degrees?[286]

> It is the inalienable and sole right and duty of a Christian [local Baptist] church to administer the ordinances, Baptism, and the Supper ... certainly another and different body can not perform them—e.g., the rites of Masonry belong to the respective lodges; they can not be performed outside, or independent of, the lodge by any number of Masons: the officers are mere ciphers so soon as the lodge adjourns, and Odd Fellow lodges certainly can not administer the rite of initiation for a Masonic lodge, or vice versa.[287]

> If the officers and members of a Masonic lodge were all Christians, the lodge could not therefore be called a church of Christ, because not scripturally organized as a church. We may unchurch an organization, then without unchristianizing its members—*i.e.,* declare a body [such as Presbyterians or Methodists], to be destitute of the marks or qualifications of a church of Christ, without calling in question the Christian character of its members.[288]

And the capstone:

> You will grant that there is only one body on earth that can celebrate a *Masonic* rite, admit a member into a Masonic Lodge, or confer the Master Mason's Degree. That body is a Masonic

> Lodge. An Odd-Fellows' Lodge, or a Grange Lodge can not do it ... If a body can masonically perform Masonic rites, and confer Masonic Degrees, that body is a Masonic Lodge. The body that can make Masonic officers, whose acts are legal in the order, is most certainly, "to all intents and purposes," a Masonic Lodge. A wayfaring man, though a fool, can understand this. Now apply this common sense to churches. There is but one organization on this earth that can authorize a man to preach the gospel—*i.e.*, confer *scriptural ordination*—and that body is a scriptural [local Baptist] church. There is but one organization on earth that is authorized to administer Christian baptism or the Lord's Supper, and that is a scriptural [local Baptist] church. There is but one body on earth that possesses Christian, or Evangelical, or gospel ministers, and that body is a scriptural [local Baptist] church.[289]

The acts of the local *Lodge* conclusively prove that the local Baptist church alone has authority to act in Christ's behalf on earth? As the Masons, so the Baptists, said the man who taught Southern Baptists to believe they had the only scripturally sound church government, officers, members, ordinances, practices, and beliefs.

When the South didn't rise again

Thus, with monumental resolve, my ancestors across the South fought to keep the Cotton Kingdom alive. Proudly, they gave their loyalty to God—and to cotton and to the Confederacy and to Freemasonry and to the local Baptist church and to every other structure that promised to produce a Solid (but strictly segregated) South.

Yet no matter what combination of gods Southern people bowed before, they did not resurrect a golden age of Southernness, for no such age had existed, except in their imaginations. Halting between two opinions, they robbed themselves of the true identity the Lord Jesus had given his life to restore to them. They robbed themselves of the resurrection power his resurrection had bequeathed them.

Desperate to justify themselves and the Lost Cause for which they had fought, the church led the way in connecting the dead Confederacy with the dead Christ. When the South didn't rise again, the church resigned itself to acting like Jesus hadn't either.

In a land devastated by war, brutalized by Reconstruction and the power struggles afterward, where economies did not rally and dead sons did not come marching home again, the church that boldly preached the cross got stuck there. The church wed to the South used the Lord's sacrificial death to legitimize the lifelessness and stupor of the Bride.

Dispirited ministers preached sermons and dispirited congregations sang hymns that gloried in the cross (a good thing). Ah, but these same sermons and hymns gave only a brief nod to the resurrection—then longed for heaven, confessing that nothing but hardship and woe lay between. Deeply confused as to who they were, deeply traumatized by what they'd experienced, deeply bitter over what they perceived as rejection and abandonment by the world, the people of God across the South became content to live like the disciples in the Gospels, rather than the church in Acts.

"This is as good as it gets"

In the Gospels, the men and women who followed Jesus yearned for what they saw in him. Going where he went, they listened to what he said, watched what he did, practiced what he taught.

Yet during Jesus' earthly life, the disciples were notably undiscerning, unempowered, and unaligned with his character. Oh, they had moments when they looked startlingly like Jesus. In those moments, they received revelation. They spoke truth. They worked miracles. But oh how inconsistent their behavior, how little their faith, how impotent their attempts to usher in his kingdom! The Holy Spirit had not yet been given; and their flesh, though willing, was weak.

In Acts, from the moment of Pentecost, disciples filled with the Spirit of Christ looked and thought and acted like *Yeshua*. They demonstrated his character. They displayed his authority. They worked miracles. They loved with his love. Individually and collectively, they revealed his righteousness, his justice, his discernment, his truth, his mercy, and his superabounding grace.

Oh, they didn't reflect him perfectly. They were always becoming. They still had to be warned about double-mindedness and idolatry. They strayed into sin, division, and error, and had to be called to repent. Yet beginning the moment of Spirit baptism, the first generation of Christ-followers showed themselves to be radically different from who they had been even days before.

During the Great Awakenings, the US church tasted what the early church demonstrated and the apostle John described: *"In this world we are like Jesus"* (1 John 4:17). After the Second Great Awakening fizzled, the US church collectively returned to looking, not like the Christ-filled church in Acts, but like the conflicted disciples in the Gospels. People the Holy Spirit had visited no longer displayed his authority, love, or miracle-working power. Though many yearned to please Jesus and a few looked startlingly like him, the church that proclaimed the gospel of Jesus Christ was notably undiscerning, unempowered, and unaligned with his character.

After the Civil War, Southern ministers assured their confused, devastated congregations, "This is the height of Christianity. This is as good as it gets." Surely some who read their Bibles saw the discrepancy between the dynamic early church and the debilitated church of their day. Surely some wondered: "We preach the same gospel. Why don't we have the same explosive power, fruitfulness, and life?" Yet, traumatized and terrified that any self-examination would bring condemnation and shame, they wanted an explanation that would exonerate, not one that would expose.

As the twentieth century dawned, Southern Christians—along with dispirited, Bible-believing Christians across the US—were ripe for the dispensational teachings of the Scofield Reference Bible, teachings that told them, "It's *supposed* to look hopeless; and the church, lukewarm; until Jesus comes again."

"Things will only get worse"

In the late 1880's, C. I. Scofield the shyster became C. I. Scofield the minister, and it's questionable whether he ditched the first identity in order to adopt the second. The popular story back in the day was that Scofield was a raging alcoholic until Christ turned his life around. Credible accounts show, not a raging alcoholic, but the consummate con man. Once Scofield began moving in Christian circles, this much we can say for sure:

He hung out with the right people—people known for their genuine, unimpeachable faith. But discrepancies in his words and doings long after his life was supposedly turned around leave huge question marks as to the character of Scofield himself.

As a young man born in Michigan but living with his sisters in Tennessee, Scofield served in the Civil War on the side of the Confederacy.

A brief biography of Scofield's life by Emma Moore Weston relates these details: When war began in April 1861, 17-year-old Cyrus Scofield gave his age as 21 and enlisted in the Seventh Regiment of the Tennessee Infantry.

> In April 1862, he was listed as a patient in a hospital in Richmond, Virginia. There was no mention of a wound, so he may have become ill.
>
> In July, he wrote to the Confederate Secretary of War asking for exemption from further duty stating that he was a minor and a citizen of Michigan. He also claimed that he had been visiting his sister in Tennessee when he enlisted, that he had never voted in the South and that his health was broken by exposure and battle fatigue. He promised that in a short time he would enter the militia in Tennessee.
>
> On September 5, 1862, Cyrus was with the Tennessee Regiment when they crossed the Potomac during heavy fighting. A discharge was issued for Private Scofield in 1862 after one year of service. There is no definite record of where he was for the next four years.[290]

In another brief online biography of Scofield's life, Dr. Glenn R. Goss, professor of Bible at Philadelphia College of Bible, wrote: "When the Civil war began, [Scofield] was in Tennessee with his sisters. While there, he enlisted in the Confederate army. Military records show he fought in the Confederate Army for over a year in 1861–1862, then was discharged by reason of not being a citizen of the Confederate States, but an alien friend. Scofield told his biographer Charles Trumbull that he served through the war, and that he was awarded the Confederate Cross of Honor."[291]

The Life Story of C. I. Scofield, written by Charles Trumbull, was published in 1920, 11 years after publication of the Scofield Reference Bible. Scofield himself was still living and was highly respected as a Christian leader. Trumbull faithfully reported the tall tale the esteemed Scofield had told him:

> Young Scofield had gone into the Confederate Army, as a matter of course, with his boyhood friends and associates. Though not seventeen, he was a big fellow, tall, strong, though slender, and practically never sick in his life. "Raised on a horse," he was a perfect horseman, and naturally enough he was often called upon for orderly work. Learning how to carry vital messages, scrawled on a scrap of paper with the pommel of a saddle as a writing-desk, while shells and bullets were falling, gave him a disciplinary training in carrying through difficult commissions. His position as orderly, while he continued as only an enlisted man throughout the war, threw him constantly with the officers and others constituting the staff, with all the influences and associations that this would mean to an impressionable boy.
>
> Before he was nineteen young Scofield had been under fire in eighteen battles and minor engagements. The Cross of Honor was awarded to him for bravery at Antietam [1863]. He was twelve miles from Appomattox when Lee surrendered to Grant [April 1865]. Dr. Scofield today enjoys telling the incident of Lee's having said to Grant ...[292]

Amazing! Scofield won prestigious medals for, and overheard the top-ranking generals' conversations in, battles fought well after he was discharged from military service.

Trumbull wasn't the only one to fall for Scofield's con. Even today, a website that carries the text of Scofield's message, "Rightly Dividing the Word of Truth," includes these statements about Scofield from *The Wycliffe Biographical Dictionary of the Church*, published by Moody Press, 1982: "Scofield, Cyrus Ingerson (1843–1921), Bible student and author ... Fought in the Civil War from 1861-1865 under General Lee, his distinguished service earning him the Confederate Cross of Honor."[293]

What Scofield did or didn't do during the Civil War happened well before any conversion to Christ. But the flagrant lies he told about his war service long after he had become a renowned Christian leader are just one evidence of a con man still alive and well.

The Scofield Reference Bible gave conservative Christians an explanation why it was okay, and even right, to go through the religious motions without expecting to see results remotely akin to those in the New Testament church. In Scofield's theology, the seven churches of Revelation speak of seven dispensations of church history, occurring one after the other in chronological order. Scofield taught that history has brought us to the last dispensation and that we today are the Laodicean church, the lukewarm church, "the church in its final state of apostasy."[294]

Scofield's teachings convinced the American church that "things are only going to get worse" until Jesus returns. Therefore, the more lukewarm and apostate the church becomes, the more we hasten the day of Christ's coming! People who identify themselves with Christ but look nothing like Jesus, who are joined together into a fractured and compromised Bride, can rest assured our Lord will sweep in one day and deliver *us* from the seven terrible years of tribulation all the rest of the world will have to endure.

Yes, the theology C. I. Scofield popularized fit perfectly with the "get saved, then wait for heaven" mentality the dead Confederacy bequeathed to the Southern church.

"The Lord—he is God!"

"Things are getting gloriously dark," I often hear church folk say. Watching news of world events, we nod with a sort of grim satisfaction, convinced it's all inevitable, believing our sole responsibility lies in making sure that we (and a few others, if possible) are "saved." We lament the fact that so few seem to want to get saved these days. But we count that too a sign of the times. It's what's *supposed* to happen. Certain that God's kingdom will gain no real ground until after Jesus' return, we hope we'll get raptured out before suffering any real loss.

"This is the Laodicean church age, you know." As we of the Southern Zion try in varying degrees to be good Christians and wait for a mass escape, the Bride of Christ around the world moves in fire and miracles, life and love. As our numbers diminish and our nation declines, we in the conservative US church culture try in vain to hold the line. We attribute our inability to make positive change to the current dispensation, but God trumpets a different message: Our impotence results from a divided heart.

We confess! What a bloody, tangled mess we've made!

We wait for God to tell us it's not that bad. But he doesn't. He lets the truth fully, deeply, sink in. He lets the laser-like conviction of the Spirit do its work. He lets us feel the weight of our sin, the depths of his grief.

Yet, even when deeply convicting, God the Spirit does not condemn. He does not condemn us who know him. For "there is now no condemnation for those who are in Christ Jesus" (Rom. 8:1). He does not condemn those who don't yet know Jesus as Lord. "For God did not send his Son into the world to condemn the world, but to save the world through him" (John 3:17).

Confronting us with the hard truth, the Lord does not shame us. Rather, he comes to reveal the "shame on us." He exposes our reproach in order to roll it away. He exposes our divided hearts to return us to himself.

In Elijah's day, a three-year drought and famine in Israel *resulted from* divided hearts. For many years, God's people had wavered between two opinions. They had looked to God and to the Baals for rain and food. In so doing, they themselves had chosen to restrict the flow of life and blessing into their land and their lives. They had subjected themselves to gods who had proven to be incredibly cruel and deceiving taskmasters.

In Elijah's day, the drought and famine in Israel *revealed* divided hearts. With no rain in sight, how would the people respond? Blame God and cry to Baal? Turn from Baal and cry to God? Continue appealing to both? Desperation offers God's people strong incentive to confront hard questions, to see the consequences of wrong choices, and to choose to embrace right ones. Yet, month after weary month, the Israelites could not bring themselves to renounce any of the gods to which they'd looked for provision for so long. They kept hoping resolution and relief would come without their having to choose.

How, then, did God respond? Did *Yahweh* leave in disgust, looking for another people who would love him with all their hearts? No, he did not. Did *Adonai* decide to overlook the double-mindedness, to put up with it, counting lukewarmness the best he could hope for from such a stiff-necked people? No, he did not. Did *Yud-Heh-Vav-Heh* grovel, pleading for the people's love? No, he did not.

In the third year when the famine was severe, the prophet Elijah summoned Israel's king Ahab to meet with him. The king went.

"When he saw Elijah, he said to him, 'Is that you, you troubler of Israel?'"

Divided hearts bring devastating consequences. Yet, like Ahab, we typically do not want to see the connection. We do not want to know that *this* results from *that*. And thus, we may label anyone exposing the truth as "the one causing the trouble." Ah, but Elijah did not agree to the lie.

"'I have not made trouble for Israel,' Elijah replied. 'But you and your father's family have. You have abandoned the Lord's commands and have followed the Baals'" (1 Kings 18:17, 18).

Boldly, Elijah identified Ahab as the one who had led Israel into idolatry. Then, Elijah told Ahab to summon the Israelites and the prophets of Baal and Asherah to Mt. Carmel. Again, the king complied!

On the mountaintop, Elijah set the agenda. First, the prophets of Baal and Asherah prepared an altar and a sacrifice to their gods. All day, they shouted and danced. They slashed themselves with swords and spears. They cried for their gods to send fire to consume their sacrifice. Nothing happened.

At the time of the evening offering, Elijah "built an altar in the name of the Lord" (1 Kings 18:32). He laid wood and a sacrificial bull atop the altar. He drenched it all with water. Then Elijah prayed, briefly, passionately:

"Lord, the God of Abraham, Isaac and Israel, let it be known today that you are God in Israel and that I am your servant and have done all these things at your command. Answer me, Lord, answer me, so these people will know that you, Lord, are God, and that you are turning their hearts back again."

Scripture says, "Then the fire of the Lord fell and burned up the sacrifice, the wood, the stones and the soil, and also licked up the water in the trench. When all the people saw this, they fell prostrate and cried, 'The Lord—he is God! The Lord—he is God!'" (1 Kings 18:36–39).

An ever-increasing kingdom

Jesus died on a cross and rose again. In him, we have the glorious hope of heaven. We also have his resurrection life now. Jesus is coming again—but he's not coming to give an escape chute to a church so lukewarm it makes him gag. He's returning for a Bride who "has made herself ready" (Rev. 19:7). He's coming for a people whom he "gave himself up" to make holy and whom he will present to himself "as a radiant church, without stain or wrinkle or any other blemish, but holy and blameless" (Eph. 5:27).

The evil spirits who crave our worship know their time is short. Frantic and filled with rage, they're not going to let up. However, the God of the covenant Name, whose kingdom will never end, has declared unequivocally that, from the time of Christ's birth, his kingdom will never stop increasing:

> For to us a child is born,
> to us a son is given,
> and the government will be on his shoulders.
> And he will be called
> Wonderful Counselor, Mighty God,
> Everlasting Father, Prince of Peace.
> *Of the increase of his government and peace*
> *there will be no end.*
> *He will reign on David's throne*
> *and over his kingdom,*
> *establishing and upholding it*
> *with justice and righteousness*
> *from that time on and forever.*
> The zeal of the Lord Almighty
> will accomplish this (Isa. 9:6–7).

The Son given to us, the Lord *Yeshua*, has taught us to pray, "Our Father in heaven! May your Name be kept holy. May your Kingdom come, your will be done on earth as in heaven" (Matt. 6:9–10 CJB).

I don't begin to know all that these verses mean. But I know that, in the midst of the world's turmoil and darkness, evidences of Christ's ever-increasing kingdom are there, for those with eyes to see. I know that, in places where God's people wholeheartedly love him, his will is being done in incredible measure on earth as in heaven. I know these Scriptures do not mean: "Pray for God's kingdom to come, but in this world, expect to see only the opposite. Tolerate and participate in the church's lukewarmness as the avenue to a quick escape. Let the world go to hell in a handbasket because that's the way to usher in Christ's millennial reign."

Because of our deeply confused identities, because of our deeply divided hearts, we've settled for a whole lot less than what our King and Bridegroom has purchased.

When our hearts are wholly his, he shows us his ever-increasing kingdom. He invites us to participate with him in answering the prayer he himself taught us to pray.

A people holy to the Lord

"If your very own brother, or your son or daughter, or the wife you love, or your closest friend secretly entices you, saying, 'Let us go and worship other gods' (… gods of the peoples around you, whether near or far, from one end of the land to the other), do not yield to them or listen to them … for you are a people holy to the Lord your God. Out of all the peoples on the face of the earth, the Lord has chosen you to be his treasured possession" (Deut. 13:6–8; 14:2).

With so many potential idols out there to worship, with people we respect and love enticing us to give our allegiance to lesser things that masquerade as God, with worship-hungry spirits working every angle to capture our hearts, it may seem impossible to love Jesus alone, without another love or two creeping in.

But when we yield to Jesus Christ as *Lord*, when his Spirit baptizes us and continually fills us, he creates in us a clean, new heart that beats in sync with his. In our inmost being, we *are* love, as he is love. It's our new, true nature to love HIM with all our heart and mind and soul and strength.

If, however, we let patterns from our old life continue, if we let other lovers draw away our hearts, our Bridegroom will not sit idly by and watch it happen. He will take extreme measures, if needed, to expose and remove our reproach and to return us to himself. He will act so we will know that HE is God, and that HE is turning our hearts back again.

8—Display of His Splendor

> I will build them up and not tear them down; I will plant them and not uproot them. I will give them a heart to know me, that I am the Lord. They will be my people, and I will be their God, for they will return to me with all their heart.—Jeremiah 24:6–7

> They will be called mighty oaks, a planting of the Lord for the display of his splendor.—Isaiah 61:1–3

Beloved of God, you've pressed in through seven chapters. In them, the Lord has exposed much we haven't wanted to see. You may be reeling from all he's revealing—about your bloodline, your region, your church culture, your life. Behind the appearance of godliness lie bloodguilt, unholy blood covenants, grave injustices, deep-rooted wrongs. You may have begun realizing the profound implications for you and those you love.

You may be crying, "No. No! Not my church. Not my denomination. Not my people. No! We would *never* cooperate with any of that. If we realized. If we knew."

Angrily, you ask: "If all this is true, why hasn't God intervened sooner? Why is he telling us now?"

Mulling such bad news, you may feel ashamed, confused, and trapped. You may not feel the least bit courageous or able or wise. "What in the world do we do with all this?" you wonder miserably. "If it's true, how can we possibly escape such a sticky and deceptive web?"

Stop. Take a deep breath. Humble your soul. Become strong in spirit. Hear the voice of *Yeshua*, bringing glorious news. His words are for you personally, but they're also for his people collectively:

You and your ancestors have lived in bondage because you didn't know who you were. What your church culture has experienced is not the abundant life I offer. Following me doesn't look like you've been told. Your experience of me so far is not all there is. I have much, much more for you—for all of you. Come out! Be free!

Don't stand, looking around you. Regardless what anyone else does, you follow me. I'll take you out from this cramped place—this frustrating, ill-fitting box—into your true identity, the identity I purchased that you've never really known. You've tried to be a "good Christian." But I call you, Wholly Devoted to Me. That's who you are. That's who you'll become if you will follow me. Loving me, you will learn to love others. You will treat individuals and whole groups of people in ways that reflect who I am. You will honor and serve others, not because that's your "place," but because that's who you are. You will spend and be spent for their sakes.

I AM angry at what the enemy has done to your bloodline, physical and spiritual. I AM angry that my Name and my Word have been co-opted to keep you in a system that does not reflect my ways. I have come to deliver you. I have come to shift the present and transform the future, but also to redeem the past. My deliverance is so complete that I will use even the ungodliness that you and your ancestors have agreed with, submitted to, and been brutalized by to catapult you into victory and life.

The way out

Embracing the good news requires receiving the bad.

Don't falter, beloved of the Lord. Continue to invite him, "tell us about past events, so that we can reflect on them and understand their consequences" (Isa. 41:22 CJB). Let faith rise up in you. Listen from your inmost being. Hear as *Jehovah* speaks.

Our history explains our story. As God reveals the past, we see why we have not been able to conquer the things crippling our families, our churches, our communities, our lives.

Our history reveals God's glory. As he reveals the past, we see how desperately we have missed and misrepresented him. Yet, wonder of wonders, he has not forsaken us.

The God who is love, the God who keeps covenant, has shown us great mercy. He's extended great grace. Yet he cannot just look the other way. The foundation of his throne is righteousness and justice. He will not remain silent while the systems, the kingdoms, the identities we've agreed with continue to shred us, his people, and to maul his Name.

The way out of the morass will be painful. It will take time. It will require violent renunciation and tedious renovation.

Even to begin, we'll have to summon courage we didn't think we had. Following our God, we will step past our offense and anger, order down our fear, and give ourselves permission to look, and look again, at the things from our past our Redeemer is uncovering. As we look at what his light exposes, the structures created to protect the strongholds will instead reveal them. If we'll continue to press in past our deep discomfort and desire to defend, the Spirit of God will free us from what has held us captive for so long.

A tale of two houses

The following story may seem random. But for that very reason, it may shed light where we least expect it—and most need it. The LORD bless you with eyes to see.

A nice house

Suppose you own a house, a nice house where you live alone. One day, an aunt you really like asks to come live with you. After giving the matter some thought, you answer, "Yes."

Your aunt moves in, time passes, and the arrangement appears to be working well. The two of you get along marvelously. She's a wonderful encourager, counselor, and friend—offering advice when asked, but not meddlesome at all. She's responsible, too, willing to tackle whatever you need her to do. She contributes her share to the household finances, and even helps you out personally if funds get tight near month's end.

One day you leave the house to go to your job. Returning home at the day's end, you turn onto your street to see trucks and equipment parked near your house. Getting closer, you see equipment and workmen in your yard. Pulling into your driveway, you realize they've bulldozed one end of your house! Rubble lies everywhere.

Parking quickly, you run into the yard, screaming, "*Stop!* Stop! What on earth are you doing? Who's in charge here?"

The captain of the work crew ambles over. "Calm down, ma'am," he says. "I'm in charge. We were hired to renovate this house, and we started today."

"*I* own this house!" you cry. "Who in the world hired you?"

"*She* did," the man says, pointing across the yard to your aunt.

Pause. Consider: What would you think? How would you feel? Why?

A wrecked house

You own a house. But you haven't been able to make the payments. In fact, you owe so much that bank officials have notified you they're coming to foreclose.

What's more, you haven't kept up the place. Quite honestly, it's a wreck. Doors hang off the hinges. The plumbing doesn't work. Clutter and dust lie everywhere. You stand in the midst of the mess, seeing for the first time how desperate your situation is, how helpless you are to do anything about it.

Then, you hear a knock. You open the door, expecting to see someone from the bank. Instead, your aunt stands there. "I hear you're in a little trouble," she says.

"Yes, I am," you reply, inviting her in.

Briefly she surveys the sad scene. "I've come to make you an offer," she says.

"I'm listening," you reply.

"I have some money in savings. I'll use it to pay your debt in full. I'll move in, and we'll renovate. I'll provide the funds. We'll work together. We'll transform this place from the ground up. I can already see how it will look! When we get finished, this house will be so beautiful you won't even recognize it."

You're amazed, delighted, ready to shout, "I accept!" when your aunt adds, "There *is* one condition."

"What's that?" you ask.

"That you sign the deed to the house over to me."

Oh. Standing in the entry to your house, you take a long look around. Your aunt stands quietly beside you, waiting for you to choose. Are you desperate enough? Do you trust her enough? Will you sign over the deed to your house?

Let's suppose you do. As promised, she pays your debt. Immediately, she moves in. The arrangement works well; the two of you get along marvelously. Several weeks later, you leave your filthy wreck of a home to go to work. At the end of the day, you return, to see trucks and equipment in front of the house. One end of the house has been bulldozed, and rubble lies everywhere. Renovation has begun.

Pause. Now, what do you think? How do you feel?

The guest

Many people in our culture have tried to "invite Jesus into their heart" in much the same way as the aunt was welcomed in the first story. They realize they've done some things wrong. They need help. Someone tells them Jesus can give them peace and joy. He died for them. If they'll trust him, he will meet their needs now and make sure they go to heaven later.

So they ask Jesus to be their Savior. They expect him to bring everything into the relationship a heavenly Lifeguard should bring. They would never say it, not even to themselves, but they also expect him to know his place—staying in the background when not summoned, yet ready to listen whenever they talk, ready to jump whenever they call.

They've been told it's important to talk to Jesus, so they go to him, regularly or occasionally, to tell him what they need. They ask him to "save" by changing the people or circumstances causing them pain. They want him to comfort and encourage, to fix what's wrong, to assure them everything will be all right.

Ah, but if at any point he starts meddling in areas they've declared off limits, if he starts bulldozing walls to initiate major changes in *them*, they get upset. They accuse him of not caring, not having their best interests at heart. He's stepped way out of line! After all, it's *their* life.

Many have asked Jesus to come into their heart and be their Savior, as one might welcome a long-term, live-in guest. But the word of God never says Jesus will come in that way.

The owner

As in the second story, Jesus knocks on your door about the time you realize you aren't the nice, "basically good" person you may have thought. God the Spirit has done his convicting work, and suddenly you see it: You're a mess! Your situation is desperate: Death and hell are on their way to foreclose, and there's nothing you can do to stop them.

Jesus makes you an offer: He has laid down his life in order to pay your debt. He literally, physically died and literally, physically rose again. Alive forever, he will live with you from now on. That is, he'll live inside you, and at the same time, you will live in him.

Yet he does insist on two things, and he's adamant about both. First, when he comes in, he comes to renovate. He'll start with a new foundation and build from the ground up. Oh, you won't have to provide the wherewithal for that. He'll draw up the plans. He'll oversee the work. And he promises to complete it. In fact, once you're his, Jesus refers to you as his "masterpiece"—even before the work begins, even in the messy middle.

Paradoxically, it's critical that you trust and cooperate. Sometimes, you'll feel sure that he's going too far, too fast, or that he's tearing out things it wouldn't have hurt to keep, or that you're never going to see the beauty on the other side of the mess.

In those seasons, it's crucial that you keep trusting, keep cooperating. If you do, even as the work progresses, your life will begin to look so beautiful, you won't even recognize it. You will radiate with his splendor.

And the other thing he's adamant about? His one, non-negotiable prerequisite: You must sign the deed to your life over to him.

How often have you heard Romans 10:9? If you've grown up in church, probably more times than you can count. But hear it now from your spirit as if you've never heard it before: "If you confess with your mouth that Jesus is Lord and believe in your heart that God raised him from the dead, you will be saved" (NLT).

Jesus becomes your Savior when you confess him as *Lord.* Confessing Jesus as Lord means signing over the deed to your life to him. From that point on, it's not "your" life any more. He's comes in, not as guest, but as owner.

That's why Jesus makes his offer as the Spirit shows you the truth—about who he is and who you are. As long as you think, deep down, that your house is pretty nice—that you're a basically good person, able to handle your own life—you'll welcome a guest, but you will not give up ownership. As long as you question Jesus' commitment to your best interests—if you think, deep down, he's a tyrant looking for another slave—you will not give him ownership.

Confessing Jesus as Lord is not carrying your own weight and looking to him for help when you can't quite make it. That's double-mindedness. That's a divided heart. Confessing Jesus as Lord requires seeing and saying the truth: "I'm broken. I fall short of the glory of God, the glory for which he created me." Confessing Jesus as Lord requires more than mental assent to his death and resurrection. It requires thrusting your entire weight—spirit, soul, and body—onto him.

When you sign your life over to *Yeshua*, he does exactly as promised: He pays in full the monstrous debt you owed to God. He moves in to stay, working such a fundamental change within you that you're instantly "created anew." He starts the progressive work of transforming every aspect of your life into the masterpiece he already knows you to be.

Under renovation

We have much to confess. Yet, for you personally and for all of us collectively, one confession is key. From the heart, by the Spirit, you declare with your lips and with your life: *Jesus is Lord.* Of the same mind, by the same Spirit, we confess together: *Jesus is Lord.*

That's the key to entering and fully experiencing covenant with the Lord your God. It's the key to annulling unholy covenants we or our ancestors have made. It's the key to being cleansed from bloodguilt. It's the key to loving the Lord with all your heart. It's the key to eradicating unrighteous roots and nourishing godly ones. It's the key to becoming who God made us to be. It's the key to living lives that profoundly honor him.

The Lord renovates—indeed, re-creates—those who have signed the deed to their life over to him. He purifies and builds up those who have entered covenant relationship with him on the basis of his shed blood. He builds us together into a holy temple. He forms us into his spotless, radiant Bride.

"Yes, in union with him, you yourselves are being built together into a spiritual dwelling-place for God!" (Eph. 2:22 CJB). *Yeshua* is the cornerstone. He is the foundation (1 Cor. 3:11). He was dead and is alive. He has paid the debt in full.

When you know him as Lord, "You are not your own; you were bought at a price" (1 Cor. 6:19–20). He has moved in: "Christ lives in you. This gives you assurance of sharing his glory" (Col. 1:27 NLT).

When you know him as Lord, you have entered the most deeply intimate of all relationships, your life inter-commingled with the God of the covenant Name. You can hear his voice. You can know his ways. Deeply, deeply, you love and are loved. At the same time, you have a deep and growing sense of his holiness, his entirely-other-than-ness. He alone is LORD. You're not afraid of God. He never terrorizes you, nor causes you to live in even a moment of anxiety. But you experience in your very depths the reverential awe no words can fully express. You walk in the fear of the LORD.

Wholly surrendered to him, you do not become his clone. He doesn't strip away your uniqueness. Rather, he unveils it. He nurtures it. Becoming who you are, you rightly connect with others. You delight and honor your Lord.

Wholly surrendered to him, you do not become his robot. He never exerts dictatorial control. God is sovereign. He is not a tyrant. He rules righteously, out of all that he is. Anything or anyone else you bow before draws its power from the other kingdom, the rebellious kingdom. Those gods, too, rule out of all they are.

If the Jesus you're serving is a dictator, that's another Jesus, not Jesus the Lord. If the Jesus you're bowing before expects endless, frantic, exhausting activity—instead of giving rest—that's a tyrannical spirit, not the Son of God. If the Jesus you're following requires you to stay "in your place" in a system that keeps you boxed in, isolated even from those closest to you, and weighted down with religious rules, that's a cruel taskmaster, not the covenant-keeping Lord.

The book of Galatians strongly warns us not to subject ourselves to a system that results from perverting God's word into legalism. Jesus was "born into a culture in which legalistic perversion of the *Torah* was the norm, so that he might redeem those in subjection to this legalism and thus enable us to be made God's sons … In the past, when you did not know God, you served as slaves *beings* which in reality are non-gods. But now you do know God, and, more than that, you are known by God. So how is it that you turn back again to those weak and miserable *elemental spirits*? Do you want to enslave yourselves to them once more?" (Gal. 4:4–5, 8–9 CJB).

But also, if the Jesus you're serving is benevolent to a fault, letting you make your own rules and redraw every boundary, that's lawlessness, not liberty, and its author is not Jesus the Lord.

It's tyranny in disguise that makes you think you're free while systematically enslaving you to "all kinds of passions and pleasures" (Titus 3:5). The result isn't pretty, and it isn't fun. "Your eyes and heart are controlled entirely by your greed, your desire for shedding innocent blood, oppressing and extorting," wrote Jeremiah (Jer. 22:17 CJB). "For you are a slave to whatever controls you," Peter said (2 Peter 2:19 NLT).

Jesus could move us like marionettes on a string, if he wanted. But he does not. Every moment, every day, he sets before us choices. This moment, this day, will we honor him as Lord?

> See, I set before you *today* life and prosperity, death and destruction. For I command you *today* to love the LORD your God, to walk in obedience to him, and to keep his commands, decrees and laws; then you will live and increase, and the LORD your God will bless you in the land you are entering to possess. But if your heart turns away and you are not obedient, and if you are drawn away to bow down to other gods and worship them, I declare to you this day that you will certainly be destroyed. You will not live long in the land you are crossing the Jordan to enter and possess. *This day* I call the heavens and the earth as witnesses against you that I have set before you life and death, blessings and curses. *Now choose life*, so that you and your children may live and that you may love the LORD your God, listen to his voice, and hold fast to him (Deut. 30:15–20).

That's Old Testament, you say. It is indeed. It's God's word to his people, the Jews. He's given them a day-to-day choice to love him and obey him individually, but also to do so collectively. If they do not, as a people, honor him alone as LORD, consequences and judgments happen to them as a nation and happen on this earth. Yet because God is in covenant with the Jews and because he is a covenant-keeping God, he never allows their utter destruction. Any evil that comes on them, he uses redemptively, to draw them back to him. And emphatically, he declares woe to any nation or people that afflicts them.

So does Deuteronomy 30 apply at all to us? In this New Testament era, does it matter if our hearts turn away and if we bow down to other gods, or is all that already covered by Jesus' blood? Yes, yes and yes. "We have been made holy through the sacrifice of the body of Jesus Christ once for all" (Heb. 10:10). Yet the paradox is also true: It matters, a lot, what choices we make day to day.

Remember Paul's admonition in Romans 11:20–22: "Do not be arrogant, but tremble. For if God did not spare the natural branches, he will not spare you either. Consider therefore the kindness and sternness of God: sternness to those who fell, but kindness to you, provided that you continue in his kindness. Otherwise, you also will be cut off."

Paul wrote to the church in Rome. He speaks to us today—individually, collectively, generationally.

Individually, confessing Jesus as Lord is both a once-for-all thing and a moment-by-moment thing. It is not running down an aisle, praying a prayer, and then spending the rest of your life hoping you can coast into heaven. It is not completing half the renovation, then refusing the rest: "continue in his kindness."

Collectively, God's people are not just random individuals. We're his family. We're being formed into his Body, his army, his temple, his Bride: "As you come to him, the living Stone—rejected by human beings but chosen by God and precious to him—you also, like living stones, are being built into a spiritual house to be a holy priesthood, offering spiritual sacrifices acceptable to God through Jesus Christ" (1 Peter 2:4–5). When we collectively make choices that dishonor the Lord, and do so stubbornly and repeatedly, the results affect the whole group, and often the generations that follow.

Remember *Yeshua*'s startling words to the church at Ephesus, the group of believers he commended for persevering, enduring hardships and not growing weary. Speaking to the church, he said: "I have this against you: The love you had at first is gone. Remember how far you have fallen. Return to me and change the way you think and act, and do what you did at first. I will come to you and take your lamp stand from its place if you don't change" (Rev. 2:4–5 *GOD'S WORD*).

We see from history that God has indeed removed the lampstands of churches and entire church cultures that have turned aside from loving Jesus wholeheartedly and serving him alone. We have not seen how much our culture—the Bible-believing, missionary-sending, conservative US church—needs to heed Jesus' warning to the church in Ephesus and Paul's warning to the church in Rome.

"I will come to you and take your lamp stand from its place if you don't change."
"If God did not spare the natural branches, he will not spare you either."

Generationally, it doesn't matter what your mama or daddy did with regard to Christ. Yet it matters very much. Confessing Jesus as Lord is a personal choice. If others in your lineage made that choice and lived it out, you may find it much easier to do so. If others in your lineage made that choice, but did not live it out consistently, you may be very confused. If others in your lineage tried to be good Christians without ever surrendering to Jesus as Lord, you may be trying to play along, and wondering why it's not working out so well for you, or you may be totally turned off by what you perceive Christianity to be. But no matter what picture of Christianity your forebears painted, no matter how well or poorly they lived it out, you know *Yeshua* only when *you* receive him, on *his* terms.

On the other hand, choices made by the generations before you have a huge impact on the type and scope of the renovations needed in your life and in the church in your culture. Inheritance doesn't just happen physically ("she has her father's nose") and materially ("he inherited his parents' debts"). The inner stuff collected by generations before us gets passed down too. It's passed down through spiritual bloodlines, as well as natural bloodlines.

If your ancestors didn't get rid of their stuff, you inherited it! That includes the good things, the blessings they accrued. It also includes the bad stuff they could not bring themselves to deal with or let go of. You may not want their junk, but you got it, and you cannot get rid of it by denying it's there. You get rid of it by signing your life over to *Yeshua* and cooperating fully in the wonderful, radical, and sometimes remarkably painful, process of becoming who you are.

Treasures hidden in darkness

"We are God's masterpiece. He has created us anew in Christ Jesus, so we can do the good things he planned for us long ago" (Eph. 2:10 NLT).

The One who comes in only where he is Lord never would have died, if he had not chosen to do so to pay our debt. He conquered death to redeem for you the identity God designed before the foundation of the world. He does have your best interests at heart.

In his love for us, his commitment to complete renovation, and his determination to free us from the junk passed down by unsuspecting generations that went before, **JHVH** has taken us down into the basement, up into the attic, and into the dark closets of the church culture rooted in the Deep South. Smack in the midst of the darkness, he has treasures to reveal—valuable treasures we didn't know existed—treasures we'll uncover as we cooperate in exposing and hauling away the junk.

"I will give you treasures hidden in the darkness—secret riches. I will do this so you may know that I am the Lord, the God of Israel, the one who calls you by name" (Isa. 45:3 NLT).

Yeshua describes some of those treasures in Isaiah 61. Read his words aloud:

The Spirit of the Sovereign Lord is on me,
because the Lord has anointed me
to proclaim good news to the poor.
He has sent me to bind up the brokenhearted,
to proclaim freedom for the captives
and release from darkness for the prisoners,
to proclaim the year of the Lord's favor
and the day of vengeance of our God,
to comfort all who mourn,
and provide for those who grieve in Zion—
to bestow on them a crown of beauty
instead of ashes,
the oil of joy
instead of mourning,
and a garment of praise
instead of a spirit of despair.
They will be called mighty oaks,
a planting of the Lord
for the display of his splendor.

They will rebuild the ancient ruins
and restore the places long devastated;
they will renew the ruined cities
that have been devastated for generations …
Instead of your shame
you will receive a double portion,
and instead of disgrace
you will rejoice in your inheritance.
And so you will inherit a double portion in your land,
and everlasting joy will be yours.

"For I, the Lord, love justice;
I hate robbery and wrongdoing.

> In my faithfulness I will reward my people
> and make an everlasting covenant with them.
> Their descendants will be known among the nations
> and their offspring among the peoples.
> All who see them will acknowledge
> that they are a people the LORD has blessed" (Isa. 61:1–4, 7–9).

Our Lord hasn't yet brought out into the light all that's hidden in the darkness, both bad and good. But he's shown us enough so we can choose: resist this major renovation he's setting about, in individual lives and in his Body—or take a deep breath, roll up our sleeves, and fully cooperate with him.

I've written this book to declare that the Anointed One is here, moving in this time and place, to bind up the brokenhearted and set the captives free—free from bloodguilt, free from unholy blood covenants, free from unrighteous roots, free from injustices hidden in plain sight, free from everything that holds us in an identity we know in our deepest being to be false. I've written this book with a cry in my heart that we will, individually and collectively, humble ourselves, seek God's face, and so submit to the renovation process that he will be highly honored and his kingdom greatly furthered.

As we confess with our lips and our lives, "Jesus is Lord," we discover to our utter shock: *we* are the treasures that were hidden in the dark. As we become who our LORD created us to be, as we do what our Father re-created us in Christ Jesus to do, we highly honor and powerfully reveal the mysterious **JHVH**. As we display his splendor, he makes for himself a glorious Name.

9—Bless Our Hearts!

Foolishly, we've thought of blessings as sweet little things. They're not. The blessings of the LORD flow from the white-hot radiance of his glory. They enlarge our human spirit, setting it ablaze. They enlarge our capacity to know and honor HIM, to become who we are in HIM and, from that place of identity and intimacy, to join HIM in bringing his ever-increasing kingdom from heaven into the earth.

I will bless those who have humble and contrite hearts, who tremble at my word.—Isaiah 66:2 NLT

In the South, you know you're in trouble when someone says, "Bless your heart!" It means, by translation, "Wow! What a hopeless mess you're in!" or, "Wow! What a hopeless fool you are!" or, "Wow, am I glad I'm not *you*!"

Maybe you did something really dumb or really bad. Maybe you got caught. Bless your heart! Maybe you've shipwrecked yourself by a series—even a lifetime—of poor choices. Maybe other people relentlessly knock you down. Bless your heart! Maybe you've had a run of really rotten "luck." Then again, maybe you're just having a bad hair day, or one of your perfectly manicured nails just broke. Bless your heart!

The person who speaks the "blessing" may feel genuine sympathy for you. More often, they want to say something belittling in a "nice" way.

Unaware, the belittling blessers fulfill Scripture! "With their mouths they bless, but in their hearts they curse" (Ps. 62:4). They put you in your place.

By this point, we of white Southern origin may feel God is saying to the lot of us, "Bless your hearts!" And, truly, he is. But he's not slapping us down. He's slapping us awake from a dangerous stupor. He's jolting our hearts back into sync with his. While we may turn blessings into curses, he offers us blessings that truly bless.

Get ready to be blessed

God never minimizes the mess we've made or the damage it's done to his holy name. *But also,* God never minimizes his covenant love and faithfulness and his capacity to restore. "I am the Lord, the God of the whole human race," he says. "Is anything too hard for me?" (Jer. 32:27).

Before he points out any flaw, he's made the way to correct it. The moment he shows us what we don't want to see, he announces his intent to redeem. "I will cleanse them of bloodguilt which I have not yet cleansed," he cries (Joel 3:21 CJB). I will "bestow on them a crown of beauty instead of ashes, the oil of joy instead of mourning, and a garment of praise instead of a spirit of despair," he promises (Isa. 61:3). "They will rebuild the ancient ruins," he declares (Isa. 61:4).

Yeshua stands at the door and knocks. We can let him in, or we can refuse to answer. We can cooperate in the replanting, rebuilding, renewing process, or we can defy it. We can also try to cooperate, but fail, because we're trying to accomplish the will of God apart from the ways of God. Wanting what our Lord offers, how do we receive it?

God's renovation process includes key aspects: forgiving, grieving, returning, repenting. We can watch for and press into each aspect as he introduces it. But we cannot approach these like a checklist. God's ways are not our ways. His ways are more circular than linear. His ways are interconnected, not isolated. His ways often offend our minds. We think *we* know better. "We've already done that," or "*I* don't need *that*!" we insist. Yet his ways are higher than ours. His ways alone lead in the paths of life.

To walk in God's ways, we need his blessings, the blessings Christ purchased for us with his blood. Romans 10:12 says, "the same Lord is Lord of all and richly blesses all who call on him." Ephesians 1:3 proclaims, "Praise be to the God and Father of our Lord Jesus Christ, who has blessed us in the heavenly realms with every spiritual blessing in Christ."

In Christ, every spiritual blessing has been deposited to our account. Yet we may want a blessing, may go to the bank attempting to make a withdrawal—and find the transaction has failed. What hinders us from appropriating the blessings already ours in Christ, or releases their fullness to us, is the attitude of our hearts.

"I will bless those who have humble and contrite hearts, who tremble at my word," says the Lord. "But those who choose their own ways—delighting in their detestable sins—will not have their offerings accepted … I will send them great trouble—all the things they feared. For when I called, they did not answer. When I spoke, they did not listen. They deliberately sinned before my very eyes and chose to do what they know I despise" (Isa. 66:2–4 NLT).

God will bless those who have humble, contrite hearts. We open ourselves to restoration as we keep our hearts in a place to be blessed.

At Sinai, as the Lord finished spelling out the terms of his covenant with Israel, before he led them toward the Promised Land, he told the priests to bless his people with these words:

> **JHVH** bless you
> and keep you;
> **JHVH** make his face shine on you
> and be gracious to you;
> **JHVH** turn his face toward you
> and give you peace (Num. 6:24–26).

The God of the covenant Name commissioned this profound blessing in order to put *his Name* on his people. He declared, "They will place my name on the People of Israel—I will confirm it by blessing them" (Num. 6:27 MSG). The Lord's blessings release his Name—his covenant character, his multi-faceted glory, his unfathomable ways—in each of us individually and in all of us collectively. As he blesses our humbled hearts, we honor him. We fully follow. We become who we are.

The first generation to whom God gave the Aaronic blessing didn't come close to receiving its fullness, because they didn't humble their hearts. Standing at the edge of Canaan, they chose their own ways over God's ways. They turned back, rather than risk the confrontations that going forward would require. From that point on, they lived miserable, purposeless, petty lives. Ah, but the children did what their parents did not. The next generation humbled their hearts, received the blessing, and took the land.

Lord, you have blessed us with every spiritual blessing! You richly bless all who call on you! You've put your name on us! Yet, time and again, we and the generations before us have chosen our ways over yours. Time and again, we've turned back rather than confront in ourselves what we must confront in order to go forward with you. What a mess we're in! Lord, bless our humbled hearts!

When *Jehovah* turns toward us to bless, we may expect to see a benevolent smile, like Santa Claus wears. Instead, fire blazes from *Yeshua's* eyes. Gazing into his eyes is like looking at a thousand-times-brighter sun. Yet what we think will blind us, he intends to open our eyes and humble our hearts to receive his outpoured grace. What we think will consume us, he intends to consume what is not of him in us, to give us peace, to make us whole.

Foolishly, we've thought of blessings as sweet little things. They're not. The blessings of the Lord flow from the white-hot radiance of his glory. They enlarge our human spirit, setting it ablaze. They enlarge our capacity to know and honor HIM, to become who we are in HIM and, from that place of identity and intimacy, to join HIM in bringing his ever-increasing kingdom from heaven into the earth.

The blessings of the Lord enlarge our capacity to carry his glory. Humility and a contrite heart open us, moment by moment, to be blessed.

Jesus is Lord

Be blessed to confess with your lips and your life, Jesus Christ is Lord.

God always initiates covenant between people and himself. Be blessed to enter his covenant and to know in your innermost being it is done: "declare with your mouth, 'Jesus is Lord,' and believe in your heart that God raised him from the dead" (Rom. 10:9).

From the moment you first confess Jesus' lordship, the Father sets to work to renew the *you* he created (the *you* the enemy mutilated). He sets to work re-forming you into one who is whole in him and wholly devoted to him. Already seeing the masterpiece, he starts the renovation that produces it. Be blessed with God-given desire and power to live from that place.

Romans 12:1–2: "Therefore, I urge you, brothers and sisters, in view of God's mercy, to offer your bodies as a living sacrifice, holy and pleasing to God—this is true worship. Do not conform to the pattern of this world, but be transformed by the renewing of your mind. Then you will be able to test and approve what God's will is—his good, pleasing and perfect will."

Philippians 1:6: "And I am sure of this: that the One who began a good work among you will keep it growing until it is completed on the Day of the Messiah Yeshua" (CJB).

1 Corinthians 3:10–15: "But let each one be careful how he builds. For no one can lay any foundation other than the one already laid, which is Yeshua the Messiah. Some will use gold, silver or precious stones in building on this foundation; while others will use wood, grass or straw. But each one's work will be shown for what it is; the Day will disclose it, because it will be revealed by fire—the fire will test the quality of each one's work. If the work someone has built on the foundation survives, he will receive a reward; if it is burned up, he will have to bear the loss: he will still escape with his life, but it will be like escaping through a fire" (CJB).

Romans 12:1–2: "So here's what I want you to do, God helping you: Take your everyday, ordinary life—your sleeping, eating, going-to-work, and walking-around life—and place it before God as an offering. Embracing what God does for you is the best thing you can do for him. Don't become so well-adjusted to your culture [including your church culture!] that you fit into it without even thinking. Instead, fix your attention on God. You'll be changed from the inside out. Readily recognize what he wants from you, and quickly respond to it. Unlike the culture around you, always dragging you down to its level of immaturity, God brings the best out of you, develops well-formed maturity in you" (MSG).

Be blessed to cooperate fully in the renovation process.

Remember: You're in process. We're in process. God is committed to complete the process. Yet, moment by moment, he gives you choices: You can thwart the process. You can sabotage the process. You can build on the right foundation in the wrong way. I bless you, even in the most painful seasons, with grace to press in to the process and, even on your hardest days, to delight in him who is re-forming you. I bless you with building on the right foundation with materials that are precious and pure. I bless you with honoring God's inscrutable timing and his unfathomable ways.

You don't do major renovation in a day. And you don't do major spiritual renovation in the order or timeframe you might want. My niece Christy says that, every time she tells God, "Don't even talk to me about *that*," *that* is exactly what God pinpoints. The Lord is heading up this project. He determines what closet or room to tackle next. He determines what unrighteous root to uproot, what righteous root to replant. Your job is to cooperate with him.

In the process, he will expose *you*, and he will continue to expose *us*. As you allow him to deal with you personally, you will gain authority to intercede for the Bride collectively. As you are being more fully changed into his image, you'll become a catalyst for changing others. Be blessed with seeing and acting on what God is showing you about *you*, and so becoming one he can trust to stand in the gap for his Bride.

The Lord is the Spirit

Be blessed to know in your deepest being that "the Lord is the Spirit." Be blessed to live from this reality: The Spirit within you is Christ in you.

1 Corinthians 2:9–10, 14–15: "No one's ever seen or heard anything like this, Never so much as imagined anything quite like it—What God has arranged for those who love him. But you've seen and heard it because God by his Spirit has brought it all out into the open before you. The Spirit, not content to flit around on the surface, dives into the depths of God, and brings out what God planned all along … The unspiritual self, just as it is by nature, can't receive the gifts of God's Spirit. There's no capacity for them. They seem like so much silliness. Spirit can be known only by spirit—God's Spirit and our spirits in open communion. Spiritually alive, we have access to everything God's Spirit is doing" (MSG).

Be blessed to respond to God, spirit-to-Spirit. Be blessed with reversing the "natural" order of trying to live: "body, soul, spirit"—because that order keeps you pulled in many directions. That order keeps you forever frustrated in the quest to do God's will. That order cuts you off from all the unimaginable things God has prepared for those who love him. Learn God's wonderful kingdom order: "spirit, soul, body"—your spirit in open communion with God's Spirit and your humbled soul and spirit-trained body following in line.

Galatians 5:16: " … run your lives by the Spirit. Then you will not do what your old nature wants" (CJB).

Galatians 5:16: " … Live your life as your spiritual nature directs you. Then you will never follow through on what your corrupt nature wants" (*GOD'S WORD*).

Tragically, we who believe in God the Three-in-One often treat the Spirit with more suspicion and less respect than Father or Son. Fearful, we may ignore the Spirit or dictate what he can and cannot do. Grasping, we may welcome the Spirit but seek for selfish ends the power he displays.

We think of the Father and the Son as persons, but may think of the Spirit as an appendage or "force"—emanating out from God, bringing us his messages, giving us his gifts, imparting to us his power, but void of personality and somehow shy of full deity. Even the term "the Holy Spirit" sounds to us, not the name of someone we can know personally, but a label for an unknowable "it."

Yet, the Hebrew Old Testament repeatedly reports the working of the third person of the Trinity with two compound names. In English translations, both names seem rather to be labels or titles. One name, *Ruwach 'Elohiym*, (rue-ahkh el-o-heem) is usually translated "the Spirit of God." The other, typically rendered, "the Spirit of the Lord," includes that unpronounceable covenant Name **JHVH**. The Interlinear Bible renders this name, *Ruwach Yahweh.*

The Spirit's name is *Ruwach*, alternately spelled *Ruach*, meaning "spirit" or "breath." But also, the One we treat with open suspicion and try to use for our own ends, the One we seek to control or manipulate, as if a lesser god, is the God of the covenant Name. The Spirit is the Lord.

Jesus Christ came to earth, lived, died, and rose again to give abundant, eternal life to those who confess him as Lord. Some think they can surrender to Jesus while ignoring the Spirit, or giving him only a cursory nod. But just as Scripture teaches, "Jesus Christ is Lord" (Phil. 2:11), so it also teaches, "the Lord is the Spirit" (2 Cor. 3:17). And, as 1 Corinthians 12:3 declares, "No one can say, 'Jesus is Lord,' except by the Holy Spirit."

You cannot withhold yourself from *Ruwach* and know *Yeshua* as Lord. No matter how much you pray to, talk of, and sing about someone named Jesus, apart from the Spirit of Christ you cannot not know Christ. If you stiff-arm the Spirit, you will misunderstand and misrepresent Jesus.

By the same token, you cannot walk by the Spirit apart from confessing Jesus as Lord. No matter how freely you worship or how numerous the spiritual gifts you manifest, if you're trying to host Jesus as a *guest*, you're not being filled with the Spirit. If you sidestep surrender to *Yeshua*, you will misunderstand and misrepresent *Ruwach*.

Some of my ancestors tried to make Jesus their Savior without surrendering to him as Lord. Some of them confessed Jesus as Lord, but then balked in the midst of the renovation process. They quenched and grieved the Spirit. They rebelled against *Yahweh*.

Refusing the voice of the Spirit, they also silenced their human spirits, with which God the Spirit communes. Thus "dispirited," they tried to live the Christian life from the *soul*, the "unspiritual self, just as it is by nature." Depending on their bent, our ancestors trusted logic or emotion to show the way. Yet, "Spirit can be known only by spirit" (1 Cor. 2:14 MSG).

When *Ruwach Yahweh* pursued them, when he manifested in order to turn their hearts, they typically did one of three things: They rejected him, sometimes even attributing his working to the devil. They sought to control him, setting boundaries as to what he could and could not do. They tried to use his astonishing power for their own purposes. All three choices blocked the flow of God's blessings and continued to halt his transformation of his people.

Even in places where Holy Spirit came in power and the people fully, gladly received him, over time they began to resist, as he began to confront what they didn't want to confront.

Be blessed to break free from blinding, binding cycles of dishonoring the Spirit, cycles set in motion by our forebears. Their concerted, repeated choices to grieve God the Spirit quenched the Second Great Awakening. The repetition of the cycle in succeeding generations has aborted or sabotaged every awakening among us since. Quenching *Ruwach*, we blind ourselves. Grieving *Ruwach*, we imprison ourselves.

Isaiah 49:8–9: "This is what the Lord says: 'In the time of my favor I will answer you, and in the day of salvation I will help you; I will keep you and will make you to be a covenant for the people, to restore the land and to reassign its desolate inheritances, to say to the captives, "Come out," and to those in darkness, "Be free!"'"

2 Corinthians 6:2: "I tell you, now is the time of God's favor, now is the day of salvation."

Yahweh has accomplished what he decreed. The time of his favor has come. *Yeshua* has been made a covenant for the people. He has arrived to restore this land, to distribute inheritances that have lain desolate far too long. *Ruwach* calls, "Come out! Be free!" *Be blessed to hear and answer from a humble, contrite heart.*

Forgive—and be released

The Lord bless you with superabundant grace to forgive.

Ephesians 4:30–32: "And do not grieve the Holy Spirit of God, with whom you were sealed for the day of redemption. Get rid of all bitterness, rage and anger, brawling and slander, along with every form of malice. Be kind and compassionate to one another, forgiving each other, just as in Christ God forgave you."

Luke 11:4: "Forgive us our sins, for we also forgive everyone who sins against us."

Be blessed, masterpiece of God, to get rid of all bitterness, rage, and anger against *yourself.* By his grace, quit uttering harsh, slanderous words about yourself. As your Lord convicts of specific sins, as you confess and he cleanses, be blessed to forgive yourself. Be blessed to recall and retract any judgments and vows with which you've hogtied yourself. When you confess the wrongs you've *done*, you yield to the Holy Spirit of God. You grieve him when you declare yourself to *be* what Jesus has delivered you from.

Be blessed to get rid of all bitterness, rage, and anger against *God*. The Lord is good. He cannot do evil. If you feel he has betrayed you or not treated you justly, acknowledge those feelings. Don't try to hide them: God knows they're there. Once you've confessed your feelings, let the Spirit judge them. Let him show you the root. Let him show you the truth. Feelings we entertain in seasons of trauma and pain may produce judgments about God that leave us stranded, unable to move forward with him.

Jeremiah the prophet succumbed to such feelings. God had made Jeremiah promises that it looked very much like God had not kept. Faithfully, Jeremiah had followed God, yet no one received his message. Brutally, repeatedly, the people with whom Jeremiah pleaded tried to force him to shut him up.

At one point, Jeremiah cried out to God, "Why is my pain unending and my wound grievous and incurable? You are to me like a deceptive brook, like a spring that fails."

Jeremiah didn't try to pretend. He expressed his anger and confusion to God himself. Then, God could get him back on track. The Lord answered Jeremiah, "If you repent, I will restore you that you may serve me; if you utter worthy, not worthless, words, you will be my spokesman" (Jer. 15:18, 19).

Be blessed to forgive God for causing you pain. He has good and loving reasons you don't yet know. Renounce and repent for judgments by which you've slandered him in your heart.

Be blessed to get rid of all bitterness, rage, and anger against *everyone*. No matter who has hurt you or your generations, no matter how deep the wound, be blessed to forgive them just as God has forgiven you.

The first mention of forgiveness in most Bible versions occurs in the last chapter of Genesis, as the story of Joseph draws to a close. In his youth, Joseph was sold into slavery in Egypt by his brothers. Think of that! His own brothers plotted against him. They closed their ears to his frightened, desperate cries. Their father Jacob had abused their respective moms, using each of the three women as breeders for sons. Now, the 10 bitter sons saw their chance to get back at their dad and to get rid of the favored son of the wife Jacob had loved. Delighting in Joseph's pain, they sold him.

Twenty-one years later, after Joseph had risen to second in command in Egypt, he and his brothers were reunited. The next year, in the midst of severe famine, Joseph brought his whole family to Egypt to live. Seventeen years after that, Jacob died. The family journeyed to Canaan to bury Jacob's body, then returned together to Egypt. Genesis 50 records what happened 39 years after Joseph's brothers committed the terrible sin of selling him as a slave.

> But now that their father was dead, Joseph's brothers became fearful. "Now Joseph will show his anger and pay us back for all the wrong we did to him," they said. So they sent this message to Joseph: "Before your father died, he instructed us to say to you: 'Please forgive your brothers for the great wrong they did to you—for their sin in treating you so cruelly.' *So we, the servants of the God of your father, beg you to forgive our sin.*" When Joseph received the message, he broke down and wept. Then his brothers came and threw themselves down before Joseph. "Look, we are your slaves!" they said. But Joseph replied, "Don't be afraid of me. Am I God, that I can punish you? You intended to harm me, but God intended it all for good. He brought me to this position so I could save the lives of many people. No, don't be afraid. I will continue to take care of you and your children." So he reassured them by speaking kindly to them (Gen. 50:15–21 NLT).

The Bible teaches that one-on-one forgiveness is crucial. Just as crucial, yet often forgotten, is the need to extend forgiveness to whole groups of people, as Joseph did to his brothers.

As you've read *We Confess!*, have you at any point felt a sharp sting deep within? Did any of the revelation from the past stir up a "hornet's nest" inside? You might have blamed this book for your pain. But God's revelations only "stir up" what's already there. His words uncover anything deadly lurking within. Any stings you felt reveal unhealed wounds infected by unforgiveness. In those wounds, hornets of anger and bitterness have built a nest. The whole nest needs to go, and the only way to get rid of it is to forgive.

Maybe the anger surprised you. Maybe the stings revealed an inheritance of deep-rooted bitterness that you hadn't even known previous generations had passed down to you. Maybe the stings exposed bitterness you still feel over hurts in your own life you thought you had laid to rest long ago. Maybe this look at the sins of the fathers shed light on injustices you're facing now. Maybe the hornets' stings felt as fresh and raw as your experiences of this week.

Maybe you've believed that harboring bitterness somehow gives you an edge over those who've caused you and yours such pain. Maybe you've believed forgiving would mean letting the bad guys win. Remember Joseph. He suffered greatly for many years because of his own brothers' cruel act. Yet he trusted God to judge and to punish. And he chose to forgive his brothers decades before they asked.

Freed from bitterness and unforgiveness, Joseph was able to step fully into his birthright. He walked the path of life. God blessed his humble heart. In time, the Lord promoted Joseph. Joseph, in turn, used his new authority, not to get revenge on his family, but to save them. Forgiveness in Joseph's heart opened the way for God to bring a profound work of redemption from a whole group's evil acts.

Forgiveness never negates justice. Rather, it entrusts justice to an utterly just God. Forgiveness releases you, and the generations after you, from living with deadly hornets inside, stinging, destroying, at will. Forgiveness uses the very pain the enemy meant for evil to catapult you into God's overcoming good.

For your own life and the sake of the generations to follow, choose to forgive. Choose to forgive now. Choose to forgive as often as needed until the last of the hornets is gone. Forgiveness isn't a feeling. It's an act. Your "unspiritual self" cannot do it, but spirit-to-Spirit you can. You accomplish it by choosing it and speaking it: "Father, in Jesus' name, I forgive (name the person or group) for (name the offense)."

Forgive *individuals*. Forgive me for telling you an array of things you didn't want to know.

But also choose to forgive *whole groups*. Forgive your ancestors for the wrongs they did. Forgive the people who did wrong to them. Forgive the Yankees. Forgive the abolitionists. Forgive the carpetbaggers. Forgive the "whole world" for turning against the South. Forgive Native Americans. Forgive African Americans. Forgive the organizers of vicious slave revolts. Forgive white Southerners, who named the name of Christ yet so badly misrepresented him. Forgive slave owners. Forgive those who didn't own slaves but did not stand up against slavery. Forgive the ministers who led the way to secession and war and, afterward, led in forming covenants with death. Forgive men. Forgive women. Forgive the Southern Baptist Convention. Forgive the local Baptist church. Forgive whatever denomination or church divided your heart and abused your spirit.

Get as specific, or as broad, as Holy Spirit shows you that your bitterness extends. *Whatever* person or group sets those hornets to buzzing and stinging deep inside you, choose to forgive the lot of them. You'll know you've forgiven when you can think of the person or group, and even the specific situations, without feeling the sting.

That may take time. It may take work. It will require God's blessings poured out on a humble, contrite heart. The Lord may dredge junk from your darkest closets, reminding you of specific incidents or revealing generational offenses, not so you can wallow in bitter anger, but so you can be radically freed from it all. At times, you may struggle to get to the place in the Spirit where you can say, "I forgive."

Be blessed with astounding grace from Holy Spirit to get to that place again and again. Be blessed with such a strong, clear Spirit-to-spirit connection that you fully cooperate to get rid of all bitterness, rage, and anger—against yourself, against God, and against everyone else. Be blessed to forgive as God in Christ forgave you, regardless whether the offender repents. Be blessed with a profound Joseph anointing, to show genuine kindness and compassion to those who have hurt you most deeply. Be radically, richly blessed to live free from the hornets' torment, and to see God turn what others meant for evil into astonishing, life-saving good.

Grieve—and be comforted

The Lord bless you with godly grief and his incredible comfort.

Everyone experiences grief. It enters with loss or betrayal, including veiled losses we do not recognize as loss. It arrives with sorrows experienced years ago, even in earliest childhood. It comes through distressing situations in our family background or ethnic history from which earlier generations never healed.

Whether grief sneaks in, or bursts in, whether it comes early or late, it does not simply dissipate with time.

If left unacknowledged and uncomforted, grief remains. Inside us, it becomes like the can of tomato sauce that sat unnoticed on a cupboard shelf for years. The ruined sauce ate a hole in the can, and black gunk spewed on everything around.

Emotionally, many of us have closets full of ruined tomato sauce. Yet, we have not identified and removed the sources of the gunk corroding every aspect of our lives.

We of white Southern ancestry have inherited *much* ungrieved grief from those before us who lived through Civil War on their land. Defeated, resilient, looking to God, determined to survive, Southerners traumatized by war and Reconstruction stuffed their grief. Proud, defiant, bitter, unrepentant, they glorified the bloodshed, instead of mourning the loss.

To mourn, fully, deeply, they had to admit what they would not even give themselves permission to think: Their wrong beliefs, their wrong behaviors, had brought about their massive loss—property trashed, livelihood destroyed, land defiled, women raped, sons and husbands killed in battle; young grieving widows dead in childbirth; their babies stillborn. Devastating physical wounds; excruciating emotional wounds; joy, peace, hope all gone, gone, gone.

I confess. My ancestors adamantly refused to face the connection between such tragedy and their corporate sin, terrified that to do so would launch them headlong into condemnation and despair. Tragically, the path of avoidance they took spirals downward. The way they could not bring themselves to go—the way they thought would send them over the cliff—is the one path to comfort, deliverance, and life.

2 Corinthians 7:10: "Godly sorrow brings repentance that leads to salvation and leaves no regret, but worldly sorrow brings death."

2 Corinthians 7:10: "Pain handled in God's way produces a turning from sin to God which leads to salvation, and there is nothing to regret in that! But pain handled in the world's way produces only death" (CJB).

Desperate to avoid grief, my ancestors opted to paint their loss as gain: The war purified the South! The blood of Confederate soldiers washed the region clean!

Of course, you don't grieve *gain*. You applaud it. You relive the story again and again, relishing the part where, even in defeat, you win. But if the gain you're celebrating was actually unspeakable loss, a whole lot of black gunk gets stuck down inside, spewing everywhere. If you never find it and remove it, your children inherit it, then their children, and theirs.

In 2005, Gayden Metcalfe and Charlotte Hays published a book titled, *Being Dead Is No Excuse: The Official Southern Ladies Guide to Hosting the Perfect Funeral.* A combination of humorous anecdotes and recipes, this amazing little volume gives a telling glimpse into grief avoidance in the South even today.

In the first chapter, titled, "Dying Tastefully in the Mississippi Delta," Metcalfe and Hays write, "Almost everybody who attends the burial automatically stops by the house afterward, and it's a social occasion." "'You get the best food at funerals,' we always say, and it's true ... A legion of friends working behind the scenes, coordinating the food, makes sure that the essential Delta death foods are represented in sufficient quantities." The burial itself "is solemn though rarely entirely devoid of humor."[295]

Try to imagine someone from another region writing a book that pokes fun at their area's death customs and gives recipes for its "death foods."

We in the South come to the large wake before the funeral, the reception afterward, and the funeral itself in an effort to console and encourage. We joke and laugh for the same reason. Yet, without realizing it, we often use the crowds, the food, the humor, even the encouragement, to help each other avoid grieving. Deeply uncomfortable with mourning, fearful it's not a Christian thing to do, we send the subtle message, to others and to ourselves, "Cheer up!"

We don't mind a few tears, discreetly shed. But we expect the Christians shedding them to quickly affirm God's presence and goodness. If someone weeps excessively or can't immediately get the faith words out, we tell each other they're "not doing well."

After the funeral, we expect one another to dispense with grief altogether and to reenter life as usual as soon as possible. We see the dangers of wallowing in grief. We know how unhealthy, how destructive it is to keep drowning in loss, never able to accept a hand up. Yet, valiantly trying to avoid the grief that leads to despair, we bypass the path to comfort and joy.

Scripture check

The Bible tells those who know Christ as Lord not to grieve as those "who have no hope" (1 Thess. 4:13). But it does not tell us not to grieve. In fact, our Lord himself says in Matthew 5:4, "Blessed are those who mourn, for they will be comforted."

Further, Romans 12:15 instructs us to "mourn with those who mourn," not to goad them to instant cheer.

Isaiah the prophet described the genuine comfort God gives, the comfort we're able to minister to one another by his Spirit: "The Spirit of the Sovereign Lord is on me, because the Lord has anointed me … to bind up the brokenhearted, … to comfort all who mourn, and provide for those who grieve in Zion—to bestow on them a crown of beauty instead of ashes, the oil of joy instead of mourning, and a garment of praise instead of a spirit of despair" (Isa. 61:1–3).

David the shepherd-king experienced this comfort. He cried to God, "You have turned my mourning into joyful dancing. You have taken away my clothes of mourning and clothed me with joy, that I might sing praises to you and not be silent" (Ps. 30:11–12 NLT).

Notice, though, on whom God bestows this beauty, dancing, joy, and praise: on the despairing, the grief-stricken, the heartbroken. The blessings come to those who walk a path that looks anything but blessed.

Paul the apostle wrote, "Praise be to the God and Father of our Lord Jesus Christ, the Father of compassion and the God of all comfort, who comforts us in all our troubles, so that we can comfort those in any trouble with the comfort we ourselves receive from God" (2 Cor. 1:3–4).

Notice: We cannot comfort others until we ourselves receive God's comfort. And we cannot receive God's comfort until we face and feel grief.

Blessed are those who *mourn. They* will be comforted.

Short-circuiting grief

Ah, but in our church culture, we often count expressions of grief as sin, and suppressing grief, a virtue. We expect the God-fearing mourner, whether ourselves or someone else, to skip mourning and instantly assume the role of comforter.

Eager not to dishonor God, distress others, or embarrass ourselves, we have thus perfected the art of short-circuiting grief.

Notice how the *American Heritage Dictionary* defines *short circuit*: "A low-resistance connection established by accident or intention between two points in an electric circuit. The current tends to flow through the area of low resistance, bypassing the rest of the circuit."

A quicker way to a desired end sounds like a good thing, especially when the quicker way appears to avoid pain. But when an electric current finds a shorter path of very low resistance, the current becomes very strong. Damage, overheating, and fires result.

Thus, in electricity, short-circuiting temporarily takes a shorter route to complete a circuit. Yet soon, short-circuiting destroys the circuit and shuts down anything dependent on it.

In a similar way, short-circuiting grief may temporarily appear to resolve it. Yet denying and stuffing grief—thus taking the path of least resistance—only strengthens the "current" beyond what you were wired to handle, bypassing resolution, impeding healing, and causing damage you would not have suffered if you had given yourself permission to grieve.

My ancestors collaborated together to short-circuit grief. After the Civil War, they took the path of statue-building and stoicism. But what they thought would bypass grief instead shut them down. It left them and the generations afterward stuck in the very place they were trying desperately to avoid.

The only way to get past grief is to *grieve*, to go with God through that narrow, painful place. "The Lord is close to the brokenhearted and saves those who are crushed in spirit" (Ps. 34:18).

In times of loss, your Lord comes very near. Ah, but so do self-pity and despair. Reject the urge to try to skip grief. But also be blessed to embrace *godly* grief. In your sorrow, turn toward the Lord and away from despair. Bring him your broken heart. Don't pretend it's already fixed. Accept the pain of the healing process. Denial, numbness, anger, all will come. But do not take up residence with any of them. Go through them in him. Refuse to wallow. Refuse to short-circuit. Trust the Comforter to take you all the way through.

"Heavens, raise the roof! Earth, wake the dead! Mountains, send up cheers! God has comforted his people. He has tenderly nursed his beaten-up, beaten-down people" (Isa. 49:13 MSG).

As God has shown me terrible choices that my ancestors made and huge losses that resulted, I've had to stop again and again to grieve. Sometimes I've wept. Sometimes I sat or lay before the Lord, deeply distressed, holding out to him what I'd learned. As I've realized how generational strongholds have ravaged my own life and family, I've grieved. What loss! What needless loss!

Again and again, God has comforted. He has held me, like a mother holds her child. He's spoken tenderly. He's poured his healing ointment into the deep, gnawing ache. And then, when I least expect it, he's swapped sorrow for joy. Once again, my heart sings. My feet dance.

This book may have revealed losses you need to mourn, losses in the present, losses of the past. *Be blessed to give yourself permission and time to grieve.*

As you turn to the Father of compassion—your heart broken, humble, contrite—be blessed with godly sorrow. By grace, reject the lies: that mourning shows a lack of faith, that it dishonors God, and that you can skip the grieving process. By the Spirit, walk all the way through the grief. Your Father will guide you to face the truth of loss, and the implications of loss, without plummeting into condemnation and despair. You will experience again and again the supernatural exchange by which the God of all comfort turns your mourning into dancing, your ashes into a crown of beauty, and your heaviness into a garment of praise.

You will become a blessing, comforting others with the comfort with which God has comforted you. Your joyful dancing will be contagious. It will encourage many others to go with God through the pain until they're leaping and dancing in a spacious place. Comforted one, become a blessed catalyst for releasing the ungrieved grief that has gripped a people and a land far too long.

Weeping turned to joy

Mary and Martha sent word to Jesus: their brother Lazarus was sick. Jesus headed for his friends' home in Bethany, but only after deliberately delaying two days. When the Lord reached Bethany, Lazarus had been in the tomb four days. Ultimately, Jesus would raise Lazarus from the dead. But first, Jesus helped two women he loved to forgive and to grieve.

John 11:20–27 shows how Martha responded to Jesus in her loss:

> When Martha heard that Jesus was coming, she went out to meet him, but Mary stayed at home.
>
> "Lord," Martha said to Jesus, "if you had been here, my brother would not have died. But I know that even now God will give you whatever you ask."
>
> Jesus said to her, "Your brother will rise again."
>
> Martha answered, "I know he will rise again in the resurrection at the last day."
>
> Jesus said to her, "I am the resurrection and the life. Anyone who believes in me will live, even though they die; and whoever lives by believing in me will never die. Do you believe this?"
>
> "Yes, Lord," she told him, "I believe that you are the Messiah, the Son of God, who was to come into the world."

We tend to think of Martha as a woman obsessed with serving. Yet this passage shows her as one learning from her Lord. After Lazarus' death, Martha did what we might not have expected. She focused on grieving, not serving, when the whole town arrived for her brother's wake.

Hearing that Jesus was near, Martha might have refused to see him, or she might have waited until he arrived. Instead, she left all her guests to go to him. Candidly, she told him, "If you had been here, my brother would not have died." Even as she expressed her confusion and disappointment, Martha called him "Lord." Even when she didn't understand, Martha forgave the friend who appeared to have done her family great wrong. She forgave the one who could have prevented her brother's death.

Sometime before, Jesus had visited the two sisters, and Mary had left Martha to do the serving alone. That day too, Martha had taken her complaint to Jesus. That day, she'd asked, "Don't you care?" This time, in a far more serious situation, Martha didn't ask that question. In her disappointment and grief, she refused to entertain the lie that Jesus' apparent inaction meant he didn't care.

Instead, she expressed faith: "But I know that even now God will give you whatever you ask." Jesus fanned that little spark of faith: "Your brother will rise again."

Martha answered: "I know he will rise again in the resurrection at the last day." True! But Jesus kept fanning. He wanted to reveal more of who he is. He wanted to show more of his ways. He wanted to increase Martha's faith. He wanted her to know that what we will experience most fully "at the last day," we can also experience in breathtaking ways "even now."

"I am the resurrection and the life," he said. "Do you believe this?"

In response, Martha made a confession of faith almost identical to the one Peter made in Matthew 16: "I believe that you are the Messiah, the Son of God, who was to come into the world."

Martha's profound confession hung in the air. What revelation she'd received! What faith she'd expressed! Yet, Jesus did not immediately raise Lazarus. Instead, Jesus sent Martha back for the sister who had not chosen to come out.

Not taking offense, still buoyed by faith, Martha "went back and called her sister Mary aside. 'The Teacher is here,' she said, 'and is asking for you.' When Mary heard this, she got up quickly and went to him. Now Jesus had not yet entered the village, but was still at the place where Martha had met him … When Mary reached the place where Jesus was and saw him, she fell at his feet and said, 'Lord, if you had been here, my brother would not have died'" (John 11:28–32).

Mary handled loss differently from Martha. Too grieved and disheartened to go out to Jesus, Mary stayed in the very house where she had previously sat at his feet. When Martha came to him alone, Jesus didn't castigate Mary. Instead, he called for her. As soon as Martha delivered the message, Mary went. Seeing Jesus, she fell at his feet. Like her sister, Mary expressed her deep disappointment. Yet Mary spoke no words of faith. Did Jesus reprimand her? No. He received her.

He welcomed her honesty. He knew that the woman humbling herself before him and calling him "Lord," had forgiven what she could not fathom. Surprisingly, Jesus did not say, "Cheer up! I'm about to fix this." Though he knew what lay ahead, he didn't tell Mary to stop crying. Instead, he wept with her. Mary may have felt ashamed when her tears wouldn't stop and the faith words wouldn't come—until she felt Jesus' teardrops splash on her shoulders.

In their loss, Mary and Martha forgave. Mary and Martha grieved. Each sister went to Jesus, expressing her confusion, but also her surrender to him and her faith in him. Then, *Yeshua* turned his dear friends' mourning into dancing. He called forth Lazarus from the grave.

Return—and be restored

The Lord *bless you with grace to see and turn back from idolatry.*

1 Kings 18:37: "Answer me, Lord, answer me, so these people will know that you, Lord, are God, and that you are turning their hearts back again."

Lamentations 5:21: "Restore us to yourself, Lord, that we may return ..."

1 Samuel 15:23: "For rebellion is like the sin of sorcery, stubbornness like the crime of idolatry" (CJB).

1 Samuel 7:2–4: "Then all the people of Israel turned back to the Lord. So Samuel said to the whole house of Israel, 'If you are returning to the Lord with all your hearts, then rid yourselves of the foreign gods and the Ashtoreths and commit yourselves to the Lord and serve him only, and he will deliver you out of the hand of the Philistines.' So the Israelites put away their Baals and Ashtoreths, and served the Lord only."

Physically, few of us have carved out an image and bowed before it. Spiritually, many of us have done exactly that. We who are called by *Yeshua*'s name can see the blatant idolatry of those who reject Christ. Yet we rationalize, minimize, and deny the hidden idols in our own hearts. We need God's blessings! We cannot see our divided hearts, unless he reveals them. We cannot renounce and relinquish our idols apart from his amazing grace.

Similarly, we cannot see false worship we've inherited from our ancestors, unless *Ruwach Yahweh* exposes it. We will not recognize the gods our fathers served or the ways those gods still oppress our lives and families, unless our Lord gives us eyes to see.

Of all the things we may not want the Lord to show us, this is the revelation we want the least. This, the Holy Spirit conviction we most stubbornly reject. Outside of salvation itself, this is the place most difficult and most crucial to approach God with a humble, contrite heart.

Only as we humble ourselves to see the ways our hearts and the hearts of our ancestors have become divided, only as we let God expose the unholy covenants that our divided loyalties have produced, can we fully experience the cleansing and re-creation bought for us with Jesus' blood.

Hear my heart here, because mentally, theologically, you could argue the statement I'm about to make. My words can't fully convey what my spirit knows is true. Certainly, we must *repent* (change our minds) before we can *return* (re-establish unbroken fellowship with God). And yet, just as surely, we must return before we can repent.

Suppose we recognize that something's out of sync in our relationship with our Lord, individually or collectively. Suppose we take the courageous path of repentance. Personally, we confess and try to turn from the sins most bothering our conscience. Collectively, we gather for "identificational repentance," and we renounce the sins of whole groups of people we in some way represent. But if genuine change does not result from those confessions, if the "After" picture still looks pretty much the same as the "Before," it's often because we've tried to repent without returning: We've tried to uproot wrong attitudes and behaviors without first making sure our hearts are wholly devoted to the Lord Jesus Christ.

A heart not wholly devoted to the Lord has given place to idols. "Therefore, return to your God" (Hos. 12:6 NASU).

You who have confessed Jesus as Lord, be blessed with superabundant grace to return to Jesus as Lord. In the moment he saved you and his Spirit entered you, you loved him with all your heart. Return to your first love. Don't assume you're already there. Lay aside your Christian checklists and credentials. Go to Jesus empty-handed, with a humble heart, and let *him* make that call. Affirm his full authority to clean out every residue of attachment to any other god.

You may want to excuse or deny whatever he shows you. Instead, taste the grief you have caused your Bridegroom. See the insult to your Father's holy name. From a deeply contrite heart, agree with what he says. Ah, then, let your tears turn to laughter as he power-washes you clean. Let his great love flood you, sweeping away any other lover. Reverence him and worship him with your whole heart.

As the fear of the Lord and the love of the Lord fill you, receive God's words to Gideon as your assignment too: "tear down your father's altar to Baal, and cut down the symbol of the goddess Asherah, which is beside it. Build a well-constructed altar to the Lord your God" (Judg. 6:25–26 GNT).

In Gideon's day, the Midianites had oppressed Israel for seven years, repeatedly destroying the crops and impoverishing the people. Intimidated and overcome by an army as thick as locusts, the Israelites hid in caves while the oppressor ravaged their land. At some point, the Israelites began to cry out to the Lord to free them from the Midianites. In response, God sent a prophet to say: their divided hearts had opened them to oppression. God called to them to return to him.

Then, the Lord appeared to Gideon—a fearful man, threshing wheat in a winepress in order to hide from the Midianites; a man angry with God for seeming not to care; a man with no credentials for leading an army except the credentials God himself supplied.

God began the conversation by speaking his own Name. In one brief greeting, he revealed his identity. He revealed Gideon's identity. And God revealed the relationship by which Gideon would become who he was: "The Lord is with you, mighty warrior" (Judg. 6:12).

Immediately on telling Gideon his true identity, God gave him a new mission. "The Lord turned to him and said, 'Go in the strength you have and save Israel out of Midian's hand. Am I not sending you?'" (Judg. 6:14).

Gideon would do that impossible mission the same way he would become a radically different person. The Lord said: "*I will be with you*, and you will strike down all the Midianites together" (Judg. 6:16).

When Gideon wondered, "So how do I know you're really God?" the Lord confirmed his identity to Gideon in the same way he showed himself on Mt. Carmel to the people of Elijah's day: God sent fire to consume Gideon's sacrifice. He revealed himself to Gideon, not only as **JHVH**, the God of the covenant Name, but also **JHVH** *Shalom*, the Lord Is Peace.

Relying on the Lord's wild plan and miraculous power, Gideon did free Israel from the Midianites. But first God commanded him to tear down his father's idolatrous altar and to build an altar to the Lord.

When Gideon obeyed that command (by night because he was afraid), the people of his town demanded Gideon's death. But his father intervened, saying to the crowd, "You're defending Ba'al, are you? It's your job to save him? … If he's a god, let him defend himself!" (Judg. 6:31 CJB).

Remarkable: The one who owned the idolatrous altar was the first to let it go! Yet Gideon's father didn't give up his idols until his frightened son made a violent renunciation of them, smashing and burning what the family and the community had allowed to usurp God's place in their hearts. And Gideon didn't smash the idolatrous altars until he met and bowed before the Lord.

The Lord is with *you*, mighty warrior. You may hear yourself replying, "Who, me?" But *Adonai* hasn't gotten the wrong address. He hasn't approached the wrong person. He sees in you an identity you do not see. He's prepared exploits for you to do. Becoming who he created you to be, you will set oppressed people free. Don't worry. He has the strategy. He'll make the way. He is the way. He is with you always, even to the end of the world. What's more, he is in you, empowering you to become and to do.

But don't go charging out to battle just yet. You have another assignment first.

Tear down your ancestors' altars to any god other than the Lord. He himself will show you what, where, and how.

A. W. Tozer said, "It takes a violent act of renunciation to deliver us from the hidden idol." Just to be clear: This violent act in no way involves damage to any persons or their property. We've done way too much of that already! The Lord may tell you to get rid of an object you own, but his law of love demands that you treat other persons with love and respect, including respecting private or public property. This violent act is a renunciation you personally make.

Remember: If your forebears didn't get rid of it, you inherited it. "It" may well include idols you're still defending, still trying to save. Even if you have never bowed before a god your ancestors served, if no one in your bloodline has renounced that idol, its altar still stands, and the evil spirit attached to that idol still has an open door to attack your family and your life.

Tear those altars down. Even if you're afraid, seek God as to how to do it, and tear those altars down.

But also, *build an altar of wholehearted worship to the Lord your God.* From that place of worship, God will lead you to war victoriously to set captives free. Remember: wholehearted worship flows from loving God and fearing God with all your heart. As already said, this worship may not look like what you've thought.

Paul wrote in Romans 12:1–2: "So then, my friends, because of God's great mercy to us I appeal to you: Offer yourselves as a living sacrifice to God, dedicated to his service and pleasing to him. This is the true worship that you should offer. Do not conform yourselves to the standards of this world, but let God transform you inwardly by a complete change of your mind. Then you will be able to know the will of God—what is good and is pleasing to him and is perfect" (GNT).

Offering your life as a living sacrifice to God is a decisive act of worship. You cannot take this step if you have competing altars in your life. Thus the need to deal with those altars first. As God reveals any idolatrous altar, shatter it and decisively return to him. As an act of worship, establish his altar as the only altar in your life, and on that altar yield yourself completely to him.

Letting God transform you inwardly is an ongoing process of worship, a gradual metamorphosis that highly honors your Lord. It's the emerging of the new, true nature that Father bequeathed you, Jesus redeemed for you, and Spirit is maturing in you. It's cooperating with the wild plans and miraculous power of God to conquer stronghold after stronghold. It's walking free from oppression, step by step. This process involves day-to-day repenting—seeing life more and more from a Kingdom perspective, recognizing attitudes and behaviors that do not reflect who God is or who you are in him, and exchanging the corrupt for the true.

The ongoing process of Romans 12:2 hinges on the decisive act of Romans 12:1.

Repenting follows returning. First, eradicate idolatry. Return to Jesus as Lord. Then, Jesus in you will guide you to war victoriously against the swarm of oppressors that have kept you, and us, impoverished and defeated. Renovation will move forward unhindered in your own life. But also, you will have great authority to set other captives free.

Be forewarned: When your violent renunciation and radical transformation becomes evident, people who still want to worship at altars erected by your ancestors may be up in arms. They may believe you're against them when, in fact, you've acted for them. Rest in *Yahweh Shalom*. He is your peace. Remember Gideon: The night he shattered his father's altars, he surely thought his father would be the person most upset. Yet his father led everyone else to let the idols go.

Do not think you can march out to conquer the oppressors without first re-establishing true worship. We've tried that for 150 years. We don't have authority to drive out our oppressors until we first destroy our fathers' idols and re-establish uncontested covenant worship with the Lord.

That's why God is drawing this book to a close. He has much more to show us about all that's oppressed us, and how to drive every oppressor out. He has much to say about the deeply tangled unrighteous roots that have held us in a false identity—the threefold taproot of greed, pride, and power; the complex snarl of immorality and violence; division, rejection, and rebellion; deception and fear. He's stored up for us profound insight into the astounding qualities of the righteous root, the oak taproot, that is ours in him. He stands ready to lead us in the ongoing process of taking off the old and putting on the new.

"I have many more things to say to you," he declares, "but you cannot bear them now" (John 16:12 NASU).

For now, he announces the outcome: "In their righteousness, they will be like great oaks that the Lord has planted for his own glory. They will rebuild the ancient ruins, repairing cities destroyed long ago" (Isa. 61:3–4 NLT).

For now, he will give us a taste of the process involved in getting there. He'll paint the process in broad brush strokes in the section on repentance below. But if he were to address those unrighteous roots in detail in this volume, we would try to move on to *repenting* (for individual sin issues) before we've fully *grieved* (the devastating losses that generations of unrepented sins have caused) and fully *returned* (to Jesus Christ as Lord).

"O Lord, bring us back to you, and we'll come back. Give us back the life we had long ago" (Lam. 5:21 *GOD'S WORD*).

> "Return, faithless Israel," declares the Lord,
> "I will frown on you no longer,
> for I am faithful," declares the Lord,
> "I will not be angry forever.
> Only acknowledge your guilt—
> you have rebelled against the Lord your God,
> you have scattered your favors to foreign gods
> under every spreading tree,
> and have not obeyed me,"
> declares the Lord (Jer. 3:12–13).

"'Even now,' declares the Lord, 'return to me with all your heart, with fasting and weeping and mourning.' Rend your heart and not your garments. Return to the Lord your God, for he is gracious and compassionate, slow to anger and abounding in love, and he relents from sending calamity" (Joel 2:12–13).

In Old Testament times, God's people tore their clothes when fasting. But God said to the people of Joel's day, as to the people of Isaiah's day, as to his church today, that he wants a different kind of fast from what we've done. The fast he has chosen requires that we rend our *hearts*. By his grace, we rip out every piece of our hearts that we've offered up to other gods, trusting our Lord to re-create in us hearts that are clean, whole, and true.

Therefore, "Let us examine our ways and test them, and let us return to the Lord" (Lam. 3:40).

Dearly beloved of the Lord, be blessed with eyes to see the hidden idols you inherited from previous generations. Be blessed with quickly recognizing when you have given any part of your heart to another god. Be blessed with courage and superabundant grace to make the violent renunciations needed to uproot every idol from your bloodline and from your heart.

Be blessed with eyes to see any unholy covenant that you or your ancestors have made. Be blessed to look, with grief, but without flinching, on the terrible bondage such covenants have brought on your forebears, your family, your culture, and on you. Be blessed with fully releasing every false loyalty and clinging only to the blood of the Lamb, as he annuls even the strongest of ungodly blood covenants on the basis of the higher, better covenant in his own blood.

Be blessed to make the decisive act of offering yourself a living sacrifice to God. Be blessed to cooperate in the ongoing process of being inwardly renewed and changed. In so doing, you will become a blessing. As you return every piece of your heart to your God, your humble, delightful, wholehearted devotion to Christ will give strong impetus to others to return. As you tear down your ancestors' altars and build an altar of worship to the Lord, you will become who you are—a valiant warrior in the kingdom, warring in the Spirit's power, delivering the oppressed.

Take the covenant meal

The Lord bless you with supernatural grace to take the covenant meal in spirit and in truth.

Jesus and his disciples reclined at table in an upper room, eating the Passover meal. "While they were eating, Jesus took bread, and when he had given thanks, he broke it and gave it to his disciples, saying, 'Take and eat; this is my body.' Then he took the cup, and when he had given thanks, he gave it to them, saying, 'Drink from it, all of you. This is my blood of the covenant, which is poured out for many for the forgiveness of sins'" (Matt. 26:26–28).

The disciples didn't understand any of it until after Jesus' crucifixion and resurrection.

But they and we have a covenant sealed with the blood of the Lamb. They and we have a command to participate in his covenant meal. Again and again until he returns, Jesus calls us to eat and drink in his Presence, commemorating his death, communing with him. Most believers have taken the Lord's Supper. But in the partaking of the bread and the cup, few of us have experienced the living Presence and the profound nourishment to our spirit, soul, and body that God designed his meal to provide. Most of us haven't even known that anything beyond what we've experienced exists.

In his book on blood covenant, Henry Trumbull wrote, "The inter-commingling of blood by its inter-transference has been understood as equivalent to an inter-commingling of natures."[296]

Jesus himself said in John 6:56: "Those who eat my flesh and drink my blood live in me, and I live in them" (GNT).

Paul affirmed, "But anyone united to the Lord becomes one spirit with him" (1 Cor. 6:17 NRSV).

In John 6, Jesus repeatedly referred to himself as "the bread"—"the bread of God," "the bread that comes down from heaven and gives life to the world," "the bread of life" (vv. 33, 35, etc.).

When he said, "This bread is my flesh, which I will give for the life of the world," the Jews became highly offended. "How can this man give us his flesh to eat?" they cried (John 6:51, 52).

Unperturbed, Jesus kept pressing in: "Very truly I tell you, unless you eat the flesh of the Son of Man and drink his blood, you have no life in you. Whoever eats my flesh and drinks my blood has eternal life, and I will raise them up at the last day. For my flesh is real food and my blood is real drink. Whoever eats my flesh and drinks my blood remains in me, and I in them. Just as the living Father sent me and I live because of the Father, so the one who feeds on me will live because of me" (John 6:53–57).

If you don't understand all that—if, in fact, it bothers you—you're in good company. Jesus' words are mystery. On hearing them, "many of [Jesus'] disciples said, 'This is a hard teaching. Who can accept it?'" and they "turned back and no longer followed him" (John 6:60, 66).

Like the Jews of Jesus' day, we're incredibly uncomfortable with mystery. It contradicts logic, defies explanation, and creates offense. When Jesus called for people to eat his flesh and drink his blood, he spoke of the mystery of trusting in him. But he also spoke of the mystery of the meal he would initiate:

Matthew 26:26–28: "Take and eat; this is my body … Drink from it, all of you. This is my blood of the covenant."

Mark 14:22, 24: "Take it; this is my body … This is my blood of the covenant."

Luke 22:19–20: "This is my body given for you … This cup is the new covenant in my blood, which is poured out for you."

1 Corinthians 11:24–25: "This is my body, which is for you … This cup is the new covenant in my blood."

John 6:55: "For my flesh is real food and my blood is real drink."

In 1 Corinthians 10:16, Paul asked, "When we bless the cup of blessing aren't we sharing in the blood of Christ? When we break the bread aren't we sharing in the body of Christ?" (*GOD'S WORD*).

The Message renders the same questions this way: "When we drink the cup of blessing, aren't we taking into ourselves the blood, the very life, of Christ? And isn't it the same with the loaf of bread we break and eat? Don't we take into ourselves the body, the very life, of Christ?"

In 1215, more than one thousand years after Jesus walked the earth, the Roman Catholic Church officially adopted the doctrine of *transubstantiation*, the teaching that in Communion the elements of the bread and wine literally, physically, change into the body and blood of Christ. Three hundred years later, when the Reformation swept Europe, the Protestant leaders with one voice rejected that teaching.

But in the swing away from an unscriptural doctrine, we beached ourselves. We began treating the bread and the cup as a picture to admire, rather than experiencing the life-giving, covenant-deepening, mystery of sharing in the body and blood of our Lord.

And so, periodically, we sip the juice or wine, swallow the bite of cracker or bread, respectfully remember the cross, and go our way without having drunk deeply of the resurrection life of Christ. We miss the rendezvous with God to which he has invited us. We bypass the deeper experience of the inter-commingling of natures that his covenant meal offers us.

But that's not all. Consider again Paul's warnings to the Corinthian church:

1 Corinthians 10:14–21: "Therefore, my dear friends, flee from idolatry. I speak to sensible people; judge for yourselves what I say. Is not the cup of thanksgiving for which we give thanks a participation in the blood of Christ? And is not the bread that we break a participation in the body of Christ? Because there is one loaf, we, who are many, are one body, for we all partake of the one loaf. Consider the people of Israel: Do not those who eat the sacrifices participate in the altar? Do I mean then that food sacrificed to an idol is anything, or that an idol is anything? No, but the sacrifices of pagans are offered to demons, not to God, and I do not want you to be participants with demons. You cannot drink the cup of the Lord and the cup of demons too; you cannot have a part in both the Lord's table and the table of demons."

1 Corinthians 11:27–32: "So then, whoever eats the bread or drinks the cup of the Lord in an unworthy manner will be guilty of sinning against the body and blood of the Lord. Everyone ought to examine themselves before they eat of the bread and drink of the cup. For those who eat and drink without discerning the body of Christ eat and drink judgment on themselves. That is why many among you are weak and sick, and a number of you have fallen asleep. But if we were more discerning with regard to ourselves, we would not come under such judgment. Nevertheless, when we are judged in this way by the Lord, we are being disciplined so that we will not be finally condemned with the world."

Do you understand that the covenant meal is not to be taken lightly? In giving it, God set before us life and profound blessings, but also the potential to eat and drink judgment to ourselves. Choose life! Heed the strong warnings Scripture gives. From a humble and contrite heart, repent for every time you have desecrated the body and blood of the Lord by taking them in an unworthy manner. Ask the Lord to cleanse you from all bloodguilt that's resulted from your taking his covenant meal while any idols or unholy covenants remained in your life or your bloodline. Be blessed to receive the forgiveness and cleansing God has promised you in Christ.

Be blessed to eat the bread and drink the cup of the Lord from a heart wholly devoted to him. Every time you do so, experience the life of Jesus in new measure in your spirit, soul, and body. Hear his words in John 6:55–57: "My flesh is real food and my blood is real drink. By eating my flesh and drinking my blood you enter into me and I into you. In the same way that the fully alive Father sent me here and I live because of him, so the one who makes a meal of me lives because of me" (MSG).

Actively receive the inter-commingling of natures that is yours by the new covenant in Jesus' blood. I bless you with embracing the mystery of the covenant meal.

You do not have to wait until someone designated "clergy" offers communion. As you seek the Lord, seek his times for taking the bread and the wine, times alone with him, times together with other members of his Body. In particular, take the covenant meal in conjunction with the decisive acts of annulling unholy covenants, forsaking idols, and returning to Jesus as Lord. Then, as you seek to know him, to "progressively become more deeply and intimately acquainted with Him" (Phil. 3:10 AMP), commune with him again and again.

Be blessed to take the cup as one sharing in the blood of Christ. Be blessed to break the bread as one sharing in the body of Christ. As often as you eat and drink it, take into yourself the very life of Christ.

Repent—and be renovated

Be blessed to embrace the total renovation your Lord has set out to accomplish in you personally and in his people collectively.

I once passed a building that had housed a chain restaurant. A sign out front read, "Closed for Remodeling." Yet, obviously abandoned, the place was vandalized and in disrepair. Sometimes our lips and our lives give a similarly conflicting report. We tell each other, "Please be patient; God isn't finished with me yet"—but actually we quit cooperating with God's renovation process long ago. Though the Spirit will pursue us and convict us and allow us to experience the consequences of our stubbornness, to bring us to our senses, he will not proceed with the process as long as we say, "No."

Be blessed to live in the place of repentance, welcoming the continuing process by which you appropriate what Jesus has already done. Be blessed with pressing in, and not turning aside, when his kingdom confronts the big issues in your culture, in your church culture, and in you. Be blessed with demolishing sin strongholds your ancestors built and generation after generation has strengthened. Be blessed, day-by-day to send your oak roots deep. Be blessed to join the swelling ranks of the wholly devoted, working shoulder to shoulder to "rebuild the ancient ruins."

2 Chronicles 7:14: "if *my people, who are called by my name,* will humble themselves and pray and seek my face and turn from their wicked ways, then I will hear from heaven, and I will forgive their sin and will heal their land."

Revelation 3:3: "Remember, therefore, what you have received and heard; hold it fast, and repent."

Revelation 3:19: "As many as I love, I rebuke and chasten. Therefore be zealous and repent" (NKJV).

1 Corinthians 15:34: "Come back to your senses as you ought, and stop sinning."

Proverbs 1:23: "Repent when I reprove—I will pour out my spirit to you, I will make my words known to you" (CJB).

Acts 3:19: "Repent, then, and turn to God, so that your sins may be wiped out, that times of refreshing may come from the Lord."

Romans 12:2: " … let God transform you into a new person by changing the way you think" (NLT).

By now, I hope you've glimpsed how brutally the sin strongholds of our ancestors continue to rule and to ravage us. "Our fathers sinned and are no more, but we bear their iniquities" (Lam. 5:7 NKJV).

In the book, *Deliverance: Rescuing God's People,* Pat Legako and Cyndi Gribble write, "Sin and iniquity are not the same. Sin is an offense against God and is called 'missing the mark.' An iniquity includes the warped deeds of sinners, but has a broader definition that encompasses an evil bent or crooked direction toward sin. In other words, iniquity is the propensity to sin, while sin is the act."

Legako and Gribble describe persons who have "a strong propensity to a particular sin in their family line," but because of the hand of the Lord on their life, or perhaps because of their own self-discipline, they haven't committed the sin. "However, the iniquity is an open door for that individual and his children."[297] The bent to sin remains. So does the weight of all the accumulated generational junk that iniquity has brought.

In Leviticus 26:40–42, the Lord says, "But at last my people will confess their sins and the sins of their ancestors for betraying me and being hostile toward me ... then at last their stubborn hearts will be humbled ... Then I will remember my covenant ... and I will remember the land" (NLT).

Even now, Lord? Even here? Some insist we've already done it. With regard to the past sins of the region, sincere Christian people have asked, "Haven't we repented enough?"

Repentance means more than saying something is wrong. Repentance means making a U-turn powered by an humble and contrite heart. I ask you: Has the US church bowed before God with an humble, contrite heart, agreeing with him regarding our sins? Have we radically changed direction and begun to look astonishingly like the radiant, pure, whole, and holy Bride of Christ?

If not—if we're still going a way that misses and misrepresents our Lord—we still need to repent.

In recent years, different individuals and groups have confessed and tried to turn from racism or another of the sins so evident in our region's past. But identifying and attempting to sever a strand or two from a web of root sins hasn't accomplished much. As we return to the Lord with all our hearts, shattering the hidden idols he reveals, he will open the way to uproot the whole mess—the whole deep-rooted tangle of sin strongholds that grips the people of a region, the church in that region, and to a significant extent, the church in the US.

On his timetable, in his way, God will guide each of us in an extreme personal makeover. As we cooperate, he will orchestrate our transformation from the inside out. Our Lord will also guide us in an extreme makeover of his house.[298] He will lead us through repentance, not on behalf of the nation, but for the generational sins of the church.

Typically, our experiences with repentance are pretty awful. Sometimes, we repent from our *minds*. That is, we mentally identify some things we've done as "sin," as if checking off the boxes on a church visitors' form. Sometimes, we repent from our *emotions*. With tears, we admit something we feel really bad about having done (or having gotten caught doing). Genuine repentance will involve our minds and emotions. But any "repentance" that starts from our soul, instead of our spirit, brings only a temporary change, at best.

Typically, our attempts to repent are one-sided. We turn from sin, or at least attempt to do so—and stop there. Genuine repentance will tear out whatever needs to go, but will not stop with a torn-down mess.

Being made new

Genuine repentance is a renovation process. Renovation, by definition, makes new.

Ephesians 4:22–24: "You were taught, with regard to your former way of life, to put off your old self, which is being corrupted by its deceitful desires; to be made new in the attitude of your minds; and to put on the new self, created to be like God in true righteousness and holiness."

Colossians 3:5–10: "Therefore, put to death the earthly parts of your nature—sexual immorality, impurity, lust, evil desires and greed (which is a form of idolatry); for it is because of these things that God's anger is coming on those who disobey him. True enough, you used to practice these things in the life you once lived; but now, put them all away—anger, exasperation, meanness, slander and obscene talk. Never lie to one another; because you have stripped away the old self, with its ways, and have put on the new self, which is continually being renewed in fuller and fuller knowledge, closer and closer to the image of its Creator" (CJB).

Psalm 37:27: "Turn your back on evil, work for the good and don't quit" (MSG).

Repentance renovates. We turn from and turn to; tear down and build up; reject one kingdom and embrace another, put off the old self and put on the new. Godly repentance always demolishes in order to rebuild. It never stops halfway through.

Genuine repentance is a birthing process. The process is not heavy and depressing, but wonderfully life-giving. God's Spirit births a new thing in our spirit that changes the direction of our life.

2 Corinthians 3:17–18: "This Lord is the Spirit. Wherever the Lord's Spirit is, there is freedom. As all of us reflect the Lord's glory with faces that are not covered with veils, we are being changed into his image with ever-increasing glory. This comes from the Lord, who is the Spirit" (*GOD'S WORD*).

Repentance begins with *revelation*. Revelation happens Spirit-to-spirit: We see in our inmost being what we haven't seen before, as *Ruwach* shows us sin, as *Ruwach* shows us righteousness.

The Spirit reveals the written Word. He leads us to the Scripture. He opens the Scripture to us. Apart from him, we can read Scripture all day. We can quote whole biblical books from memory. But we won't correctly distinguish what God adores and what he abhors. Apart from the Spirit, we will repeatedly, vehemently, call good, evil; and evil, good.

The Spirit reveals the living Word, who became flesh and lived among us. Jesus said, "My sheep listen to my voice; I know them, and they follow me" (John 10:27). He said, "the Spirit of truth … will guide you into all truth … He will bring me glory by telling you whatever he receives from me" (John 16:13–14 NLT).

When he speaks, Spirit-to-spirit, we don't just nod mental assent. In fact, our minds may try to rationalize or dissuade. Our emotions may steel themselves against surrender. But deep within, we know what the Lord has shown us. Astonishingly, what overwhelms us most when God exposes iniquity and sin is not guilt, but godly grief. We see how our wrong choices have hurt others, how they've hurt us. Most of all, in the deepest part of us, we know what our wrong choices have done to our Lord. Holy Spirit touches our human spirit at the point of his grief.

The moment we receive the revelation in our spirit is like *conception*. Afterward comes *gestation*, which may take seconds or minutes or days or months, as the understanding of the truth develops within us, as our mind and emotions come into alignment with what the spirit has embraced. Then, in quick succession, come *confession* and *repentance*.

Confession is to repentance as labor is to giving birth. Confession that springs from the revelation and deep grief God's Spirit has implanted births repentance. If we try to confess apart from revelation, or if we confess too soon, before the gestating work of the Spirit is done, we'll birth nothing. If we utter loud cries of confession, but then do not follow through with repentance, we abort the good thing confession promised to bring forth. Like labor and childbirth, confession and repentance are often exceedingly hard, but always incredibly worth it. The process involves pain, sometimes even wailing. But when completed, it always only yields life and joy.

In Isaiah 6, the prophet saw the Lord seated on his throne, surrounded by worshiping angels. Immediately, Isaiah also saw that he and his people had sinned with their lips. As Isaiah confessed that sin, the hot coal of God's grief touched Isaiah's lips. As we confess from humble and contrite hearts, a coal from God's altar touches the thing in us that has grieved him. We utter a last, loud cry, and *birth* occurs. Our innermost being experiences the searing pain of his grief, followed by intense relief and unspeakable joy, as Christ is formed in us. (See Gal. 4:19). In each birthing, a new aspect of our new nature in him comes forth.

Repentance is a process by which God cleanses and transforms individual believers. It's a process by which God cleanses and transforms his Bride.

In Christ, we're new at the core—and we're being made new. Individually and collectively, we're becoming who we truly are. Accepted in the Beloved, we're learning to see and to live from his unshakeable, eternal, ever-increasing kingdom. We're learning to live from the astonishing truth that Christ's kingdom is here. It's in us. And it is superior, both to the unseen rebellious kingdom and to the visible, material realm.

Repentance is the means by which we cooperate with Jesus in that process. It's moving with him, learning from him, growing in him. It's giving him *carte blanche* to expose any ways we are missing and misrepresenting him. It's cooperating as he exchanges the old for the new. It's refusing to try to dictate what we will or won't change.

Repentance is *not* revisiting the same issues again and again, decrying the wrongs but never seeing real change. That's spiritual bulimia.

Repentance is following Jesus fully, yielding to the Spirit's voice, honoring the Father's holy name. It's locating every sign we've posted, saying, "No further!" or "Do not touch!"—throwing down the signs and going with God.

Paul described repentance when he wrote, "whenever anyone turns to the Lord, the veil is taken away. Now the Lord is the Spirit, and where the Spirit of the Lord is, there is freedom. And we all, who with unveiled faces contemplate the Lord's glory, are being transformed into his image with ever-increasing glory, which comes from the Lord, who is the Spirit" (2 Cor. 3:16–18).

Repentance is continuing to turn to the Lord and turn to the Lord and turn to the Lord, until every veil is taken away. It's gazing into the eyes that blaze with fire and finding that the fire doesn't destroy you, but rather burns up whatever is not of God in you.

The repentant continually approach the Lord with a humble, contrite heart. As a result, they're blessed. Their lives are a blessing.

Be blessed to be counted among them. Fix your eyes on Jesus. Don't turn away when his gaze burns right through you. Press past the pain into the joy. You will not burn up. You'll become a fire!

The psalmist cried to the Lord, "You make … your servants flames of fire" (Ps. 104:4 *GOD'S WORD*).

Jesus cried to the Father, "glory has come to me through them" (John 17:10).

May glory come to Jesus through you. Be exponentially blessed to break free from every iniquity that has bound your generations. Run, leap, and dance into a spacious place, where you blaze with the glory of the God of the covenant Name.

Instead of pride, walk in humility. Instead of greed, contentment. Instead of deception, truth. Instead of fear, faith. Instead of seeking to control and manipulate, delight in submitting to God and, mutually, to one another. Instead of violence and immorality, live from God's purity and peace. In place of division, rejection and rebellion, be blessed with unity in the Spirit growing ever more complete.

Day by day, face the junk—and find the treasure! Uncover riches you never knew existed, unclaimed realities already yours in Christ. Individually and collectively, embrace the process that continues until the Bride is radiant and whole.

The LORD bless you
and keep you;
the LORD make his face shine on you
and be gracious to you;
the LORD turn his face toward you
and give you peace (Num. 6:24–26).

10—Confession

> We know our wickedness, O LORD, The iniquity of our fathers, for we have sinned against You. Do not despise us, for Your own name's sake; Do not disgrace the throne of Your glory; Remember and do not annul Your covenant with us. —Jeremiah 14:20–21 NASU

> But at last my people will confess their sins and the sins of their ancestors for betraying me and being hostile toward me ... then at last their stubborn hearts will be humbled ... Then I will remember my covenant ... and I will remember the land.—Leviticus 26:40–42 NLT

Confessing requires seeing. To come out, to be free, we must see.

Seeing, we agree that what God has revealed is true. Agreeing, we go where we previously could not.

To run free, we must see.

I confess: Even as a Christian—a committed Christian—I didn't know what I didn't see.

My Confession

Since childhood, I've known Jesus Christ and desired to honor him. Growing up in a genuinely Christian home, becoming a Christian at age 8, actively participating in church, eagerly studying the Bible, marrying a Christian man, rearing our two daughters to know and follow God, living out God's call to write and speak what he was teaching me—I experienced blessing upon blessing, grace upon grace.

At the same time, other loyalties competed with my loyalty to Christ. Incredibly, I did not recognize these as rival loyalties. I did not see the subtle, yet dramatic, difference between *loyalty to things connected with Christ* and *loyalty to Christ himself.* Genuinely loving Christ, I prayed to honor him. Fooled by the counterfeit, I could not see where religious-looking but wrong motives, attitudes, and patterns intermingled with godly ones.

Even so, God loved me and acted to answer my prayer. Beginning in 1998, he took me where I didn't want to go to reveal what I desperately needed to see. Since then, he has gone to great lengths to show me himself, myself, and us.

Seeing God

Here's where words fail.

I knew Christ before, and wanted to know him more, but a veil covered my eyes. I saw him, yet something like gauze or a hazy film clouded the image.

I wear corrective lenses. Without those lenses, I can still see, but everything's blurry. When I look at people, I may recognize them, especially if I know them well, but I can't clearly see their features.

Before getting my first pair of glasses in fifth grade, I thought blurred vision normal. Now I know: It's not. So with my perception of Jesus Christ. I could recognize him. I could tell you much about his nature and his ways. But a veil of religious preconceptions kept me from seeing him clearly. Not having experienced life without the veil, I didn't see how much I didn't see.

Long ago, a man named Job had an eye-opening encounter with God. When Job entered a season of great suffering, his "friends" repeatedly, relentlessly insisted that all Job's losses had resulted from something terrible he had done. Job insisted he had remained true to God (and he had). He also began to accuse God of betraying him (God had not). Eventually, God showed up to remove the veil that kept his servant Job from seeing him clearly.

Afterward, Job said to God, "Surely I spoke of things I did not understand, things too wonderful for me to know … My ears had heard of you but now my eyes have seen you" (Job 42:3, 5).

Isaiah the prophet wrote, "In the year that King Uzziah died, I saw the Lord" (Isa. 6:1). Ezekiel said, "In my thirtieth year, in the fourth month on the fifth day, while I was among the exiles by the Kebar River, the heavens were opened and I saw visions of God" (Ezek. 1:1).

After Mary Magdalene encountered the risen Christ, she "went to the disciples with the news: 'I have seen the Lord!'" (John 20:18).

Isaiah and Ezekiel, Job and Mary already knew the true God. Yet, at a specific time, God did a profound work in each of their lives. He brought a previously fuzzy picture into focus. They saw him as they had not seen him.

If you see a new glow on my face, it's because I have seen the Lord! He looks *GOOD*! As never before, I've seen his radiance, his power, his compassion, his indignation, his faithfulness, his fullness, his suffering, his resurrection, his mystery, his love.

Seeing me

I've seen myself, too. What a sobering picture! And yet, what a beautiful one! All those years, I settled for much, much less than what Jesus had purchased. All those years, I looked at myself through a distorted mirror, a lens that simultaneously puffed me up and put me down.

Wanting to please Christ, I bowed before a system that promises everything Christ promised, but always holds it just out of reach; a system that propels us into activity, rather than drawing us into rest; that applauds pivotal involvement in God's purposes, yet relegates to the periphery all but a chosen few.

I wore the veil this system handed me. I accepted the place this system assigned me. Deep inside, I longed to fulfill my true identity in Christ, but the real and the counterfeit so commingled that I couldn't tell where one ended and the other began. When my true identity did try to express itself, a system I associated with Christ used any means it found convenient—persuasion, promises, bribes, threats, intimidation, accusation, attack—to readjust the veil.

Yet, God kept going after that veil. When he removed it, I saw.

Seeing the Lord, Job said of himself, "Therefore I despise myself and repent in dust and ashes" (Job 42:6). Visiting one of Job's friends, the Lord said, "I am angry with you and your two friends, because you have not spoken of me what is right, as my servant Job has" (Job 42:7).

When Job repented, God didn't leave him groveling in the dust. Picking Job up, dusting him off, calling him, "my servant," God vindicated Job, blessed him, and restored twice as much as he had lost. My, my, my! Job was looking good!

As Job, Isaiah, Ezekiel, and Mary learned, the more clearly we see God, the more clearly we see ourselves. The opposite is true, too. The same veil that blurs our view of Christ hides our true identity in him—from ourselves and from others.

"But whenever anyone turns to the Lord, the veil is taken away" (2 Cor. 3:16). Praise God!

"Now the Lord is the Spirit, and where the Spirit of the Lord is, there is freedom" (2 Cor. 3:17). Hallelujah!

Today, as never before, I "with unveiled face" am "beholding as in a mirror the glory of the Lord" and "being transformed into the same image from glory to glory, just as from the Lord, the Spirit" (2 Cor. 3:18 NASU). Whoopee! I'm looking *good*!

Seeing us

Speaking of sobering—and beautiful—pictures, I've also seen *us*. God has shown me, up close and personal, the state of his church and the inner workings of the Western church culture that we all too often believe to be the same thing. It's epidemic, this confusing of *loyalty to things connected with Christ* with genuine *loyalty to Christ*. It's epidemic, this business of settling for much, much less than what Jesus has purchased.

Living on the resurrection side of history, we're demonstrating little of the authority, power, love, and life that characterized the church in Acts—while telling ourselves this is the best we can hope for, this side of heaven.

We can list many good things we're experiencing and doing, blessing upon blessing, grace upon grace. Yet if we removed the veil, we'd see that we're like people trying to function inside a network of Plexiglas prisons. Being invisible (to us), these prisons appear to provide freedom, purpose, and community. Being prisons, they keep us isolated, irrelevant, and bound.

Great news! Jesus Christ loves us. He is committed to freeing us even from prisons we do not see. He has promised to transform all his people from every nation into "a radiant church, without stain or wrinkle or any other blemish" (Eph. 5:27). We will indeed look *good*!

Reflecting glory

The path of life takes us through death because that's where the veil falls away.

Job lost everything. His friends who came to comfort only kicked him while he was down.

Isaiah had never known a king other than Uzziah. How devastating for God's prophet to watch the godly king who ruled Judah for 52 years, in the end, fall to pride, be stricken with leprosy, and die, unrepentant.

Ezekiel was preparing to enter the priesthood when an ungodly nation conquered his unrepentant one. Along with 10,000 other people of Judah, Ezekiel was carried away into exile in Babylon.

Mary Magdalene watched the man who had changed her life, the Messiah in whom she had put her hope, die a brutal, disgraceful death.

On the cross, "Jesus uttered a loud cry, and breathed His last. And the veil of the temple was torn in two from top to bottom" (Mark 15:37–38 NASU). Yes!

When Job and Isaiah, Ezekiel and Mary let go of everything except God himself, they saw.

Seeing, they became who God had created them to be.

As long as we're semi-comfortable with our perceived lot in life, we won't risk seeing and being seen. We may not even realize there *is* more—to see, to experience, to possess. We'll accept as "enough" the blessings and the grace already received and chalk the rest up to "living in a fallen world." We'll squelch any voice, inward or outward, that suggests otherwise.

Ah, but when things get really, really uncomfortable, we're just a breath away from watching the veil fall. If we'll let it go—and not snatch it back up and not put it back on, regardless how afraid or intimidated or exposed we may feel—we're on our way to seeing clearly.

Seeing, agreeing, we take another step toward becoming who we are.

Our Confession

We in the Southern church culture and in the conservative US church culture didn't see what we didn't see. We were afraid that, if we looked, we'd be humiliated. We were afraid we'd lose our identity.

The God of the covenant Name has come to remove our veils of pride and fear, deception and shame—to dress us in his righteousness, to crown us with his joy. He gives us grace to see what we could not see before. He gives us courage to say what we could not previously say.

He reminds us, "If you grasp and cling to life on your terms, you'll lose it, but if you let that life go, you'll get life on God's terms" (Luke 17:33 MSG). "For if you want to save your own life, you will lose it; but if you lose your life for my sake, you will find it" (Matt. 16:25 GNT).

Trying to hold on to our identity, we've lost it. Releasing our identity for *Yeshua's* sake, we find it! For our Bridegroom, who delights in us, has given us his Name.

We confess who you are

Father, Son, Holy Spirit, you are the Lord, the God of the whole human race. Is anything too hard for you?[299]

You are the Lord our God. You are one. You are *Jehovah, Yahweh, HaShem, Adonai, Yud-Heh-Vav-Heh*—God of the covenant Name. You are *Ruwach Yahweh,* Spirit of the Lord, Spirit of truth. You are *Yeshua*, our Redeemer, the Lord who saves.

You are holy. You are faithful. You are merciful. You are love.

You are the Lord Almighty, the King of glory. You have established your throne in heaven, and your kingdom rules over all. "Righteousness and justice are the foundation of your throne; grace and truth attend you. How happy are the people who know the joyful shout! They walk in the light of your presence, *Adonai*. They rejoice in your name all day and are lifted up by your righteousness, for you yourself are the strength in which they glory" (Ps. 89:14–17 CJB).

You rule an ever-increasing kingdom. Your ruling authority will grow, and there will be no limits to the wholeness you bring. You rule an everlasting kingdom. How great are your signs! How powerful your wonders! You rule all generations.

"You are worthy, our Lord and God, to receive glory and honor and power, for you created all things, and by your will they were created and have their being" (Rev. 4:11). We are your handiwork, your workmanship, created in Christ Jesus to do the good works you prepared in advance for us to do. We have been justified by your blood, Lord Jesus. How much more will we be delivered by your life!

We are your Beloved, your Body, your Bride; your temple, your army, your sons. What love you've lavished on us! You've made us new. When you appear, we will be like you; because we will see you as you really are. Having this hope within, we continue purifying ourselves, since you are pure.

Even now, we confess what we cannot fathom: In this world we are like Jesus. We have an identity that Father bequeathed to us, Jesus redeemed for us, and Spirit is maturing in us. We live in you, Lord, and you in us. We contemplate your glory with our faces unveiled. We are being transformed into your image with ever-increasing glory, from the Lord, who is the Spirit.

Lord Almighty, you have promised to pour out "a spirit of grace and supplication." No matter how many promises you've made, Lord, they are "yes" in Christ. Through him, then, we say "Amen." So be it. We ask: Pour out a spirit of grace and supplication on *us*.

You've told us what happens next, Lord. You said, "They will look on me, the one *they* have pierced, and they will mourn for him as one mourns for an only child, and grieve bitterly for him as one grieves for a firstborn son" (Zech. 12:10).

How painful it is, Lord, for us to see and confess what calls forth such deep grief. But by your Spirit, we will look on you. We will confess the ways *we* have pierced you. Remember, Lord, what you have promised:

> On that day a fountain will be opened … to cleanse them from sin and impurity.
>
> On that day, I will banish the names of the idols from the land, and they will be remembered no more.
>
> On that day living water will flow out … half of it east … and half of it west.
>
> The Lord will be king over the whole earth. On that day there will be one Lord, and his name the only name (Zech. 13:1–2; 14:8–9).

We confess what we've inherited

As we look on you, Lord Jesus, the one *we* have pierced, we confess: We and our ancestors have sinned. Individually and collectively, we've missed and misrepresented you. We've agreed with who we are not.

Our ancestors tried to serve the Cotton Kingdom *and* the Kingdom of God. They received Jesus, yet refused to show genuine love to all people. They fell before God the Spirit, then spent decades resolutely quenching and grieving him. They believed the Bible, but convinced themselves they alone understood it aright.

They entered blood covenant with the Lord Jesus, and then brought a staggering burden of bloodguilt on themselves and the generations to come.

They forced the relocation of Native Americans, seizing their lands, breaking their hearts, breaking every covenant made with any tribe, and provoking the needless loss of tens of thousands of lives.

Men demeaned and devalued women, narrowly defining their "sphere," controlling them through counterfeit honor and socially acceptable disrespect, and subjecting them to devastating trauma, violation, and loss on pretext of protecting them. Women agreed with all of this, outwardly demure yet often clawing one another to get the one sliver of pie allotted to them.

Together, men and women colluded in a societal system that destroyed or profoundly wounded millions of African Americans—spirit, soul, and body—in countless ways. Our ancestors called slavery "godly" and "biblical" and refused all pleas to end that violent, immoral system.

They deliberately or heedlessly separated slave families, used slave women as breeders and sexual objects, were unfaithful to their own spouses, and rejected their own daughters and sons. In all these ways and others, they wreaked havoc in countless bloodlines.

They provoked a civil war to preserve an identity not from you. They trusted God *and* King Cotton to give them victory. When neither did, they defied surrender long after defeat was assured, multiplying the needless bloodshed.

After the war, our ancestors pledged allegiance to the Lost Cause, equating the death of the Confederacy with the death of Jesus Christ. They erected thousands of monuments exalting the Confederate "baptism of blood." They did not hate the war's bloodshed, but rather adopted a pattern of glorifying the bloodshed that still continues today. In all these ways, they sinned against the blood of Jesus, by which alone we are atoned.

They led the church to wed the culture, when the church is to be wed to Christ alone.

They declared both Jesus and Freemasonry, the Light. In public, they preached Christ. In secret, they swore oaths to the Craft, pledging their highest allegiance to their Masonic brothers, willingly taking curses on themselves, their families, and the generations to come.

Bouncing between two identities, they lived like Jesus had not resurrected and the Spirit had not come. Yet, they considered their culture a Southern Zion, a prototype for Christians everywhere.

The confusion and compromise our ancestors embraced still impacts us today.

We see glaring ungodliness in our nation. But how can we uproot unrighteousness when we're bound by unholy covenants to the same sins? We say we oppose abortion. We say we oppose domestic violence. We say we oppose sexual immorality. But our lips and our lives declare two different things. How can we lead the nation into purity and life when we have not hated bloodshed, have much uncleansed bloodguilt, and are bound by blood covenant to a violent and immoral root?

We decry oppressive religious systems. We denounce corruption in government, education, and business. We lambaste ungodliness in the media and the arts. But how can we hope to overcome evil with good in our culture while ignoring the evil strongholds in the church? How can we demonstrate godly love and honor to a watching world, while clinging to an identity that can only counterfeit both?

How can we convince people to follow God fully when we're deeply double-minded? How can we interest them in loving the Lord with all their hearts when we don't have a clue how that looks?

We confess our sins

Lord our God, we confess: We and our ancestors have sinned. We have agreed with the bewildering meshing of a godly identity and an ungodly one. We have been deeply confused as to our identity, deeply divided in our hearts. We've lived with double-mindedness so long we've accepted spiritual schizophrenia as the normal state of the church.

Like our ancestors, we've resigned ourselves to looking like the disciples in the gospels, rather than looking like *Jesus* and acting in the power, life, and anointing of the church in Acts.

We've lived our lives sometimes believing what you say, Lord—about who you are and who we are—and sometimes believing the opposite. We've lived our lives obeying some of what you command, but refusing obediences that appear to cost too much. We've lived our lives wanting to please you, and trying to please people too.

We've confused loyalty to Christ with loyalty to something we link with Christ. In every case where we've tried to give our first allegiance to Jesus *and* to anyone or anything else, we've moved away from our true identity—and into idolatry.

Individually and as a church culture, we have gone to great lengths to save our idols, while at the same time telling ourselves that we're trusting in Christ alone.

Because you love us, you look right into us, with your eyes of fire. You expose our divided hearts. You show us, not to shame us, but to burn away the shame. You show us to restore us to yourself.

Looking into your eyes, Lord Jesus, we confess our idolatry. We renounce every rival to Christ in our hearts, inside or outside our church culture. We renounce loyalty to any denomination, church, ministry, or position that competes with our loyalty to Christ. It is sin to mix worship of you with worship of anything or anyone else. We renounce the entwining of Christianity with exaltation of the Confederacy. We renounce participation in Freemasonry as a seeking for "light" apart from Christ and a seeking of power through worship of Baal.

We embrace the violent act of renunciation required to tear our idols from our hearts. We recognize that this renunciation is not a word-only act. It is a spirit, soul, and body act. The words reflect the relinquishment we make from our whole being, with our whole heart. We understand that generic confessions will not do. Lord, you are pinpointing the idols our ancestors worshiped and never turned from, as well as the idols we ourselves have embraced. As you reveal, we look and do not turn aside. We listen and do not close our ears. We agree with what you say. We name what you name.

You declare that it's of first importance that we love you, the Lord our God, with all our heart and soul and mind and strength. We cry from humble, contrite hearts: *We want to be wholly devoted to* YOU.

We renounce the checklist method as the means to that end. We say with the apostle Paul, "that old rule-keeping, peer-pleasing religion [is] an abandonment of everything personal and free in [our] relationship with God."

Deuteronomy 30:6 promises, "The Lord your God will circumcise your hearts and the hearts of your descendants, so that you may love him with all your heart and with all your soul, and live." Circumcision is painful, Lord, but it is essential for wholly loving you and for living lives that reflect our new, true identity in you. We give you permission to do it. We yield to it.

Looking into your eyes, Lord Jesus, we confess our bloodguilt. Your word says that shedding of innocent blood, needless shedding of blood, and not hating bloodshed bring bloodguilt. Your word says that sexual sin and whatever injures or destroys a family's bloodline bring bloodguilt. Your word says that sinning against the blood by which we're atoned brings the greatest bloodguilt of all. We and our ancestors have done all these things, all of them.

The Civil War should not have happened. The abolition of slavery could have been accomplished another way. Our ancestors, your church, should have led out in wise, just, and peaceful solutions, instead of leading the way into war. They did not hate the war's bloodshed, nor the bloodshed of Indian removal, nor of slavery. The consequences you declared in Ezekiel 35:6 have happened: bloodshed has pursued us.

Today, casualties of legal abortions in the US number 52 million and counting. Collectively, we in the church have agreed with abortion, as our ancestors agreed with Indian removal, slavery, and civil war—some participating, most tolerating. Collectively, your Body has been paralyzed—unable to rescue innocent babies and desperate moms we have not made up our minds to love; unable to take kingdom authority over bloodshed we have not made up our minds to hate.

We've colluded in similar ways with other sins that involve bloodshed and defile bloodlines, including premarital sex, adultery, homosexuality, pornography, exploitation and every kind of abuse—physical, sexual, emotional, verbal. What we say in Sunday School about sexual immorality and abuse often bears little resemblance to what we do behind closed doors. We acknowledge the grievous wrong of continuing in any behaviors you call improper. We acknowledge the grievous wrong of actively or passively approving those who do.

In all this, Lord, we do not condemn. We *confess*. We do not accuse others. We agree with what you've exposed in *us*. We refuse the lie that these revelations put shame on us. The shame is already there. Trying to deny it, to hide it, and to compensate for it has kept us isolated, burdened, terrified, and exhausted. You reveal in order to remove the burden, in order to set us free.

We confess our bondage to unholy covenants. Our ancestors bound themselves, by the shed blood of Confederate soldiers, to an identity not from you.

Such covenants trample the Son of God underfoot, treat as an unholy thing the blood of the covenant that sanctifies us, and insult the Spirit of grace. These unholy covenants have continued to bind succeeding generations, for they do not fade away with time. The covenant in the blood of the Lord Jesus alone can annul them.

We renounce all covenants with death that our ancestors made. We renounce any dependence on any blood except Jesus' alone for redemption, sanctification, and atonement. We who have Southern Baptist ties renounce the written oaths of allegiance to the Confederacy that the Southern Baptist Convention made. We confess that we ourselves have sinned against the body and blood of the Lord. We've eaten the bread and drunk the cup of the Lord in an unworthy manner. Unawares, we have taken your covenant meal while hidden idols and unholy covenants remained undealt-with in our bloodlines and our lives. Taking the bread and the cup with divided hearts, we've eaten and drunk judgment on ourselves.

Lord, remember your promise in Joel 3:21: "I will cleanse them of bloodguilt which I have not yet cleansed" (CJB). We cry to you for that cleansing, Lord, as we turn from the iniquities you name. In Isaiah 28:18, you declare, "Your covenant with death will be annulled; your agreement with the realm of the dead will not stand." We agree with that annulment, Lord. We cry for it. We cling to one covenant only, and that is the new covenant in Jesus' blood.

Lord our God, we confess: We and our ancestors have sinned. *We have agreed with grave injustices spawned by unrighteous roots.*

We renounce *pride*, in our ancestors and in us, that has kept our egos central. Pride has lashed us to an identity not from you. Pride has led our ancestors and us to embrace the lie, embodied in Landmarkism, that we alone have got it right. Pride prompted the co-opting of Scripture, using the Bible as a "belt" to keep people in line. Pride prompted the church to lead the way into secession and war. Pride prompted the equating of the Confederacy with Christ. Our ancestors did not humble themselves to receive rebuke, but rather became defensive and defiant. Pride drove them to erect structures alongside your altar—man-made structures they trusted to validate and preserve them. We have walked in their ways. Pride has divided our hearts.

We renounce *greed*, in our ancestors and in us. Like them, we've been mastered by what you have given to serve us. Our ancestors bowed before cotton and tobacco and other things that promised wealth. They nurtured a passion for more, always more; more than others, more than they already had. Loving gain, they deeply feared loss. They fasted and prayed and went to war to keep from suffering loss. When the war produced exponentially greater and more insurmountable loss than they otherwise would have known, they gloried in lack. We, their children, continue to pursue *more*, while always expecting, deeply fearing, and often provoking, *lack*. How often in these uncertain economic times have we prayed and taken action, telling ourselves we did it for you, Lord—yet you knew we acted either from a deep yearning for gain or an equally profound fear of loss? Greed has divided our hearts.

We renounce the *desire to control*, in our ancestors and in us. It is sin to refuse to submit to you, Holy Spirit. You are God. It is sin to treat another race, another region, another gender, or another person as lesser. It is sin to create systems built on the premise that our group must be the one to rule. It is sin to circumvent laws and moral boundaries and to trample the law of love, in order to keep people in "their place." The very fact that "they" have "a place" means we have agreed with a system of control. We renounce the pursuit of power that has divided and decimated your Body. Routinely, we have used verbal assaults, manipulation, intimidation, and force to get our own way. The desire for power has divided our hearts.

From this threefold taproot—greed, pride, power—other unrighteous roots have grown.

We and our ancestors have looked the other way when those in power committed *immorality and violence*. We've colluded with physical violence and immorality, hidden just out of sight. We've believed the lie that verbal violence, subtle or blatant, is an acceptable means to righteous ends.

We and our ancestors have cultivated *isolation, division, and rebellion*. We've bred an "us versus them" mentality. We've rejected anyone we considered, "them." We've even rejected "us."

We and our ancestors have been consumed with *fear*. Fear has enforced division, isolation, and domination. Fear has silenced any voice that's spoken up to identify the unrighteousness and injustices with which we've aligned. Fear has imprisoned us in the status quo.

We and our ancestors have lived in *deception*. We have agreed together to clean only the outside of the cup. We have agreed together to guard the appearance at all costs. Our ancestors redefined "honor" and "virtue," and passed their definitions down to us. We inherited from them a "magnificent incapacity for the real." Afraid to face the truth, we've become masters of denial. We've been deceived.

We renounce all these strongholds. We renounce the pride, fear, and denial that keep us bound to all the rest. We renounce the lie that the church in this day must be lukewarm, and that a lukewarm church will greet you when you return. We confess that you, *Yeshua*, are the Bridegroom; and we, the Bride. We embrace our highly favored status, "accepted in the Beloved." We confess that our divided hearts have left your Bride fractured and compromised. Not loving you wholeheartedly, we've not loved our neighbor as ourselves. We've not loved one another as you loved us. Yet you are returning for a Bride who has "made herself ready," a bride clothed in "righteous acts" (Rev. 19:7).

We confess with one voice from our innermost being: *"The LORD our God, the LORD is one"* (Deut. 6:4). *"The Lord is the Spirit"* (2 Cor. 3:17). *"Jesus Christ is Lord"* (Phil 2:11). In Christ, we have found the fountainhead, the cornerstone, the taproot of our true identity. Lord Jesus, you gave yourself up to make us holy, and you will present to yourself "a glorious church without a spot or wrinkle or any other blemish … she will be holy and without fault" (Eph. 5:27 NLT).

We confess our true, God-given identity

In spite of all we've wrongly aligned with, we have a covenant root, an oak taproot God himself planted. We have entered covenant with a covenant-keeping God. He says of his covenant people: "They will be called mighty oaks, a planting of the LORD for the display of his splendor" (Isa. 61:3).

When we confess and turn from the ways we've misrepresented him, he forgives us completely and cleanses us fully. He removes our sins as far as the east is from the west. He magnifies every way we've represented him well.

As we live from our oak taproot—walking out our true identity as the Body and Bride of Christ—we look like him! We keep repenting, keep making ourselves ready. With our lips and our lives, we confess who we are in truth, and who we're becoming:

We love the Lord our God with all our heart, soul, mind, and strength. We obey him, serve him, and praise him with a whole heart. Spiritual schizophrenia is gone; double-mindedness, vanquished. We're characterized by singleness of heart.

We fear the Lord our God. We walk in the reverential fear of the Lord. It's no longer important for us to appear righteous before others or to have their approval.

We honor God as God. We've quit trying to accept Jesus as our *Savior* without surrendering to him as *Lord*. We've quit calling him "Lord, Lord," but not doing what he says. We've quit trying to tell God the Holy Spirit what he can and cannot do. No longer quenched or grieved, the Spirit of the Lord moves mightily in our midst, doing all he has come to do.

We pray from our inmost being what Jesus taught us, first and foremost, to pray: "Our Father in heaven! May your Name be kept holy. May your kingdom come, your will be done on earth as it is in heaven" (Matt. 6:9 CJB). We desire above all else for the God whose Name we bear to be honored as the holy God he is. We seek first his kingdom and his righteousness. We are wed to our Lord alone.

We see what God is showing us—even the things we'd rather not see. We listen to what he is saying—even the words we'd rather not hear. We obey, trusting his grace to overwhelm us with the needed desire and power.

We treat other people well. Any hint of "us" versus "them" is gone. Any hint of superiority and inferiority, gone. We walk in humility, honoring others above ourselves. We love our neighbors as ourselves. We love one another as Christ loved us. The God who is love teaches us moment-by-moment how love looks. With his love, we spend and are spent for others' sakes.

We maintain the unity of the Spirit in the bond of peace. We discard all attempts at unity that reek of conforming, compromise, and control. Like the members of a great symphony, we each learn our God-given part. We learn to listen to one another and to follow our Conductor "until we're all moving rhythmically and easily with each other, efficient and graceful in response to God's Son" (Eph. 4:13 MSG).

We reject both greed and a poverty mindset. In humility and contentment, we access all the riches of Christ, including all the material resources needed for his kingdom purposes and every spiritual blessing that is ours in him. We act for the sake of his name and his kingdom, not from a fear of loss.

We reflect the resurrection life of Christ. When people look at us, individually and collectively, they see *his* character, *his* miracle-working power, *his* love.

We reject a fatalistic view of the future. We reject the lie that the last-days church must be a Laodicean church. We refuse to settle for looking like the disciples in the Gospels when Jesus has died and risen and sent his Spirit so that we can look like *him*. We believe the truth, that Christ's kingdom is ever-increasing. Believing, we begin to see what is already happening worldwide.

We cooperate with Christ and all his multifaceted Bride to heal lands and redeem cultures. Learning from people we previously thought we had to teach, following people we previously thought we had to lead, we do kingdom exploits with our Lord. We serve him shoulder-to-shoulder with people from every race and region, every culture, every generation. We see dramatic shifts in matters in our own culture that we've tried unsuccessfully for generations to address. We have authority in our Lord to move mountains we previously could not move. We have anointing by the Spirit to open blind eyes and set captives free.

Having confessed the unthinkable, we dance and sing with all God's people, celebrating the impossible:

> You'll get a brand-new name
> straight from the mouth of God.
> You'll be a stunning crown in the palm of God's hand,
> a jeweled gold cup held high in the hand of your God.
> No more will anyone call you Rejected,
> and your country will no more be called Ruined.
> You'll be called Hephzibah (My Delight),
> and your land Beulah (Married),

> Because God delights in you
> and your land will be like a wedding celebration.
> For as a young man marries his virgin bride,
> so your builder marries you,
> And as a bridegroom is happy in his bride,
> so your God is happy with you (Isa. 62:2–5 MSG).

At last we realize: The uncomfortable, the difficult, the devastating aspects of confessing and repenting aren't a plot to do us in. They're God's way of removing the veil so we can see and reflect his glory—splendor we cannot imagine or describe.

About the Author

Deborah Brunt was born and reared in Corinth, Mississippi, and once again calls north Mississippi home. Two of her great-great-grandfathers fought for the Confederacy, between them participating in numerous major battles, including Chickamauga, Antietam, and Gettysburg.

A Southern Baptist for 50 years, Deborah worked seven years as a leader in the denominational structure. She holds two certificates in Women's Ministry from New Orleans Baptist Theological Seminary.

Deborah earned a Doctor of Practical Ministry degree from Wagner Leadership Institute. During her doctoral studies, she began exploring underlying issues in the US conservative church culture, evangelical and charismatic. She began extensive research into the history of the church in the South.

Deborah is author of four previous books, the most recent, *Focused Living in a Frazzled World: 105 Snapshots of Life*. She has a one-and-a-half hour teaching on DVD, "We Confess! The Civil War, the South, and the Church." She and her husband have two married daughters. You can visit Deborah Brunt online at keytruths.com.

In 1994, Deborah went for a walk along Mississippi back roads. What should have been an idyllic setting was marred by all the litter people had thrown. Deborah had been meditating on the prayer Jesus taught his disciples to pray first: "Hallowed be your name." She had asked the Lord what those words meant. Seeing the littered land, she realized she was seeing the *opposite* of hallowing: What was intrinsically beautiful had been trashed.

That day, God began to show Deborah how his people, who share his beauty, have defaced their true identity and trashed his name. He told her, "I will clean up my reputation by cleaning up my people. I will pour out grace on them, so they can hallow me."

Notes

1—Celebration

1. News One for Black America, August 13, 2009, http://newsone.com/nation/throwback/news-one-staff/southerners-celebrate-150th-anniversary-of-the-civil-war/.
2. *The Murfreesboro Post*, July 27, 2010, http://www.murfreesboropost.com/state-prepares-to-celebrate-150th-anniversary-of-civil-war-cms-23934.
3. Shelia Byrd, Associated Press, *The Commercial Appeal*, December 6, 2010, http://www.commercialappeal.com/news/2010/dec/06/miss-prepares-for-commemoration/.
4. David Taintor, TPM Muckraker, December 21, 2010, http://tpmmuckraker.talkingpointsmemo.com/2010/12/south_carolianians_host_secessionist_ball.php.
5. kfrizzell, *Texas Heritage Online* Blog, January 28, 2011, http://www.tsl.state.tx.us/tho/blog/2011/01/28/events-celebrate-150th-anniversary-of-civil-war/.
6. Times Dispatch Staff, *Richmond Times-Dispatch*, January 3, 2011, http://www2.timesdispatch.com/special_section/2011/jan/03/upcoming-events-celebrating-150th-anniversary-civi-ar-749956/.
7. *Florida Travel*, February 16, 2011, http://www.miamiherald.com/2011/02/13/2057009/celebrating-150th-anniversary.html.
8. Madison County Tourism blog, January 5, 2011, http://www.madisontourismblog.com/1/post/2011/01/peterboro-to-celebrate-150th-anniversary-of-civil-war.html.
9. *Plymouth Patch*, January 28, 2011, http://plymouth-mi.patch.com/articles/plymouth-historical-museum-celebrates-150th-anniversary-of-the-civil-war-with-new-exhibit.

10. Walt Belcher, TBO.com, February 10, 2011, http://www.tboblogs.com/index.php/entertainment/comments/history-channel-to-celebrate-150th-anniversary-of-civil-war.

11. *Civil War Librarian* blog, September 3, 2010, http://civilwarlibrarian.blogspot.com/2010/09/news-is-celebrating-civil-wars-150th.html.

12. Harold Jackson, "Commemorate, Don't Celebrate Civil War's 150th," *The Philadelphia Inquirer*, January 16, 2011, http://www.philly.com/philly/opinion/20110116_Commemorate__don_t_celebrate_Civil_War_s_150th.html.

13. Wayne Washington, The State: South Carolina's Homepage, December 16, 2010, http://www.thestate.com/2010/12/16/1607696/celebrate-or-commemorate-debate.html.

14. CWSAC Battle Summaries: Civil War Sites Advisory Commission Report on the Nation's Civil War Battlefields, Technical Vol. II: Battle Summaries, http://www.nps.gov/hps/abpp/battles/tvii.htm.

15. Katharine Q. Seelye, "Celebrating Secession Without the Slaves," *New York Times*, November 29, 2010, http://www.nytimes.com/2010/11/30/us/30confed.html.

16. http://www.thetakeaway.org/2010/dec/01/south-celebrates-150-years-civil-war/, audio interview posted December 1, 2011.

17. Bruce Smith, "Civil War anniversary opening up old wounds: commemorating 150 years brings divisions of its own," December 11, 2010, http://gazettextra.com/news/2010/dec/11/civil-wars-150th-anniversary-stirs-debate-race/.

18. Jackson, "Commemorate."

19. Seelye, "Celebrating Secession."

20. Charles Reagan Wilson, *Baptized in Blood: The Religion of the Lost Cause 1865–1920* (Athens: University of Georgia Press, 1980), 112–113. Quotations from *Baptized in Blood* used with permission of Charles R. Wilson.

21. Unless otherwise noted, Scripture quotations are taken from *Today's New International Version* (TNIV).

22. "The History of Jim Crow," accessed July 15, 2011, http://www.jimcrowhistory.org/geography/violence.htm.

23. Quoted in Sarah M. Grimke, "An Epistle to the Clergy of the Southern States," 1836, 19.

24. Emphasis added. Throughout *We Confess!*, wherever Scripture quotations include italics or bold, the emphasis has been added by the author, unless otherwise noted.

2—Song of Deliverance

25. Donald Miller, *Blue Like Jazz* (Nashville: Thomas Nelson Publishers, 2003), 118.
26. Miller, 125.
27. See also Exodus 5:1; 7:16; 8:20; 9:1,13; 10:3.
28. Sylvia Gunter, "Generational Healing—Hebrews 4:15–16," *You Are Blessed in the Names of God* (Birmingham, AL: The Father's Business, 2008), 57.
29. Luther E. Copeland, *The Southern Baptist Convention and the Judgment of History: The Taint of an Original Sin*, rev. ed. (New York: University Press of America, 2002), xiii, xv. Quotations from this source reproduced with permission of University Press of America in the format Other book via Copyright Clearance Center.
30. Samuel S. Hill, Jr., introduction to *Churches in Cultural Captivity: A History of the Social Attitudes of Southern Baptists*, by John Lee Eighmy (Knoxville: University of Tennessee Press, 1972), v.
31. Terry Matthews, "Lecture 1: Spiritual Bulimia," Religion 466: Religion in the South, Wake Forest University, accessed March 1, 2007, http://www.wfu.edu:/~matthetl/south/lectureone.html. Quotations from Religion in the South used with permission of Terry Matthews.
32. Matthews, "Lecture 13: The Religion of the Lost Cause," accessed February 24, 2011, http://www.wfu.edu/~matthetl/perspectives/thirteen.html.
33. Samuel S. Hill, forward to *At Ease in Zion: A Social History of Southern Baptists, 1865–1900*, by Rufus B. Spain (Tuscaloosa: University of Alabama Press, 2003), x.
34. Hill, forward, x.
35. Hill, forward, xxi, xx.
36. Hill, forward, xiii.
37. Jesse C. Fletcher, *The Southern Baptist Convention: A Sesquicentennial History* (Nashville: Broadman & Holman Publishers, 1994), 50–51, 64–65.
38. Fletcher, 60–61.
39. Copeland, 12.
40. C. Vann Woodward, introduction to *Mary Chesnut's Civil War*, by Mary Boykin Chesnut (New Haven: Yale University Press, 1981), xxx–xxxiv, xlix.

3—King Cotton And Mighty Oaks

41. John C. Willis, *Forgotten Time: The Yazoo-Mississippi Delta After the Civil War* (Charlottesville: University Press of Virginia, 2000), 8.

42. Willis, 8.

43. "Cotton," *The New Georgia Encyclopedia*, accessed September 21, 2010, http://www.georgiaencyclopedia.org/nge/Article.jsp?id=h-2087.

44. William W. Freehling, *Prelude to Civil War: The Nullification Controversy in South Carolina, 1816–1836* (New York: Oxford University Press, 1965), 1.

45. Lee Davis Perry, Lee Davis Todman, J. Michael McLaughlin, *Insiders' Guide to Charleston: Including Mt. Pleasant, Summerville, Kiawah, and Other Islands* (Globe Pequot, 2007), 257.

46. "Cotton," *Encyclopedia*, emphasis added.

47. James Henry Hammond, *Selections from the Letters and Speeches of the Hon. James H. Hammond, of South Carolina* (New York: John F. Trow & Co., 1866), 316–317.

48. Shashank Bengali, "Mississippi Delta: The Land Economic Recovery Never Revisits," McClatchy Newspapers, posted April 11, 2010, http://www.mcclatchydc.com/2010/04/11/91778/in-mississippi-delta-recession.html.

49. Willis, 9.

50. C. C. Clay, "An Address before the Chunnemygee Horticultural Society," reported in *De Bow's Review,* Dec. 1855, quoted in Emily Anne Eliza Shirreff, "A Few More Words on The Chivalry of the South," Tract No. 11 (London: Victoria Press, 1864), 20–21.

51. Shirreff, Tract 11, 21–22, quoting Frederick Law Olmsted, *Journey and Explorations through the Cotton Kingdom* (1861), vol. ii, 336; and Hinton Rowan Helper, *The Impending Crisis of The South* (1857), 22.

52. "Acorns to Oaks: How to Grow Your Own Oak Trees," accessed July 16, 2011, http://www.wildbirds.org/oaks/oaks.htm.

53. Wilson, *Baptized in Blood*, 17.

54. Freehling, 125.

55. Freehling, 340–341.

56. Freehling, 341.

57. OT:3639 *kelimmah. The Online Bible Thayer's Greek Lexicon and Brown Driver & Briggs Hebrew Lexicon (Thayer's* and *BDB),* Copyright © 1993, Woodside Bible Fellowship, Ontario, Canada. Licensed from the Institute for Creation Research.

58. OT:3640. *kalam. Theological Wordbook of the Old Testament.* Copyright © 1980 by The Moody Bible Institute of Chicago. All rights reserved. Used by permission.

59. OT:8469. *tachanuwn* or *tachanuwnah. BDB.* Also, *Biblesoft's New Exhaustive Strong's Numbers and Concordance with Expanded Greek-Hebrew Dictionary.* Copyright © 1994, 2003, 2006 Biblesoft, Inc. and International Bible Translators, Inc.

60. OT:776 *'erets. BDB.*

4—The Fast God Has Chosen

61. John Lee Eighmy, *Churches in Cultural Captivity: A History of the Social Attitudes of Southern Baptists* (Knoxville: University of Tennessee Press, 1972), 24.

62. David Goldfield, "The Civil War Was a Choice," CNN Online, posted April 12, 2011, http://www.cnn.com/2011/OPINION/04/12/goldfield.civil.war/index.html?hpt=C1.

63. James Oakes, *The Ruling Race: A History of American Slaveholders* (New York: Alfred A. Knopf, 1982), 96–122.

64. Joe W. Burton, *Road to Augusta: R. B. C. Howell and the Formation of the Southern Baptist Convention* (Nashville: Broadman Press, 1976), 13–14, emphasis added.

65. [Edwin C. Holland], *A Refutation of the Calumnies Circulated against the Southern and Western States, Respecting the Institution and Existence of Slavery among Them* ... (Charleston: A. E. Miller, 1822), 22.

66. *Genius of Universal Emancipation*, October 14, 1827, quoted in Gordon E. Finnie, "The Antislavery Movement in the Upper South Before 1840," *Abolitionism and American Reform*, John R. McKivigan, ed. (Indianapolis: Indianapolis University, 1999), 161.

67. David T. Morgan, *Southern Baptist Sisters: In Search of Status, 1845–2000* (Macon, GA: Mercer University Press, 2003), 10.

68. Morgan, 10, 163.

69. See Rollin G. Osterweis, *Romanticism and Nationalism in the Old South* (Baton Rouge: Louisiana State University, 1949), 129.

70. John Albert Broadus, *Memoir of James Petigru Boyce D.D., LL.D.: Late President of the Southern Baptist Theological Seminary, Louisville, Ky.* (New York: A. C. Armstrong and Son, 1893), 139.

71. Fletcher, *Southern Baptist Convention*, 10.

72. *Alabama Baptist* (Montgomery), Nov. 28, 1889, 1, quoted in Rufus B. Spain, *At Ease in Zion: A Social History of Southern Baptists 1865–1900* (Tuscaloosa: University of Alabama Press, 2003), 83.

73. Walter B. Shurden, *Not a Silent People: Controversies that have Shaped Southern Baptists* (Macon, GA: Smyth & Helwys Publishing, 1995), 34.

74. Fletcher, 46–47, emphasis added.

75. Fletcher, 10.

76. *Southern Baptist Convention Annual, 1845*, 19.

77. Fletcher, 55.

78. Fletcher, 12–13.

79. Burton, 83.

80. *Journal of the Congress of the Confederate States of America, 1861–1865*, vol. I, May 17, 1861, accessed February 24, 2011. The entire resolution may be found on the Library of Congress website at: http://memory.loc.gov/cgi-bin/query/r?ammem/hlaw:@field%28DOCID+@lit%28cc00157%29%29. Interestingly, this resolution does *not* appear among the resolutions listed for 1861 on the official SBC website. However, the 1863 Resolution on Peace both references and reaffirms the 1861 resolution.

81. "Resolution on Peace," May 1863, SBC Resolutions, accessed February 24, 2011, http://www.sbc.net/resolutions/amResolution.asp?ID=801.

82. Wilson, *Baptized in Blood*, 4–5.

83. See Malachi 2:1–9; Isaiah 28:14–19.

84. Fletcher, 32–33.

85. Walter B. Shurden, *Not an Easy Journey* (Macon: Mercer University Press, 2005), 204.

86. Shurden, *Not an Easy Journey*, 202–203.

87. Shurden, *Not an Easy Journey*, 202.

88. James A. Rogers, *Richard Furman: Life and Legacy* (Macon: Mercer University Press, 2001), 234, 248.

89. Rogers, 122.

90. Rogers, 152–153, 187–188.

91. Rogers, 231, 238, 249, 309.

92. Rogers, 226.

93. Rogers, 206.

94. Fletcher, 44.

95. Rogers, 54, 67.

96. Quoted in Rogers, 203.

97. Fletcher, 32.

98. Rogers, 106.

99. Richard Furman to Edmund Botsford, 12 October 1802, SCBHS, quoted in Rogers, 109.

100. *Minutes of the Charleston Association*, 1800, SCBHS, quoted in Rogers, 110.

101. Rogers, 112.

102. Richard Furman, "Address to the Churches: The State Convention of the Baptist Denomination, in South-Carolina, convened in the Village of Coosawhatchie, 4th December, 1824, … " *Minutes of the State Baptist Convention*, 1824, SCBHS, 10–11.

103. *Minutes of the Baptist General Committee at their Yearly Meeting, Held in the City of Richmond, May 8, 1790* (Richmond: T. Nicholson, 1790), 7, quoted in Donald G. Mathews, *Religion in the Old South* (Chicago: University of Chicago Press, 1979), 69.

104. Richard Furman, letter to an unidentified person, SCBHS, quoted in Loulie Latimer Owens, *Saints of Clay: The Shaping of South Carolina Baptists* (Columbia, SC: R. L. Bryan Co., 1971), 73.

105. Richard Furman, "Exposition of The Views of the Baptists, Relative To The Coloured Population In The United States In A Communication To The Governor of South-Carolina," December 24, 1822 (Charleston: A.E. Miller, 1838, 2nd Ed.), 6, online at http://history.furman.edu/-benson/docs/rcd-fmn1.htm.

106. Furman, "Exposition," 17.

107. Furman, "Exposition," 17.

108. Furman, "An Address to the Residents Between the Broad and Saluda Rivers Concerning the American War for Independence, November, 1775," quoted in Rogers, 268.

109. John 16:13, 8.

110. Freehling, *Prelude to Civil War*, 52.

111. Freehling, 76.

112. Whitemarsh B. Seabrook, *A Concise View of the Critical Situation and Future Prospects of the Slaveholding States, in relation to their Coloured Population* (Charleston: A. E. Miller, 1825), 15.

113. *Report of the Committee … [on] Religious Instruction … of the Synod of South Carolina and Georgia* (Charleston, 1834), quoted in Charles Elliott, *Sinfulness of American slavery*, vol. 2 (Cincinnati: L. Swormstedt & J. H. Power, 1850), 54.

114. Furman, "Address to the Churches," 9–10, 11.

115. Matthews, "Lecture 1: Spiritual Bulimia."

5—Restoring the Foundations

116. *American Slavery As It Is: Testimony of a Thousand Witnesses* (New York: American Anti-Slavery Society, 1839), 22.

117. *American Slavery*, iv.

118. 1740 South Carolina Slave Code. Acts of the South Carolina General Assembly, 1740 # 670. Transcription from McCord, David J., ed. *The Statutes at Large of South Carolina*. Vol. 7, Containing the Acts Relating to Charleston, Courts, Slaves, and Rivers. Columbia, SC: A.S. Johnston, 1840, 397.

119. Oakes, *The Ruling Race*, 27, 28.

120. Copeland, *Judgment of History*, 9.

121. *American Slavery*, 144.

122. Elizabeth Keckley, *Behind the Scenes* (New York: G. W. Carleton & Co., 1868), 11-12.

123. Quoted in *American Slavery*, 35.

124. *American Slavery*, 104.

125. *American Slavery*, 20.

126. *American Slavery*, 36.

127. *American Slavery*, 34.

128. *American Slavery*, 39.

129. *American Slavery*, 55, 56, 57.

130. *American Slavery*, 47.

131. James Pennington, *The Fugitive Blacksmith* (London: Charles Gilpin, 1850), iv-v, vii.

132. *American Slavery*, 52.

133. Matthews, "Lecture 8: The Convenient Sin," accessed March 8, 2007, http://www.wfu.edu:/~matthetl/south/eight.html.

134. Oakes, 57.

135. Oakes, 123, quoting John Mills to Gilbert Jackson, May 19, 1807, Mills Letters.

136. Joseph Holt Ingraham, *The Southwest. By a Yankee* (New York: Harper & Brothers, 1835), II, 91.

137. *American Slavery*, 110.

138. Oakes, 97, 98.

139. *American Slavery*, 180.

140. *American Slavery*, 178.

141. *American Slavery*, 181.

142. *American Slavery*, 23.

143. Eighmy, *Churches in Cultural Captivity*, 6.

144. "Mississippi Declaration of Secession," The Civil War Home Page, accessed August 31, 2011, http://www.civil-war.net/pages/mississippi_declaration.asp.

145. "Indian removal: 1814 – 1858," PBS Online, accessed February 17, 2011, http://www.pbs.org/wgbh/aia/part4/4p2959.html.

146. "Native Americans and the Civil War," Digital History, last modified September 1, 2011, http://www.digitalhistory.uh.edu/database/article_display.cfm?HHID=100; "Native Americans," HistoryCentral.com, accessed September 1, 2011, http://www.historycentral.com/CivilWar/people/Native.html.

147. Wilson, *Baptized in Blood*, 46.

148. Osterweis, *Romanticism and Nationalism in the Old South*, 10.

149. Mary Boykin Miller Chesnut, *Mary Chesnut's Civil War*, ed. C. Vann Woodward (New Haven: Yale University Press, 1981), 407.

150. Copeland, 92.

151. Emily Anne Eliza Shirreff, "The Chivalry of the South," Tract No. 6 (London: Victoria Press, 1864), 12.

152. Chesnut, 29.

153. Shirreff, Tract 6, 11.

154. Wilson, 46–47.

155. W. J. Cash, *The Mind of the South* (New York: Knopf, 1941), 86, quoted in Osterweis, 89.

156. SBC Resolution adopted May 13, 1861.

157. W. O. Carver, *Christian Missions in Today's World* (Nashville: Broadman, 1942), 36–37, quoted in Copeland, 39.

158. Herbert A. Kellar, ed., "A Journey Through the South in 1836: Diary of James D. Davidson," *The Journal of Southern History*, vol. I, no. 3 (Aug 1935), 355, 356.

159. James Silk Buckingham, *The Slave States of America* (London, 1842; reprinted by Applewood Books, 2008), II, 295.

160. Oakes, 57.

161. Oakes, 72.

162. Shirreff, Tract 6, 14.

163. *Christian Index* (Atlanta), July 19, 1883, 8, quoted in Spain, *At Ease in Zion*, 146.

164. Chesnut, 261–262.

165. Chesnut, 153–154.

166. *Religious Herald*, Sep. 12, 1872, 4, quoted in Spain, 94.

167. *Alabama Baptist*, Nov. 28, 1889, 1, quoted in Spain, 83.

168. *American Slavery*, 115.

169. Osterweis, 46.

170. G. W. Featherstonhaugh, *Excursion through the Slave States*, II, 340–342, quoted in Osterweis, 141.

171. "The Difference of Race Between the Northern People and the Southern People," *Southern Literary Messenger* XXX (June 1860), 401–409, quoted in Osterweis, 79.

172. Chesnut, 83.

173. *American Slavery*, 118.

174. Wilson, 61.

175. David Grimsted, *American Mobbing, 1828–1861: Toward Civil War* (Oxford University Press, 1998), 86, 98.

176. Shirreff, Tract 11, "A Few More Words on the Chivalry of the South," 28.

177. "Antebellum Slavery."

178. Gloria J. Browne-Marshall, "The Realities of Enslaved Female Africans in America," excerpted from: Gloria J. Browne-Marshall, *Failing Our Black Children: Statutory Rape Laws, Moral Reform and the Hypocrisy of Denial* (2002), accessed September 3, 2011, http://academic.udayton.edu/race/05intersection/gender/rape.htm.

179. Thomas Jefferson, *Notes on Virginia*, sixth Philadelphia ed., 251, quoted in *American Slavery*, 117.

180. "Nat Turner's Rebellion: 1831," PBS Online, accessed September 1, 2011, http://www.pbs.org/wgbh/aia/part3/3p1518.html.

181. *American Slavery*, 109.

182. John Witherspoon to Susan McDowall, January 14, 1836, Witherspoon and McDowall Papers, quoted in Oakes, 118.

183. Oakes, 122.

184. Wilson, 46.

185. Copeland, 99.

186. Duff Green, *U.S. Telegraph*, November 1835, quoted in William Dexter Wilson, *A Discourse on Slavery: delivered before the anti-slavery society in Littleton, N. H., February 22, 1839* ... (Concord: Asa McFarla, 1839), 44.

187. Freehling, *Prelude to Civil War*, 82.

188. Frederick Law Olmsted, *The Cotton Kingdom: A Traveller's Observations on Cotton and Slavery in the American Slave States*, vol. 2 (New York: Mason Brothers, 1861), 353.

189. "Charles Grandison Finney and the Revival," accessed March 31, 2011, http://xroads.virginia.edu/~HYPER/DETOC/religion/revival.html.

190. Burton, *Road to Augusta*, 50.

191. Chesnut, 25.

192. Chesnut, 20.

193. Chesnut, 241.

194. Chesnut, 436.

195. Chesnut, 195.

196. Chesnut, 167, 659.

197. Chesnut, 738.

198. Spain, 22, quoting *Christian Index* (Macon, GA), Nov. 9, 1865, 2.

199. Quoted in Spain, 74.

200. Richmond *Enquirer*, April 15, 1856, quoted in Oakes, 141.

201. Alabama, *Journal of the Senate* (Montgomery, AL, 1857), 25, quoted in Oakes, 149.

202. Chesnut, 196.

203. *American Slavery*, 123.

204. Chesnut, 761–762.

205. W. J. Cash, "The Mind of the South," *The American Mercury*, October 1929, 185, http://www.wjcash.org/WJCash1/WJCash/WJCash/THE.MIND.OFTHE.SOUTH.html#Article.

206. Cash, "The Mind of the South," 186.

207. Eighmy, 21, quoting Cash, *The Mind of the South*, 80.

208. Graham Cooke, *Coming into Alignment* (Vacaville, CA: Brilliant Book House, 2009), 161.

6—The Blood of the Covenant

209. Sylvia Gunter, *You Are Blessed in the Names of God* (Birmingham, AL: The Father's Business, 2008), 65.

210. Email sent February 15, 2011.

211. "Covenant," *Nelson's Illustrated Bible Dictionary* (Thomas Nelson Publishers, 1986), Biblesoft, Inc.

212. *Adonai*, "Pronouncing Explanatory Glossary," *Complete Jewish Bible: An English Version by David H. Stern* (Clarksville, MD: Jewish New Testament Publications, 1998), 1558.

213. Henry Clay Trumbull, *Blood Covenant: A Primitive Rite and its Bearing on Scripture* (New York: Charles Scribner's Sons, 1885), 4.

214. Trumbull, *Blood Covenant*, 202.

215. Trumbull, *Blood Covenant*, 6.

216. Hammond, Selections, 344.

217. James P. Guenther, "Your SBC Executive Committee: Part 1 of 4," accessed July 20, 2011, http://www.sbcec.net/history/SBCEC-Part1of4.asp; also see SBC Constitution, Article III.

218. *Journal of the Congress of the Confederate States*, May 17, 1861.

219. "Resolution on Peace," May 1863.

220. "Preventing Diplomatic Recognition of the Confederacy, 1861–1865," U.S. Department of State, accessed September 10, 2011, http://history.state.gov/milestones/1861-1865/Confederacy.

221. Wilson, *Baptized in Blood*, 4.

222. Wilson, 5.

223. Wilson, 5.

224. Wilson, 71.

225. Wilson, 44, quoting "George C. Harris' Address" in UCV, *Minutes of the Eleventh Annual Meeting and Reunion of the United Confederate Veterans ... 1901* (New Orleans, n.d.), 56.

226. Wilson, 29.

227. Wilson, 166–167.

228. Wilson, 44–45.

229. Wilson, 5.

230. Matthews, "Lecture 13: Lost Cause."

231. Wilson, 44.

232. Trumbull, *Blood Covenant*, 204.

233. Matthews, "Lecture 7: Division Within the Denominations," accessed February 24, 2011, http://www.wfu.edu:/~matthetl/south/seven.html.

234. Fletcher, *Southern Baptist Convention*, 78.

235. Copeland, *Judgment of History*, 13.

236. Copeland, 13.

237. Copeland, 15, emphasis added.

238. Eighmy, *Churches in Cultural Captivity*, 208.

239. Psalm 106:6, 36–40, 42–45, 47 NRSV.

240. Numbers 25:11 MSG.

7—An Undivided Heart

241. A. W. Tozer, *Man: The Dwelling Place of God* (Camp Hill, PA: WingSpread Publishers, 1966, rev. ed. 1977 by Zur Ltd.), 88.

242. Exodus 20:3, Barnes' Notes, Electronic Database Copyright © 1997, 2003, 2005, 2006 by Biblesoft, Inc. All rights reserved.

243. "Whoever doubts is like a wave in the sea that is driven and blown about by the wind. If you are like that, unable to make up your mind and undecided in all you do, you must not think that you will receive anything from the Lord" (James 1:6–8 GNT).

244. Fletcher, *Southern Baptist Convention*, 12.

245. To read the story in detail, see Joe W. Burton, *Road to Augusta*; James E. Tull, "Chapter 7: The Graves-Howell Controversy," *High-Church Baptists in the South: The Origin, Nature, and Influence of Landmarkism* (Macon, GA: Mercer University Press, 2000), and Homer L. Grice and R. Paul Caudill, "Graves-Howell Controversy (1857–62)", *Encyclopedia of Southern Baptists* (1958), 580–585.

246. Burton, 34.

247. J. J. Burnett, "R. B. C. Howell," *Sketches of Tennessee's Pioneer Baptist Preachers* (Nashville: Marshall & Bruce Company, 1919), 246–252, accessed September 2, 2011, http://knoxcotn.org/old_site/tnbaptists/howell_rc.htm.

248. James R. Graves, *Old Landmarkism: What Is It?* (Memphis: Baptist Book House, 1880), xi.

249. H. Leon McBeth, *The Baptist Heritage: Four Centuries of Baptist Witness* (Nashville: Broadman Press, 1982), 447, quoted in Fletcher, 60; Tull, *High-Church Baptists*, 123.

250. Timothy George, "Southern Baptist Ghosts," *First Things*, May 1999, 17–24, http://www.firstthings.com/article/2007/01/southern-baptist-ghosts-22.

251. Graves, *Old Landmarkism*; also Fletcher, 61–62; Eighmy, *Churches in Cultural Captivity*, 18.

252. "James Robinson Graves," Southern Baptist Historical Library & Archives, accessed September 1, 2009, http://www.sbhla.org/bio_graves.htm.

253. Burton, 145.

254. Tull, 86.

255. Burton, 144.

256. Tull, 86–87.

257. Tull, 90.

258. Burton, 161.

259. Burton, 127, 170–171.

260. Burton, 22.

261. Burton, 31.

262. Wilson, *Baptized in Blood*, 7.

263. Wilson, 37–38.

264. Matthews, "Lecture 7: Division Within Denominations."

265. Matthews, "Lecture 13: Lost Cause."

266. Matthews, "Lecture 11: Baptized in Blood," accessed March 7, 2007, http://www.wfu.edu/~matthetl/south/eleven.html.

267. Wilson, 139.

268. Wilson, 25.

269. Wilson, 38, 39.

270. Wilson, 18, 21, 22, quoting John E. Cooke, *Stonewall Jackson: A Military Biography* (New York: D. Appleton, 1876), 548–550.

271. Wilson, 24.

272. Matthews, "Lecture 12: The Challenge to Orthodoxy," accessed March 11, 2007, http://www.wfu.edu/~matthetl/south/twelve.html.

273. Wilson, 36.

274. Wm. M. Pratt, "The Early Baptist Churches of Kentucky" (1887), *Memorial Volume Containing the Papers and Addresses that were Delivered at the Jubilee of the Association of the General Association of Baptists*, Louisville (1888), 36–52, accessed September 2, 2011, http://baptisthistoryhomepage.com/kent.early.hist.pratt.html.

275. Charles G. Finney, "Chapter XIX: Relations Of Masonry To The Church Of Christ," *The Character, Claims, and Practical Workings of Freemasonry* (1869), accessed March 31, 2011, http://truthinheart.com/EarlyOberlinCD/CD/Finney/Theology/1869Freemasonry/freem_chap19.htm.

276. Finney, Chap. XIX, *Freemasonry.*

277. Finney, Chap. XIX, *Freemasonry.*

278. Graves, 25, xiv.

279. Graves, 139.

280. Albert Gallatin Mackey and H. L. Haywood, *Encyclopedia of Freemasonry, Volume 3 (1909)* (Kessinger Publishing's Rare Reprints, 1946) 1222.

281. Albert Gallatin Mackey and Donald Campbell, *A Lexicon of Freemasonry* (Philadelphia: Moss, Brother & Co., 1860), 267–268.

282. Cf. Prov. 22:28; Job 24:2 KJV.

283. Albert G. Mackey, *The Principles Of Masonic Law: A Treatise On The Constitutional Laws, Usages and Landmarks of Freemasonry* (New York: Jno. W. Leonard & Co., 1856), 87.

284. Graves, 29.

285. Graves, 123.

286. Graves, 48.

287. Graves, 51–52.

288. Graves, 28.

289. Graves, 149–150.

290. Emma Moore Weston, "The Story of Scofield's Life," condensed from J. M. Canfield, *The Incredible Scofield*, accessed April 8, 2011, http://www.gospeltruth.net/scofield.htm.

291. Glenn R. Goss, "The Scofield Bible and C. I. Scofield," accessed April 9, 2011, www.rayofhopechurch.com/scofield.htm.

292. Charles Gallaudet Trumbull, *The Life Story of C. I. Scofield* (New York: Oxford University Press, 1920), 8.

293. Elgin S. Moyer, *The Wycliffe Biographical Dictionary of the Church* (Chicago: Moody Press, 1982), 362, quoted on http://www.biblebelievers.com/scofield/, accessed April 9, 2011.

294. *Scofield Reference Bible* (New York: Oxford University Press, 1967), 1355, heading prior to Rev. 3:14.

9—Bless Our Hearts!

295. Gayden Metcalfe and Charlotte Hays, *Being Dead Is No Excuse: The Official Southern Ladies Guide to Hosting the Perfect Funeral* (Miramax Books, 2005), 3, 2.

296. Henry Trumbull, *Blood Covenant*, 202.

297. Pat Legako and Cyndi Gribble, *Deliverance: Rescuing God's People* (Tate Publishing, 2007), 87–88.

298. See Nehemiah 9.

10—Confession

299. Other Scriptures used in this section's confessions about God: Jer. 32:27; Deut. 6:4; Ps. 103:19; Isa. 9:7 MSG; Dan. 3:33 CJB; Eph. 2:10; Rom. 5:9–10; 1 John 3:2–3 CJB; 1 John 4:16–18; 2 Cor. 3:18; 2 Cor. 1:20.